THE LAMENTATIONS

The Lamentations

A REQUIEM FOR QUEER SUICIDE

Patrick Anderson

FORDHAM UNIVERSITY PRESS   NEW YORK 2024

"The Summer Day" by Mary Oliver reprinted by the permission of The Charlotte Sheedy Literary Agency as agent for the author. Copyright © 1990, 2006, 2008, 2017 by Mary Oliver with permission of Bill Reichblum.

"A Woman Is Talking to Death" by Judy Grahn reprinted with permission of the author. Copyright © 1974 by Judy Grahn.

Copyright © 2024 Fordham University Press

All rights reserved. No part of this publication may be reproduced, stored in a retrieval system, or transmitted in any form or by any means—electronic, mechanical, photocopy, recording, or any other—except for brief quotations in printed reviews, without the prior permission of the publisher.

Fordham University Press has no responsibility for the persistence or accuracy of URLs for external or third-party Internet websites referred to in this publication and does not guarantee that any content on such websites is, or will remain, accurate or appropriate.

Fordham University Press also publishes its books in a variety of electronic formats. Some content that appears in print may not be available in electronic books.

Visit us online at www.fordhampress.com.

Library of Congress Cataloging-in-Publication Data available online at https://catalog.loc.gov.

Printed in the United States of America

26 25 24   5 4 3 2 1

First edition

For all of us.

Contents

Prologue   1

I. Introitus   13
   i. Office of the dead
      (*Officium defunctorum*)   14
   ii. All flesh (*Omnis caro*)   19
   iii. And he shall be like a tree
      (*Et erit tamquam lignum*)   26

II. Dies Irae   31

III. Kyrie Eleison   51
   i. Sorrowful is my soul
      (*Tristis est anima mea*)   52
   ii. What am I, miserable, then to say?
      (*Quid sum miser tunc dicturus?*)   58
   iii. My soul is weary with my life
      (*Taedet animam meam vitae meae*)   70

IV. Lacrimosa   75

V. Offertorium 93
    i. *Through the tombs* (*Per sepulcra*) 94
    ii. Seeking me, you sat down wearily
       (*Quaerens me sedisti lassus*) 96
    iii. Let not the abyss swallow them,
       lest they fall into obscurity (*Ne absorbeat
       eas tartarus, ne cadant in obscurum*) 101

VI. Sanctus 108
    i. I kneel with submissive heart
       (*Oro supplex et acclinis*) 109
    ii. Great trembling there will be
       (*Quantus tremor est futurus*) 111
    iii. Hail, true body (*Ave verum corpus*) 128

VII. Benedictus 132
    i. Death has struck (*Mors stupebit*) 133
    ii. May the martyrs greet
       you at your arrival
       (*Adventu suscipiant te martyres*) 142

VIII. Agnus Dei 155

IX. Libera Me 174
    i. A heart reduced to ashes
       (*Cor contritum quasi cinis*) 175
    ii. When from the dust shall rise
       (*Qua resurget ex favilla*) 183
    iii. That which is hidden will appear
       (*Quidquid latet apparebit*) 196

X. In Paradisum 199
    i. Eternal light (*Lux aeterna*) 200
    ii. Perpetual light (*Lux perpetua*) 207

Coda 217

ACKNOWLEDGMENTS 225

NOTES 229

BIBLIOGRAPHY 243

INDEX 255

Liber scriptus proferetur in quo totum continetur.

> A book shall be brought forth in which all will be written.

Prologue

Permit me voyage, love, into your hands. . . .
　　　　　　HART CRANE, "VOYAGES III" (1926)

We look for the sermon in the suicide.
　　　　　　JOAN DIDION, *THE WHITE ALBUM* (1979)

On October 17, 1979, Robert Sego drove from Garland, a small suburb of Dallas, Texas, to his hometown in Haskell. Robert was a guidance counselor at North Mesquite High School, where he had worked since the school's opening twelve years earlier. He was well-liked by students, several of whom later referred to him as a "best friend." In 1979, October 17 fell on a Wednesday. It was eighty-seven degrees on that day, unseasonably hot for the Dallas area. In Haskell it was even hotter: ninety-two degrees. There was no rain as Robert drove to his grandfather's grave at the Willow Cemetery. Once he arrived, around noon, he pointed his gun at his chest, just over his heart, and pulled the trigger. A short time later, when the police arrived, he was declared dead at the scene.[1]

Two weeks before his death, on Tuesday, October 2, Robert visited a popular gay cruising site in the JCPenney men's restroom at the NorthPark Center Mall in Dallas. It was late afternoon when he and another man were interrupted by a mall security guard, who then summoned the police. The men were arrested for lewdness and released without bail. Hoping the arrest would remain quiet, Robert returned to his everyday life and work. He had declined to give the police his occupation when asked, for good reason: in the previous year, the Briggs Initiative—a ballot measure in California that would have barred gay and lesbian people from working in public schools—had failed to pass, but had inspired similar initiatives in Texas, where sex between men had been outlawed since 1860. The most recent version of Texas's criminal code, which had been amended in 1973, included Section 21.06, the basis for Robert's arrest. This section expanded earlier statutes to include all same-sex sexual practice; it criminalized "deviate sexual intercourse with another individual of the same sex. 'Deviate sexual intercourse' means any contact between any part of the genitals of one person and the mouth or anus of another person."[2] One month after

Robert's death, a man named Donald Baker would file suit against the state, challenging the constitutionality of Section 21.06 on privacy grounds, but would eventually lose his case. Texas's ban on same-sex sexual practices would remain in effect until the 2003 Supreme Court decision in *Lawrence v. Texas*.

No trial date was set for Robert's case in 1979, possibly because the charges were going to be dropped. For two weeks, his life continued without trouble. But sometime early in the week of October 15, the anonymous parent of a student at the school called a reporter at the *Mesquite Daily News* and leaked news of the arrest. The reporter called the high school's principal on Tuesday, October 16. After classes ended that day, the principal told Robert about the call and mentioned that the reporter had asked about "an incident on October 2." Robert left the school in a panic; this was the last time he was seen alive by anyone who knew him. He drove to his home in Garland and wrote a note to his sister and friends, telling them what he planned to do.[3] The following morning, hours before the *Mesquite Daily News* published a cover story outing him,[4] Robert drove two hundred miles to the cemetery in Haskell, where his body would be found shortly after noon. He was forty years old.

Stories like this one are neither rare nor extraordinary in the historical record. For decades before 1979—indeed, for centuries—the suicides of people we would today assemble under a general *queer* heading appeared in newspaper stories, legal and religious documents, police and coroner records, medical and psychiatric case reports, and a wide range of aesthetic texts, including novels, poems, plays, and films. By 1979, what I will call the *archetype* of queer suicide had long ago taken root in the public consciousnesses within many national and community contexts, so widely understood as a narrative trope that it could be reliably deployed by journalists, novelists, playwrights, filmmakers, and others without needing much exposition. Obliquely referred to as "the honorable thing" in some generations, queer suicide has played a mournful accompanying role in life stories involving loneliness, shame, isolation, familial and social alienation, religious and political persecution, arrest and incarceration, blackmail and forced outing, and many other markers of marginalization and oppression. After 1979, the resonance of queer suicide evolved as the AIDS epidemic and its public health failures left many people who had been diagnosed with HIV feeling as if they had no other option but to choose a "death with dignity." The expansion of what is variously known as the euthanasia, doctor-assisted suicide, or right-to-die movement in the 1980s and 1990s is due in no small part to the many victims of AIDS who chose to spare themselves what, at the time, was almost certain to be a slow and painful death. In the early twenty-first century, that resonance evolved again, this time to the epidemic of suicide among queer children and adolescents, many of whom had experienced relentless bullying within their schools and communities.

This is a book about queer suicide and the many forms of violence to which it responds. This is also a book about those who remain after a suicide has taken place, and the particular forms of mourning that follow in its wake. In the pages that follow, interwoven with the stories of many people who have chosen to die, I write about four deaths spread across many years of my own life: my grandfather, two of my oldest queer friends, and my best friend. I write about the archives that have structured the difficult process of grieving these losses. After the most recent of the suicides in 2019, I found myself practicing what in retrospect seems like a melancholic, queer methodology: I began rereading many of my favorite books from the long history of queer literature: *Giovanni's Room*,

The Price of Salt, Dancer from the Dance, Stone Butch Blues, The Front Runner, Sister Outsider, Oranges Are Not the Only Fruit, Conundrum, Dykes to Watch Out For, Nocturnes for the King of Naples, Tales of the City, and many more. I found that suicide seems to haunt—explicitly or implicitly—many of these texts. And so I began to collect and read psychological, sociological, and anthropological studies from the past, and early examples of nonfiction books written by gay, lesbian, and transgender authors. I ravenously began seeking and collecting stories about queer suicide from a wide variety of textual genres, including obituaries, newspaper stories, and psychological surveys. At some point, I began to think of what I was doing as a summoning of queer ancestors—so I also began to recover and reexamine the artifacts of my own queer life. These practices became like rituals for me, almost-daily enactments that oriented me differently, with each text or artifact or photograph I uncovered, to the experience of loss-to-suicide that has anchored my biography.

This is a book about those rituals, tracing the work that gets done by them, and tracing, too, the blend of sadness, nostalgia, anger, despair, regret, and hope that define what it means to survive in the shadow of queer suicide. In the pages that follow, I alternate between several different kinds of writing: I construct a history of queer suicide that, itself, moves through a wide range of institutional and social contexts; I review historical writing *about* queer suicide, particularly writing by queer authors hoping to stem the flow of queer deaths; I revisit narrative representations of queer suicide in films, theatrical productions, and other media; I relate the life stories of many queer people who have chosen to die; I recall the lives of the four loved ones whose deaths have motivated my writing; and I enact, in all of these tellings, the experience of grieving losses that almost dare not speak their own names. While writing, I have sought to fully immerse myself in that grief both to honor its raw power and, in the end, to heal myself of its most persistent and overwhelming effects. In that sense, writing this book has performed a kind of catharsis upon me, compelling me not just to *witness* the mournful profundities of surviving queer suicides but also to fully *inhabit* them, and in doing so, then, to release myself from their formidable grasp.

I have used the formal structure of a requiem for this book despite the fact that I do not subscribe to the dogma of its religious liturgies. I have chosen this structure for several reasons. First, requiems are recursive and repetitive, returning to musical and textual motifs with slight variations throughout their compositions. They share this quality with grief and mourning: the flashes of memory that replay out of nowhere, interrupting the flow of daily life; the tendency to be struck, again and again, with the freshness of loss; the repetitions of longing and regret that ebb and flow; the suddenness with which one can be overcome with weeping, no matter how many times one has wept before. The requiem structure, in its own internal cycles, both rehearses and gives voice to this quality of profound grief, its tendency to retreat or fold back on itself just as you thought it was nearing its end.

Second, in the Catholic tradition, the Requiem Mass is a formal rite, a way of marking loss with a ceremony defined by a community gathering and a performance of rehearsed practices. As rituals, such requiems are intended to provoke a transition between the immediacy of loss and a restoration of everyday life. But within their formal structures, requiems ask that we dwell with loss, give ourselves over to loss, and allow loss to infuse our very being. As we bear witness to those who have gone, we are also asked to face our own ends. This has been the method at the heart of my work on this book: to dwell in the archives of queer suicide, to center the lives of those who have died, and to give those lives access to this formal ritual from which—like all people who have died by suicide, and like queer people more generally—they have historically been barred.

Finally, in my own experience, choral and symphonic requiem compositions have often been sources of great beauty and have elicited sometimes-cathartic emotional responses from me. This is especially true for the Lacrimosa section of Mozart's *Requiem* and Gabriel Fauré's *Requiem* in its entirety, both of which I sang in my high school choir with two of the friends whose deaths appear in this book. More recent examples, like the *Cadman Requiem* by Gavin Bryars and the *Requiem for Beirut* by Rami Khalifé, also have the ability to move me to tears. I have written this book as I have grieved my losses, needing catharsis; I have written this book *as a way* of grieving my losses. Throughout, I have sought to remember the beauty of queer lives, including my own, and to expose myself to the rich, if exhausting, emotional complexity of both grief and gratitude for all of them. Writing in a requiem form has structured that process. It has also offered something like a cathartic experience, as the best kind of music always does, whether by Fauré or Khalifé or Tori Amos or Sylvester or Sinéad O'Connor or Nina Simone or Ravi Shankar or Billie Holiday or the Magnetic Fields or Odetta or Björk or Charlie Parker or Prince or Chet Baker or Sade or Sigur Rós or Patsy Cline or Johnny Cash or Everything but the Girl. These have been the soundtrack accompanying my writing, just as the formalized *Requiems* of Berlioz and Britten and Brumel have given me a formal structure in which to write.

The text for the traditional Requiem Mass (or Mass for the Dead) is drawn from the Roman Missal, which lays out the readings, prayers, chants, and other liturgical texts for many of the Catholic Church's rites and rituals; choral and orchestral Requiem compositions (including those by Mozart and Fauré) vary in how closely they follow that traditional form. For this book, I have named each of the ten sections for a text from the Requiem Mass, and each section is subdivided into smaller sections whose titles I have culled from the lines of those prayers. Each section generally (but not dogmatically) aims to fulfill the purpose of the text after which it is modeled, which I briefly describe here. The Introitus is written as an invocation and as introduction to those who have died. The Dies Irae ("day of wrath") is focused on the immediacy of queer suicide—the day of death itself—and on the shock and sudden grief experienced in the period after one receives news of such a death. The Kyrie Eleison, traditionally a plea for mercy, centers on narratives that express the aching loneliness of those who have longed for love that has been forbidden them, driving some to end their lives; following this, the Lacrimosa is written to convey the grief of those who have survived the suicides of others. In the Offertorium, I dwell with the artifacts and remainders of lost beloveds—gravesites, mementos, old photographs—and the power they hold to transfix. In the Sanctus, I consider the power of places where the absences of those who have died become especially potent and acute, the "sacred places" of queer life and queer death. The Benedictus, which is traditionally an invocation of blessedness, is focused on martyrs: I turn to the shifting meanings of queer suicide during and after the first wave of the HIV/AIDS pandemic, and the epidemic of suicide among bullied youth and adolescents after the turn of the millennium. The Agnus Dei ("Lamb of God") is a reflection on the value of companionship, in whatever form it may take. The final two sections—the Libera Me ("Rescue Me") and In Paradisum ("In Paradise")—center on the release from suffering and the restoration of peace so desperately sought *both* by those who have chosen to end their lives *and* by those of us who have survived them. Throughout all of these sections, I have woven a narrative that describes the broader history of the archetype of queer suicide, recovers many stories about queer suicides from numerous archives, and reflects on the representation of queer suicide in a variety of aesthetic and journalistic venues.

Generally speaking, I use the word *queer* as a broad category of sexual and gender identities, inclusive of many other historical terms. When writing about specific people and their lives, I use the words that they used for themselves, including terms like homosexual, gay, lesbian, bisexual, and transgender. Not everyone who appears in this book would identify themselves using any of these (or any related) terms. Likewise, not every death narrated in this book was definitively determined by forensic investigators to be self-inflicted, nor does every death fit a strict clinical definition of suicide. All of the stories included in this book, including those that could not categorically be called queer suicides, are here because they have played a role in my experience of loss, or in my seeking to understand queer suicide, or in my process of mourning the sudden deaths at the heart of this work. With that in mind, and with the exception of my grandfather, I have chosen to use pseudonyms for the people in my own life whose deaths occasioned this writing.

In his recent book *Undoing Suicidism*, Alexandre Baril describes wearing a medical bracelet with clear instructions not to provide lifesaving procedures in the event he is unconscious or unable to communicate. He frames his discussion of this bracelet by explaining that,

> I have been suicidal since the age of twelve, that I am still suicidal, and that, even on my best days when I feel good and enthusiastic about life (suicidal people can also experience positive emotions), I still wish that I were dead instead of alive.[5]

In order to obtain an official Do Not Resuscitate (DNR) certificate from the Ontario Ministry of Health and Long-Term Care, Baril describes how, in every meeting with a physician or counselor, he has had to deny these sentiments, insisting that his desire not to have his life prolonged does not correlate with suicidal ideation or intentions, which would invalidate the DNR request. This is a conundrum, he argues, that has the effect of alienating people who experience, whether in the short or long term, the desire to die. Similarly, Baril asserts that standard medical, psychiatric, and social responses to suicide, which almost universally pathologize the desire to die and focus entirely on preventing such feelings, result in "more harm and more deaths by suicide rather than prevent[ing] suicide."[6]

This is a provocative and controversial claim. Baril's ultimate intention with his book is to encourage the nurturing of what he calls "suicidal futurities, opening a space where death by (assisted) suicide can occur as well as a space to have open and honest discussions about living with a desire to die."[7] For anyone who has survived the suicide of a loved one, this makes for some rough reading: it is difficult to accept, much less embrace, the fact that someone you love longs to end their life. But Baril's argument raises an important concern for my own work in this book: how to honor the agency of people who have died by suicide, and to respect the autonomy of their choices, while also honoring the profound sense of loss and despair that their deaths occasion, centered on the wish that they had chosen to live instead—which, in its best form, is an expression of love.

Suicide has historically been treated as a shameful, immoral, pathological, and often criminal event. I do not wish to extend or participate in that kind of shaming. I hope that this book honors the lives of those whose stories it includes. I hope that in grieving the losses described in these pages, I have not failed to dignify the agency of those who have died. News of the suicide of someone intimate to oneself is—to borrow Joan Didion's pithy description of touching a massive turbine in the bowels of Hoover Dam—"so explicit as to suggest nothing beyond itself."[8] This writing—these words, these pages, this queer requiem—is my attempt to touch the turbine: to seek its inner mechanics, to feel the uneven rhythms of the work it performs, to listen closely to its restlessly doleful hum. This writing is also my attempt, as Didion put it, to find the "sermon in the suicide," as a way of "telling [myself] stories in order to live."[9] In other words, and most importantly, this writing is my effort to bear witness both to the aching experience of mourning, and to the lives of those who are mourned.

I
Introitus

At the center of his life, he remains anonymous, a displaced person, an outsider.
    MIKE WALLACE, *CBS REPORTS*, "THE HOMOSEXUALS"
                                              (1967)

One by one, they were all becoming shades.
                JAMES JOYCE, "THE DEAD" (1914)

i. Office of the dead

Officium defunctorum

A pulse of light in a darkened room, quick and cool, gleams to reveal that the room is filled with moving bodies. The light bursts and fades, here then gone, but is back again in an instant, following the beats of a bone-deep song. With each return it reveals the bodies in changed positions: there a head thrown back with eyes half-shut; there the arms shot out as if reaching for another; there a body suspended as if caught mid-leap in ice. All are drenched with sweat. With each new flash a new arrangement: the strobe captures then releases them as they dance, stills them as if in a photograph before returning them to their dark, ecstatic obscurities. And then it is back again, each flash a new composition, a new photograph, a new disappearance into each interstitial moment of dark. In this room, it could be any year in the late electrical age: the 1960s, perhaps, or sometime in the middle-nineties, or even later still. Each flash reveals something new, a hint at the eras of those who are here, but nothing resolves with definitive clarity. The pulsing light does not *follow* so much as *catch* the presence of time, its supple capacity both to disclose and to obscure. Let us say that it is 1964, and also 1994, and 1997, and 2019. Let us say that here, in this pulsing room, it is all of these years and more.

And let us call this scene an intercession: a prayer and a pleading for those who have gone. These are their bodies, sheened with the efforts of dancing. With each flash of light they are restored before slipping again into the sleeve of absence: each pulse a return to us, each fade another loss. They are both now and then; they are both here and away. These are our martyrs. These are our saints.

※ ※ ※ ※ ※

INTROITUS

For two hundred days in 1964, my paternal grandfather, Bud, and my best friend, Robin, were both alive. Robin was born in March. Bud was dead by the end of September. In 1964, I was not yet a dreamed-of thing. The teenagers who would later become my parents, busy seeking routes of escape from the southern towns they ached to leave, hadn't even met. By the time I arrived they had both left the South, only to return a few years later. In March 1964, Robin was born in Fort Worth, Texas, where his father was stationed at Carswell Air Force Base. At that time, Bud and his family, including my fifteen-year-old father and his twin sister, lived in LaBelle, Florida. As the crow flies, there are 1,030 miles between Carswell Air Force Base and my grandfather's home in LaBelle, or 1,238 miles as one might drive on today's roads. Roughly halfway along this itinerary is Birmingham, Alabama, the city where my parents eventually settled, the city where I was raised, and the city where I would later meet two of my earliest queer friends, Alec and Lana.

On the day Robin was born, the weather in Fort Worth was fair, with a high temperature of seventy-four, a low temperature of fifty-one, and no rain. On the day Bud died, the weather in LaBelle was also fair, with a high of eighty-seven and a low of seventy-two. In Birmingham, the period between March and September is typically hot and excruciatingly humid. Rain is not uncommon, though it rarely brings relief from the suffocating heat. The thunderstorms, especially in late spring, are feral and intimidating. The occasional tornados are fearsome: random and relentless in the violent etchings they carve across the land. Birmingham weather, generally speaking, is as unsettling as it is unsettled. I remember huddling in basement rooms, folded into a ball, as winds whipped ragefully through the forests outside, and as giant pines and oaks were plucked from their beds and left planked on the ground. I remember deluges so thick with incessant drumming that when I was caught outdoors in them, my entire being would be infused with their weighted significance: these rains brooked nothing except their saturations. I remember the omnipotence of weather and the catastrophes of its worst effects. Birmingham is heavy with weather.

Robin loved the renewal occasioned by rainstorms. Lana loved stomping puddles dry. Alec would sometimes stand in a downpour, letting it overtake him. I doubt Bud minded the rain. He lived on a farm. He knew its necessity.

Situated halfway along a route between the place where Robin was born and the place where Bud died, Birmingham sprawls on clay-heavy soil veined with iron ore deposits that make the dirt look red as if rusted, or as if stained from rivers of flowing blood. Red Mountain, which cuts across the southern edge of the city, is crowned with a monument to Vulcan, the Roman god of fire and smithing. He cuts a handsome figure there, gripping a hammer in one hand and hoisting a spear tip in the other. He wears a smelter's apron and sandals with ties wrapped up to the knee. From the front, his bearded face follows the line of the spear point, and his apron gapes slightly to reveal the strength of his chest. From the rear, his heavily muscled back and ample buttocks are pert with effort. In the early 1980s, when I had begun to understand myself (and had begun to be understood by others) as queer, I would watch for him to appear whenever we drove through the winding roads over which he towered, my eyes drawn to the lazy drape of the apron's bib, gaping just enough to hint at the mysteries beneath. But I never got caught staring. By then I had learned that in Birmingham, this was a secret I needed to keep.

This troubled city of sweetgum trees and Spanish moss was both the context for and the foil to my becoming. In Birmingham in the 1980s, there were no reliable models for queer identity, no accessible mentors to point a way; instead, one was left with the caricatures of lurking criminality, laughingstock simpering, shadowy despair, and painful morbidity that occasionally appeared in television or film, and that sometimes featured in the sermons of brimstone preachers. Queerness was interstitial: a slow-rolling game of stolen glances and brushed arms; memorized images from page and screen, saved for the work of fantasy; hushed mutual recognitions that only fleetingly found voice. But when, as a gangly teenager, I was sent to a school seventeen miles south (and out of view) of Vulcan, I slowly found my kin. Alec was sent here too, and later Lana. This was a place for exploration: the sprawling campus included several hundred acres of wooded land that bordered a lush state park, a lake with resident swans, student gardens and a stable, and a timetable for classes with scheduled free periods meant for wandering. Here, halfway between the place where Robin was born and the porch where Bud died, queerness could find a voice.

It's a neat little trick, to map the routes that define a life and discover constellations: my hometown exists at the center of the distance between the places where, for two hundred days in 1964, my grandfather and my best friend were alive; and in this place, I was sent to a school where I befriended Alec and Lana. These are intimate coordinates, and together they form a geography defined both by becoming and by loss. In September 1964, Bud turned a gun to his head; in January 1994, Lana drove her car into a stopped police cruiser; in September 1997, Alec attached a hose to his car's exhaust pipe; in June 2019, Robin knotted a makeshift noose. But for two hundred days in 1964, my paternal grandfather, Bud, and my best friend, Robin, were both alive, and all of the geographies I have just described were still to be mapped.

On September 23, 1964, the morning after Bud died, the *Fort Myers News-Press* published a short article: "LaBelle Man Shoots Self." This is an accurate headline, a lithe, pithy rendering of the facts. A man in LaBelle, Florida, shot himself. It was intentional, and there was "no apparent reason," though he had recently been complaining of back pain. A man in LaBelle, fifty years old, sent his two teenage children out back, and then walked out the front door and shot himself on the porch. A man was in LaBelle while his wife was away in Tacoma, Washington, to assist with the birth of a grandchild. Before the child was born, that man shot himself. "No reason could be ascribed to the shooting." There was laundry that needed hanging in LaBelle, and so a man sent his twin children to hang it in the backyard. While they did, this man turned a .22 caliber pistol to his temple. "He had been having back trouble, his daughter said." He left no note. LaBelle man shoots self.[1]

Little more than a half-century later, Robin's body would be found in his Oakland, California, home. No news articles covered this event, but stories have found their way through a series of whispered networks, and have by now concretized into a narrative: Oakland man hangs self. A neighbor was out for a walk and noticed that Robin's two cats, Desmond and Louie, were running amok. The neighbor also noticed that the front door was slightly ajar. He approached it, calling Robin's name, and then he walked inside. Oakland man hangs self. No note was left. In the days leading up to this event, a series of phone calls and text messages pointed toward its potential occurrence. This became clear in retrospect, if not in the happening. Oakland man hangs self. He left no note.

For two hundred days in 1964, my paternal grandfather, Bud, and my best friend, Robin, were both alive. I have sometimes wondered if those two hundred days—between the birth of a boy who would much later become my most intimate confidant, and the death of a man I would never meet but who would nonetheless haunt my entire life—might not be, in some strange way, my origin story, my golden days, my *once upon a time*.

ii. All flesh

Omnis caro

Here is another darkened space: a cinema's screening room. As the lights dim, a beam shoots forth from a tiny window in the back. The audience stills and hushes as the film's first images flicker and gleam from the pristine screen.

Here is the opening scene: a teenage girl wanders through an old southern family house. She seems to feel something like dislocation in every room. In the front, she listens as two young women read an erotic excerpt from *The Godfather*; they shoo her away. She moves to the kitchen, where an eccentric older woman describes an injury to her hand. The girl stands apart, an anthropologist observing, before furtively slipping out of the room. She moves hastily through a den filled with men watching football on a small television and screaming at the young children making a ruckus nearby. She emerges onto a screened porch, where a man lounges on a bench reading *Madame Bovary*. We learn from her voiceover,

> Nobody else in my family ever seemed interested in me. But Uncle Frank was different. He was a college professor, and he lived in New York City. He used aftershave. His fingernails were always clipped. And he wore a gold chain underneath his shirt. I could listen to him talk all day. He was the only adult that I knew who looked me in the eye, who was curious about what I had to say, and who liked to make me laugh.

This is *Uncle Frank*, a film first released at the Sundance Film Festival in Park City, Utah, in January 2020, shortly before the opening salvo of a pandemic closed cinemas and theaters around the world. Set in 1973, the film tells the story of Frank Bledsoe, a gay middle-aged university professor who returns to his native South Carolina for his father's funeral. As the film proceeds through its opening scene, Uncle Frank, played delicately by Paul Bettany, also finds himself hovering on the periphery of every room, drawn into focus only by his father's occasional bursts of rage. We are in South Carolina, but we might as well be in William Faulkner's Mississippi, or Carson McCullers's Georgia, or my own Alabama: time moves slowly in these scenes, and is punctuated by traumas large and small, all in the soft focus of humid nights and afternoons. Young Betty is fourteen, and she wants to be a majorette, and she wishes people would call her Beth. Of all the characters who populate her world, it is only Uncle Frank who truly sees her.

A few years later, Beth has enrolled at the university where Frank teaches literature. She meets and starts dating another student, Bruce; one night, he takes her to a party at her uncle's apartment. It is here where, as she drinks with her uncle's bohemian friends, Beth learns what the earlier clues—jewelry, aftershave, manicured nails, *Madame Bovary*—had implied: that Frank is gay. She also learns that he has been living in this apartment with his partner, Wally, for the last decade. Too drunk to return to the dorms after the party, Beth spends the night. At breakfast the following morning, Frank receives a telephone call from his mother telling him that his father (and Beth's grandfather) has died.

Frank, Beth, and Wally set out on a long drive to South Carolina. As they make their way south, and later during the wake and funeral, Frank's troubled history with his father unfolds in a jumbled series of sepia-toned flashback scenes. We learn of Frank's first love at the age of sixteen: a boy from school named Sam. We watch the friendship blossom and grow, their secret intimacy building in a crescendo until, in a horrific climax, Frank's father discovers them in flagrante in Frank's bedroom one afternoon. We hear Frank's father unleash condemnation upon him: "you're gambling with your very soul, son, opening yourself up to that sickness. . . . It's perversion. God hisself [*sic*] will turn his back on you, cast you into the lake of fire."[2] We hear his threats to kill both boys if they ever see each other again. We see Frank discover a letter Sam has left for him: "I'll never be normal. I am a pervert, I am a queer. Forgive me. Sam." We watch as Frank runs to search for him at a lake where, in previous scenes, they had swum together, entwining their arms and legs in sensual embraces. We learn that Sam has drowned himself, and that Frank has carried profound guilt and shame for this early departure throughout his life.

Although it seems in the film that he might, Frank never follows Sam's lead to suicide, even after his father's last will and testament publicly outs and disinherits him. In what reads like a fabulist's fantasy for anyone raised in the twentieth-century South, this violent rejection has the effect of restoring Frank to his family rather than casting him out. He and Wally are welcomed and embraced in the final scene: "whatever you are, no problem," his brother says. "My hairdresser is gay," says his sister-in-law; "he is the most hilarious person in the whole world." Aunt Butch tells him of a dancer she knew, a "backwards bobby" whom everyone called "the tissy pretzel." This was the best that any of them could do. "Mothers know," his own mother tells him as she wraps him up in her arms. The film closes with everyone gathered in the backyard, a reconstructed scene of familial belonging. But despite the happy ending of its final moments, the narrative message of *Uncle Frank* is clear: this story of queer emergence and reconciliation is also a story of queer suicide.

This imbrication of queerness with suicide was not a new trope when *Uncle Frank* premiered in 2020; it was as old as film itself. A century earlier, in 1919, the first film offering an explicit and sympathetic portrait of homosexuality began and ended with suicides. Produced in Germany shortly after the Great War, *Anders als die Andern* (*Different from the Others*) was written and directed by filmmaker Richard Oswald. In the opening scene, a violinist named Paul Körner (played by Conrad Veidt, who would later appear in *The Cabinet of Dr. Caligari* and *Casablanca*) is reading a newspaper. There he finds three obituaries for men who have killed themselves "for unknown reasons." Paul immediately attributes these suicides to the "sword of Damocles of [Paragraph] 175," the German law that criminalized homosexuality. He imagines the fatal impact of it and similar policies making "life impossible" for an "endless procession" of homosexual people "from all times and countries," figures who appear to him in a dreamlike vision.

At his concert that evening, Paul meets a young man named Kurt who asks to become his student. They begin to meet for lessons, and over time they seem to fall in love. But soon, a mysterious man who has watched them walking through a park arm-in-arm begins blackmailing Paul. After repeated extortions, Paul eventually refuses to continue paying him. He reports the man for "felonious blackmail," and the man reports Paul for violating Paragraph 175. At the trial, the judge rebukes the man, sentencing him to three years in prison for blackmail. The judge then sympathetically tells Paul that he is not empowered to acquit him given the explicit clarity of the law; he regretfully sentences Paul to a week in prison.

For many viewers in 1919, Paul's sentence would have recalled the trials, imprisonment, and tragic death of Oscar Wilde twenty years before. In the film, Paul leaves the courtroom to discover, as with Wilde's widely sensationalized trials, that the news of the verdict has already spread: he is shunned by friends on the street and condemned by his father, whose response is to remark, "If he's a man of honor, he'll know what he has to do now." Paul's concert tour and contracts are abruptly cancelled by the agency representing him. Exhausted and filled with despair, he slowly but determinedly swallows numerous pills. Alone in his parlor, he collapses in a chair and dies. When Kurt hears of Paul's suicide, he rushes to his deathbed. He lashes out at the others in the room, declaring his love for Paul and his intention to take his own life, too. But he is urged to reconsider by his sister, who recently attended a lecture on the "natural variation" of homosexuality by a doctor who has also come to mourn. With their encouragement, Kurt decides to "keep on living to change the prejudices whose victim—one of countless many—this dead man has become."[3]

The doctor in this climactic scene was played by the renowned sexologist Magnus Hirschfeld, who was also the film's cowriter. By the time *Different from the Others* was made, Hirschfeld had already amassed an archive documenting homosexual and transgender subcultures in numerous cities, including Berlin, Chicago, Tangier, Tokyo, and Rio de Janeiro.[4] After returning to Germany from traveling in 1897, he cofounded the Scientific-Humanitarian Committee, an organization focused on advocacy for people we would today identify as queer and trans, and especially on repealing Paragraph 175. In 1919, the same year *Different from the Others* was made, he founded the Institut für Sexualwissenschaft (Institute for Sexual Science) in Berlin. As he told it numerous times throughout his life, Hirschfeld escalated his commitment to this work early in his career because of a suicide: one of his former patients, an army officer, had written him a letter before killing himself on the eve of his wedding. Although the young man did not explicitly name his sexuality, he wrote romantically of "that which nearly strangled my heart" and noted that Hirschfeld's advocacy for the abolition of Paragraph 175 "sweetens the hour of my death."[5]

As Heike Bauer has beautifully documented in her book *The Hirschfeld Archives*, Magnus Hirschfeld's work in and beyond Berlin was transformative in producing research documenting the vast diversities of queer and trans lives, fostering education and advocacy, and marshaling resources so that queer and trans people could thrive despite profoundly oppressive legal, economic, and social obstacles. For example, Hirschfeld himself provided counseling for many, and conducted groundbreaking research on what we today categorize as gender-affirming care for trans people. At the height of its work during the Weimar era in Germany, the Institute also opened a Museum of Sex to the general public. But in the 1930s, the Institute became a particular target of the Nazi Party. On May 6, 1933, its facilities were stormed by Nazi-affiliated groups, which ransacked its archives and destroyed most of its materials at a massive book burning held several days later.

By 1919, when Hirschfeld had founded his institute, the association of homosexuality with suicide—the notion that queer people would (and for some commentators, *should*) end their own lives—was already an archetype. Historian Samuel Clowes Huneke has traced the emergence of this archetype to the nineteenth and early-twentieth centuries, when the very idea of sexual *identity*—as distinct from sexual *practices*—began to take shape in the clinical and intellectual work of sexologists like Hirschfeld. Stories of suicides eventuated by the public outing (and often the blackmail) of those who engaged in homosexual sexual practices, and those whose gender identities did not the match the gender assigned at their birth, extend much further back in the historical record. But in this era, the disproportionate incidence of suicide among people we might today describe as queer or trans was explicitly marshaled in arguments aimed at overturning policies like Paragraph 175. Huneke demonstrates how this rhetorical deployment of queer suicide—its use in constructing a political argument—"embedded itself in representations of homosexuality precisely at that moment when doctors, scientists, and political reformers were defining it as a sociomedical identity."[6] As a result, "Suicide became the hallmark of literary depictions of gay men and lesbians" in aesthetic productions of the era—poetry, novels, and visual art of various kinds—and promulgated an aesthetic currency in which queerness and suicide were not only correlated but glamorized: the archetype "crafted a narrative that not only led gay characters inexorably into death but exulted in the beauty and meaningfulness of their suicides."[7]

"As the twentieth century progressed," Huneke notes, "that correlation of homosexuality and suicide increasingly colored depictions of gay life," solidifying the archetypal status of the trope and leading to ever-more narratives of queer suicide, especially in literature and film.[8] Where queerness appeared, death was likely to follow: if not as a result of violence from others or, later, as a result of a viral plague, then as a result of the queer person's own intentions. In other words, if we carve out that long stretch of time between *Different from the Others* and the uncannily similar *Uncle Frank*, we might identify the period from 1919 to 2020 as a century of queer emergence and equally as a century of queer suicide—that is, as a century in which queer emergence was accompanied by queer suicide. The archetype became so fixed in public consciousness that even when queerness was not central to a given narrative, it could still function as a fulcrum for that narrative's plot. To cite a well-known example: in the mid-1970s, actor and director Max Baer Jr. approached country music star Bobbie Gentry about adapting her chart-topping ballad "Ode to Billie Joe" into a feature-length film, *Ode to Billy Joe*. The song, which had been released in 1967, told the story of a teenage girl learning that a local teenage boy had killed himself by jumping from the local Tallahatchie Bridge.[9] The song gives no definitive answers as to the boy's reasons for wanting to die. In order to flesh out the story, screenwriters for the film made the narrative whole by giving the suicide an explanation: inconsolable with conflicted desire and shame, Billy Joe confesses that he had had sex with his sawmill boss Dewey the previous night.[10] In other words, the trope of queer suicide was by this time so widely understood that it could be reliably instrumentalized as a simple but critical plot device in a narrative that is not otherwise queer.

But this century in which queer suicide became an archetype rings with personal resonance, too: my grandfather Bud, who would kill himself in 1964, was born in 1914; my best friend, Robin, who was born in 1964, died by his own hand in 2019. Within that stretch of time that almost exactly overlaps with the century of film between *Different from the Others* and *Uncle Frank*, other beloveds have likewise chosen to die. That roughly hundred-year span is both a collective and a deeply personal history: a current within the history of queerness itself, and the context for my own grappling for queer emergence amid sudden leavings and shadowy loss. This is the story of how those histories intertwine; this is an archive for remembering those who are gone; this is a testament to the aching labor of mourning; this is a plea for mercy.

iii. And he shall be like a tree

Et erit tamquam lignum

Once upon a time is an ancient opening. Its earliest known form, *onys oppon a daye*, was recorded as early as 1380. Its

INTROITUS

current phrasing emerged by the late sixteenth century, seducing audiences into fables and folklore and signaling a series of fanciful, sometimes frightful, happenings. In its modest, hazy turn to a distant land and a distant age, and in the precision of its uncertainty, the phrase abandons the immediacy of our present and orients us toward the fantasy of an obscure past. *Once upon a time* compels us to unmoor from the known here-and-now and give ourselves over to narrative, to the story and its telling. "Distance makes possible," writes Maria Konnikova about the etymology of the phrase, "what immediacy cannot accomplish."[11]

Once upon a time, a boy was born, and then a man died. Each was unknown to the other, but they would die in similar ways. And in the duration between those events, another soul sought its origins, but only in hindsight. He located himself, who had then not yet been born, on a road halfway between the boy and the man. There he met two others, a girl and boy who, years later, would similarly disappear. He sought to witness these disappearances again and again, one right after the other, then jumbling their original sequence, then trying them out as coterminous. He sought their ripples, the way they bent the nature of time; he plumbed the evacuations they left behind. He reconstructed their narratives, told them backward and otherwise. He gathered their meanings, intended or not. He sought to recover *once upon a time*.

Suicide compels its survivors on an endless search for previously undiscovered harmonies, which can sometimes feel like resolutions. Birmingham is halfway between Fort Worth and LaBelle. Bud died on the autumnal equinox, Robin on the summer solstice: the longest day and a day with evenly distributed light and dark, fixed in a fatal conjunction. Once upon a time, a solstice and an equinox drew apart and then converged. In orienting ourselves to the fantasies occasioned by *once upon a time*, we give ourselves over to narrative as a site of becoming that which we may not otherwise become. On the day Alec died, someone killed the largest alligator ever measured in Florida; the alligator was sixty-five years old. On the day Lana died, Queen Elizabeth II fell off her horse and broke her wrist. Some conjunctions sound like fairy tales, with or without *once upon a time*.

Suicide resonates in two temporal directions: backward, into a past defined by suppressed knowing—its survivors are haunted by all the things we should have sensed—and forward, into a future contoured entirely by absence. This quality of suicide is more haunted than regret. It is an eccentric form of melancholy, repetitively replayed, peculiar to those who, despite all our strivings toward self-forgiveness, convince ourselves that we knew, and wish that we had then acknowledged the knowing. And this quality of suicide forever alters the very texture of time: the survivor will forever be caught between that past of unclaimed knowing and that future of ineffable loss, which together become a new denotation for *the present*, a new condition for *presence*. *Suicide* may be a noun, but its resonance acts like a verb.

Once upon a time, a boy was born in the middle-west, where there were no mountains. This boy, as he grew, was frightened of the sky, and of clouds, and of the wind in particular, because there were no trees or higher lands to break its relentless pursuit, the way it followed him wherever he went. The flat horizons he saw seemed harbingers of monotonous doom—or rather, of the doom of monotony. Winters were long but at least brought snow, which altered the shapes and textures of the otherwise changeless land. The boy's father sometimes sang a song that told the story of his own father, who had been lost in a frightful flash. Like the wind, this song frightened the boy, but he grew used to it over time.

Once upon a time, he ached to leave. He knew himself then, knew that the longings that grew in his chest moved with a different rhythm than the longings of other boys. This he knew to keep secret, even at such a young age. He listened for similar rhythms in the people he sometimes met, but he didn't yet know this as *seeking*; he was merely paying attention. When, still a child, this boy's parents took him and his younger brother and moved back to their native lands, his seeking became more complex. Here, deep in the South, different dangers lurked. The sky was neither so large nor so threatening, the clouds were not so intimidating, and the wind no longer sang in solo. There were more trees, which broke up the wind's howling with their own smaller, crinklier sounds. He loved the sounds the trees made, but he feared what may be hiding within or behind them. Some years passed, and as he began to learn how to sing to his secret rhythm, his seeking became more nuanced still. Sent to a school that was built around a lake, where freedom took on a more robust vernacular, he finally heard rhythms that seemed to harmonize with his own. This began to feel like what others meant by *home*. He listened closely, and with their rhythms now in sync, two others became like kin until, with what sounded like the worst kind of silence, they suddenly took their leave.

So he left that place of loud trees for a distant city on the left edge of land, where the boy found himself among many whose rhythms sang like his own. One in particular became his friend, and together they spent many moons marveling at the beauty of their rhythms and puzzling over why they had had to hide them for so long. But one day, like his father's father and like his two schooltime friends, this friend departed without warning. After, as the boy sat in terrible wonder, seeing his friend leave again and again in a nightmare of repetitions, he began to notice the wind again, and how it followed him as in his youth when he sang alone. And so, once upon a time, having outlived his childhood, and having lost in a frightful flash friends whose rhythms had so closely matched his own, he began his seeking again, this time casting backward beyond even his long-ago birth. He sought another time for himself, before he had yet *been* himself. He remembered his father's song—and knowing that singing could sometimes solve mysteries, he began to sing one of his own: "Once upon a time, a boy was born, and then a man died. Once upon a time, the boy also died, and two others besides. They did it themselves, gone without goodbyes. No reason was given, no notes were left, once upon a time."

II
Dies Irae

But for him it was his last afternoon as himself. . . .
The current of his feeling failed; he became his admirers.
    W. H. AUDEN, "IN MEMORY OF W. B. YEATS" (1939)

Exit, pursued by a bear.
Enter a Shepherd.
    WILLIAM SHAKESPEARE, *THE WINTER'S TALE* (1623)

Let us imagine a morning, a Friday in late June. In the place where I live, a coastal neighborhood in San Diego, June days tend to begin with a shallow but tenacious marine layer of clouds that we call the Fog. Summer comes later here, building slowly to its searing peak in September. But June is a gentle month, almost timeless in its repetitions: The Fog, an ocean breeze, chills at night. In June it becomes possible to believe that the sun will never scorch you, the dry Santa Ana winds will never blow, and wildfires will be nothing more than stories from other lands. Let us imagine a morning like this: filtered gray light, ocean air winding its way up the canyon, no noise but rustling leaves. It is nine o'clock: no excuse not to be awake by now, no excuse not to have showered, made the coffee, fed the cat. Let us imagine me—though you may know not who I am or how I appear—standing at the front windows, mug in hand, watching the world outside as it shifts gently into gear.

Now let us imagine that with the suddenness of an ancient god's wrath, an earthquake occurs. This is no minor trembler, no slow-rolling shift, no jolt that is gone as soon as it strikes. The earth rips apart, splitting itself into caverns where, just before, a road stretched or a house stood. All appears, at first, as a too-ripe fig left dangling on its tree, cracked open to reveal its strange core, its peculiar flecks of flowers and seeds. Standing at the window, one can see that all has fallen but this house, this window, this quiet observer who thinks, in his shock, that he must still be asleep. This must be a dream that has slowly distorted itself, as dreams sometimes do, into a panicked nightmare, traumas layered just under the skin of its narrative lines, terrors hiding just beyond familiar forms.

Sometimes earthquakes are real, sometimes earthquakes are metaphors, and sometimes, when our world splits apart, we are unable to tell the difference. On a day in late June in 2019, just after nine o'clock in the morning, I received a telephone call that I had not anticipated. My best friend of

DIES IRAE 33

many years, Robin, had died, and his sister was calling to tell me. I turned from the front, where the windows face south, and walked quickly to a room in the back of the house, where the patio doors face east. I stood for a moment, listening to her calm but heavy voice, before crumpling to the floor. She told me he died, but she did not at first say how. "Are you sure?" I asked. She was sure. And then, without recognizing my own voice, I said, "He did it himself."

Robin's sister paused. "He did it himself," she said back to me, and at first I thought: how strange this is, a little myth—Echo and Narcissus—played out on the telephone. "He did it himself," the searcher croons; "he did it himself" from the shade. And then I gasped as the heaving breaths, the ones you only know if loss has slammed into you unawares, overtook me. Between gusty sobs, I heard myself ask, "How?" Robin's sister paused. "Are you sure you want to know?" I considered the question. "I'm sure," I said.

And then she told me.

* * * * *

In a series of diary entries written in October 1933, several months before his thirtieth birthday, celebrated designer Cecil Beaton recorded the sudden death of his younger brother Reggie. Initially in shock, Cecil described his immediate reaction as "sinisterly unmoved" until, the following morning, "I began now to react myself. A lump gathered in my throat. My eyes swelled. I could not keep back a stream of tears, wept quietly over breakfast while Daddy remained calm."[1] At the formal inquest for Reggie's death, the driver of an underground train was called to testify. This is what he said:

> At eleven o'clock I was driving my train into Piccadilly Station. About seventy-five yards from the tunnel opening stood a man without a hat. He was about

a yard from the edge of the platform, looking straight in front of him across the tracks. As I came within a few feet of him, he raised his hands to his head and dived in front of the train.[2]

Newspapers across the United Kingdom covered the story of this young pilot from the Royal Air Force who had died so suddenly. In a transcript of the inquest published by the *Liverpool Echo*, the judge asked the driver, "You know the difference between a person who makes a deliberate jump in front of a train, and a person who comes over giddy and falls?" "I think I know," the driver replied. "Was there any question of his falling?" "No, I think it was a dive." "Deliberate?" "Yes."[3]

Despite the family's hopes for a finding of accidental death, the judge at the inquest ruled that Reggie died by suicide. Cecil was distraught, unmoored by both the evidentiary facticity of the inquest and the now-public reality of the judge's ruling. He wrote of his wanderings through memories of Reggie: "I am thinking now of all the days Reggie and I spent together. We grew up in great intimacy, fighting a lot but really devoted. It was only later that we drifted apart. I felt shy of him as an adult."[4] He wrote of Reggie's sounds: "I won't ever again hear Reggie calling Becky, telephoning to young ladies or talking to Manley in a plummy voice";[5] and, later, "I remembered Reggie's heavy tread on his way up to his bedroom; his calling Manley and his rather breathless, 'Beck, Beck, Beck, Beck,' to the dog."[6] He wrote of Reggie's body: "Recently, I noticed how much less hairy Reggie's hands were than mine. I think of his wristwatch and his fingernails . . ."[7]; and "I kept seeing Reggie's fresh, clear-cut features, his good nose, his eagle, lidless eyes so direct yet soft in their gaze, his forehead wrinkled in surprise."[8]

For Cecil, who had long before acknowledged and embraced his homosexuality, surviving his brother's suicide seemed paradoxical, incommensurate with their divergent roles within their family and their places in the world at large. The day of Reggie's funeral, he wrote of being unable to sleep the night before, haunted by this conundrum:

> The whole disaster struck me now as some incongruous nightmare. It was unlike anything that could possibly happen to us. If anyone in the family were ever to have been tempted to suicide, then why not me? . . . The others, Reggie in particular, couldn't have been more normal. It was nothing short of impossible that it should be *his* face in the papers under "killed by a train." It was an absurd unreality that *he* should be the "Flying Officer" on the placards. . . . What error of fate could overnight have overwhelmed us like this?[9]

As his grief deepened, Cecil described in anguished detail the visitations from Reggie's friends, the extensive offerings of flowers and wreaths, and the funeral itself, filled with "painful kisses, silent handshakes . . . faces swollen red with tears." At the gravesite, as Reggie's casket was lowered into its vault, torrents of sobs struck Reggie's parents and siblings; of his own response, Cecil wrote simply, "I was howling."[10]

Several years later, his father sold the family's London home at 61 Sussex Gardens. Cecil mourned its dispossession, remembering how his slow self-emergence had thrived there: "I had great fun trying to make it appear as grand as we could afford. It was my ambition to make each room look like a stage set . . . a circus of many colors. Even today, I like the look of that circus." But he remembered, too, the ruin that was made of the home on the day that Reggie died, a day that had forever changed his relationship to the place: "then came the terrible night when Baba was waiting up for me. By the glow of the orange light she told me that Reggie had been killed. The house knew death: black scenes and wreaths stretching from the conservatory through to the drawing room."[11] The day of Reggie's death had occasioned a shift in the world of the home: even the warm, "familiar Italian light giving an orange glow in the hall" was hued, now, with Reggie's absence. Cecil closed his mournful goodbye with a query: "I wonder if 61 Sussex Gardens can entirely cast off our memories just because it is an inanimate thing?"[12]

* * * * *

I have heard this story told so many times, it sometimes seems like it is my story—like it happened to me. My father and his twin sister, fifteen years old, have just returned home from school. It is hot outside. Their father asks them to hang some freshly laundered bedclothes on the lines in the back. Their mother is away in Tacoma. She is visiting their older sister, who is pregnant with her second child; her first child had not lived long. And so my father and his sister, along with several other siblings, have been left in LaBelle with their father, who has rediscovered his taste for whiskey.

Their father is something of a Renaissance man: mechanically minded, he can tinker with any engine, any machine, and quickly learn its inner logics. He has built ships, wielding his welding flame as nimbly as an embroidery needle. He is deft with farming and husbandry, and once devised a system of breeding minnows that resulted in plump, perfect bait. Here in LaBelle, he has an orange grove that blooms the most fragrant flowers and pops out fruit so robust with dripping intensity that my father will spend the rest of his life trying to find approximates in the citrus sections of countless markets. And he, my father's father, can sing, his deep, voluptuous baritone resembling the texture of a well-polished mahogany plank. But on this day, having rediscovered his taste for whiskey, he is unsettled as a storm. The day before, he had collapsed into my father's arms, tightly strung with a throbbing ache in his injured back, and gasped, "Why must I suffer?" My father had had no reply, just stood and held him, then shifted to right him back on his feet.

They are whipping the bedclothes like kites, casting them up and over the line. The weather is fair and hot, a good day for drying. They are just home from school, and knowing how quickly his moods can turn, they are doing exactly what their father told them to do. They hear a loud snap, a pop, a bang. My father's twin sister looks at him, and he looks back at her. My father describes this particular moment of this particular day in precisely the same way every time he speaks of it: "We heard a sound like a firecracker. I knew what it meant." I used to wonder: What did it mean that he knew? How did he know? Or rather, why did he know? What was the prehistory of that gunpowder blast and its echo among the trees? What was its texture; what was its tone? How was it different from other sounds, from the firecrackers they sometimes lit or the trees that sometimes fell? What secret knowledge—what prior witnessing—had led him with certainty to translate the import of that sound? How did the sound disclose the scene of its creation—my grandfather slumped on the front porch of the house—and the intent that had occasioned it?

My father says that he knew. He and his sister went into the house to look for their father, who was not there. My father told his sister to wait and went out to the front porch. There his father lay crumpled in the corner, a pistol near his hand. My father backed away, afraid not of his father's ruined body but rather of the gun in reach. My father went inside. "Daddy's dead," he told his sister. "He did it himself." My father had known.

I used to wonder: how had he known? And then that day in June 2019 occurred, and Robin's sister called; and after the initial shock, I didn't need to be told: he did it himself. Where had those words come from as I collapsed on the floor staring east through the glass, and why did they take their particular form? Were they lines handed down from 1964, yawning across a continental expanse—Florida to California—and groaning like a tether? Had they inscribed themselves onto my very being, like a poem memorized as a child, like a lyric from a song that echoes long after it has played, so that on that day, a foggy Friday in June, they burst forth without hesitation as if, all along, they had been lying in wait for their inevitable cue?

* * * * *

Eighteen months before Cecil Beaton's brother dove into the path of an oncoming underground train, the young poet Hart Crane leaped from a ship on which he was traveling from Veracruz to New York, and disappeared under the waters between Havana and Miami. He was wearing pajamas and an overcoat. Several witnesses reported that he shouted, "Goodbye, everyone," before he jumped. His body was never recovered.

It was April 26, 1932. Hart had been traveling with his friend Peggy Cowley. The previous day, the ship had docked in Havana; Peggy went shopping while Hart went wandering. They planned to meet at a restaurant that Hart knew, but by some confusion, they missed one another. When they eventually reconnected back aboard the ship, Peggy was angry; she knew that Hart had been drinking, and she believed he had just forgotten her. He tried to convince her the mistake was hers: she had gone to the wrong restaurant, and he had feared that she had been abducted. The squabble was never resolved, and as Peggy returned to her berth, Hart returned to the whiskey, drinking himself into such furies that, on two occasions, the captain instructed his officers to nail shut the door to Hart's room with him inside.

Testimonies later revealed that before he had been forcibly detained, Hart had gone cruising below decks, propositioning cabin boys and sailors. At some point he was violently rebuffed: when he reemerged the following morning and found Peggy, his face and body were bloodied and bruised. The attackers had taken a ring and his wallet. Hart feared that these items would be used, once the ship docked, as evidence against him in a lewdness charge; as biographer Paul Mariani describes, he told her that "he'd really disgraced himself. Everything was lost. It was time to go."[13] In a 1988 documentary, now much older but still haunted by that day's events, Peggy recalled trying to convince Hart that perhaps some breakfast would help him feel better. "They brought in a menu to him, and I don't think he left one item out. Just an enormous meal. He wanted to be filled with something. And then I went back to be dressed for lunch, and all of a sudden the boat stopped. And I gave a scream and said 'Hart,' and I went out to the deck."[14]

After their breakfast, Hart wandered back to the promenade deck before climbing over the rails and diving into the water. His "Goodbye, everyone" confirmed what his friends and familiars already knew: he did it himself. Other passengers rushed to the edge of the deck, and several reported seeing his body just before it vanished; one claimed that he was attempting to rescue himself, swimming back toward the ship, but other witnesses denied this possibility. The captain slowed the ship, as is customary when someone goes overboard, and began circling a broad ring of waves. Searchers were sent out on lifeboats, but there was no trace of the young poet, and eventually the ship returned to its route. Three days later, hours before the ship was due to arrive in New York, the *New York Times* reported the incident, suggesting only that Hart had been mourning his father's recent death. The story included the message received by wireless three days earlier from the ship's captain: "Hart Crane went overboard at noon today. Body not recovered."[15]

* * * * *

I do not know many things about the day of Lana's death in 1994, not for sure. I know that while on the highway not far from campus, she drove straight into a police car responding to another collision. I do not know where she was going or coming from, though there are rumors. I know that there were no skid marks, no indication that she had swerved or tried to stop. I know that among those of us who had been close to her, many saw the crash as the fiery conclusion to a downward spiral of self-destruction that had defined the previous year. Whether she had intentionally driven her car into that police cruiser in a spectacular final gesture was an open question: some felt she had, others didn't. Either way, there seemed to be a tragic inevitability to this particular end. It both was and was not a suicide. It both was and was not a surprise.

I know that when I returned to my Chicago apartment one evening, my roommates had left me a series of scrawled notes near the telephone: call Kelly; call your stepmother; stepmother called again; important, call home, somebody died. I know that I called my friend Kelly first and that she did not answer. I know that I then called my stepmother, who told me what had happened, and who then put my youngest stepbrother on the phone. He was still a student at the school. He told me they had a town hall in the library that morning, and the headmaster told everyone that Lana had died. He asked me when I had last seen her—"Last month," I said, "when I was home." He told me he was sorry. I know that by then I was sitting on the floor in the hall, and I remember shivering: an arctic blast had enveloped Chicago and it was well below freezing that night, a kind of midwestern cold that infuses every atom of your body as if the sun has never shone.

I know that eleven years later, a younger alumnus of our school published a fictionalized account of her death in a young adult novel that was wildly popular, and that this novel launched what has become an enormously successful career for him. I know that he interviewed some of Lana's closest friends to gather stories about her. I know that his book was later adapted into a television series, and that this series was popular, too. I know how it felt to hear him describe the book and the series as *fiction*. I know that many of us who knew her well were made profoundly uncomfortable, and in some cases angry, by the book and later the series. In his version of events, the character based on Lana—the central and titular character in the book—died when her car collided with a police cruiser that had stopped to respond to a jack-knifed truck. There were no skid marks or other indications that she had attempted to slow, stop, or swerve. In his version of events, she had been drinking with friends on campus. She had driven away in a rush after realizing that she had forgotten the anniversary of her mother's suicide. She was driving in the direction of her mother's gravesite, and she died instantly upon impact. Upon learning of her death the following morning, the narrator begins a quest to uncover the truth of whether she intended to crash and die. He never does.

What I know about the day of Alec's death in 1997, I know from a story published in a student magazine he cofounded at his college in North Carolina. Sometime between two and four in the morning on a September Tuesday, he parked his car close to the outer wall of his apartment building. He then threaded a hose from the exhaust pipe through a window to his living room. He started the engine, went back inside, and lay down on his couch. His body was discovered later that afternoon by a student leaving a nearby painting class. The medical examiner ruled the death a suicide. At a memorial service held on the campus several days later, a German professor read from a journal Alec had kept in his seminar on Franz Kafka: "Everyone waits. I am also waiting, but I don't know what for."

When I heard the news, I was living in Chapel Hill, North Carolina, after returning from Sri Lanka, where I had spent the previous year. I was home alone one afternoon when a friend from our old school—the same Kelly as three years before—called to tell me the news. I remember confusion, the sense that I wasn't hearing her right, and then the sense that I was still asleep. I remember the shock of it once it sank in, the initial feeling that this wasn't right, that this couldn't be right. And then, as the hours rolled on, I remember feeling the first shades of what I later realized was survivor's guilt, which took the physical form of a deep, red blush every time I thought about it, like secret shame.

Because I had so recently moved back to the United States, I did not have a car. So a new friend who had never met Alec offered to drive me to the college town two hours away where he had been living and where a memorial service was being held for him. I do not remember the drive there. I do remember that when we arrived in the town, we could not find the memorial and no one we asked could help us, until eventually we realized that it was too late. The memorial was over. This was another failure, another unanswered letter or telephone call. As we turned the car back toward home, I quietly began to recite some half-remembered lines from the Irish writers Alec had loved so much, incantations that I hoped would draw him near. I recalled Auden's ode about Yeats's death: "You were silly like us; your gift survived it all," I whispered to Alec as if he could hear me, and said under my breath, "Earth, receive an honored guest." But it was the opening stanza of Auden's poem that spoke most distinctly to me: "*it was his last afternoon as himself,*" I thought, imagining the scene of Alec's apartment that day, and then, "*he became his admirers.*"[16] I felt him with me then, bequeathed to the air I breathed as Whitman had promised of his own eddied flesh. Again and again I felt myself blush, hot as coals, throughout our slow drive back to Chapel Hill.

* * * * *

One month after my grandfather died, on October 27, 1964, a young, queer dancer leaped from the fifth-floor window of a Greenwich Village apartment and fell to his death. Freddie Herko was twenty-eight years old, and he had been using amphetamines heavily for at least the previous year. He was staging a small performance. Mozart's *Coronation Mass* was playing, and Freddie's friend and former lover Johnny Dodd, whose apartment this was, sat and watched. Emerging from the bathroom, Freddie began to dance. He wore no clothes, but was scented with Johnny's cologne. He spun and whirled around the room, occasionally rushing toward the open window. As the *Sanctus* movement began—with its towering, archly dramatic instrumentals and vertiginous chorus— Freddie performed a "perfect jeté" out the window.[17] Johnny, the only spectator, claimed to have seen Freddie rise into the air outside and sail away long enough to carry him across Cornelia Street before plummeting then to the ground. He had spoken to friends before about doing a "suicide performance." Recovering from his shock a few days later, Johnny said of the scene in his flat, "It was obvious that Freddie had to do it now: the time and the place were right, the decor was right, the music was right."[18]

There are several versions of the story of the day that Freddie died, each of which has contributed to the mythology of the whole. In Steven Watson's telling, the morning of the final dance, Johnny had seen Freddie dancing frantically on a counter at a local diner. He gathered Freddie up and took him to his apartment, where Freddie drew himself a bath, pouring a bottle of Johnny's cologne into the water.[19] In Andy Warhol's telling, Freddie turned up at the apartment unannounced and climbed through a panel in the door. Johnny was there with some other friends—and after his bath, Freddie ushered all but Johnny out of the flat.[20] In Diane di Prima's version, Freddie had telephoned Johnny, and then had "come up to take a shower."[21] When he was finished, he put the *Coronation Mass* record on the phonograph and began to dance. All of these tellings end the same way: when the *Sanctus* began, Freddie performed a leap out the window, not even brushing its sill or jamb, and then flew before he fell.

Diane had met Freddie ten years earlier, in 1954. Freddie had been admitted to Juilliard that year to study piano, but upon seeing a performance of *Giselle* starring Igor Youskevitch, he decided to enroll in the American Ballet Theatre instead. After training in ballet and Merce Cunningham's modern technique, Freddie became a fixture in the downtown scene throughout the 1950s and early 1960s, a founding member of the Judson Dance Theater and the New York Poets Theatre, and a regular at Andy Warhol's Factory. Diane described their first meeting in this way: "He was sitting on a bench on the south side of [Washington Square P]ark, not far from the chess players. And crying because autumn always made him sad. Or so he said. . . . Freddie had a wit at once childlike and sardonic, a sense of play lightly colored over with a streetwise bitterness."[22] They had become fast friends, and over the course of the following decade, they would sometimes live together, share a lover, and engage each other's creative processes with an intensity bordering on obsession. Ten years after his death, she would publish a book of poems she had been writing for him since the day she first found him weeping on that bench in Washington Square.[23] In "November Poem," composed shortly after Freddie's death, she wrote, "I think of your leap a lot, the elegance of it, your brilliant fall to earth: / 'Let it come down'—our words, four days before. My tears on Sunday night. / You set me free. To dance, to make whatever can be made."[24]

In her memoir *Recollections of My Life as a Woman*, Diane remembers receiving a phone call from the artist Charles Stanley, who "flatly, but rather slowly and carefully" said, "Diane? I'm sorry to have to tell you this, but around five o'clock Freddie Herko jumped out of Johnny Dodd's window." Initially imagining a grave injury, Diane then "heard the silence around Charles' words" and realized that Freddie was dead:

> It was the finality of it I remember. A kind of stuck place—the end of the film cut off and burned so you never see it. Never know what was supposed to happen. All of a sudden it was too late to fix anything. To explain later, to let him in when Alan wasn't home. To let him use the shower. To be his friend . . . How tender and scared we both were, two battered kids trying to make sense of the world, make some beauty in it.[25]

As the news spread, friends began gathering at Diane's house, filling the rooms. Not knowing what else to do, Diane slipped out and called her friend Audre Lorde, "instinctively knowing she would know what this meant for me." Audre came and drove her "to Central Park, into a leafy, uninhabited space of trees and silence, and then she opened the car windows to let in the sharp smell of fallen leaves, and took me in her arms."[26] In the months that followed, every evening for a year after Freddie's death, Diane would light a stick of incense in her study and write to him until it had burned out. Later that fall, she wrote to him of that night:

> The day you died, I drove thru Central Park with Audre who had come to pick me up, to take me out of that house . . . so that I could come to terms somehow with the deed. We entered the park, there had been a fire, it had been so dry this fall, this summer too. The smell of the burning leaves, and of the dry leaves rotting on damp earth. A sharp, sharp smell, acrid high in the nostrils. . . . That smell in the park that night somehow closed the circle, cut me loose. A cycle was finished, a whole Odyssey. . . . It has all drawn gracefully to its natural conclusions. Like major chords at the end of a Mozart piece. . . . We buried you under the wind, the seeds were blowing.[27]

On October 28, 1964, the *New York Times* published a short description of Freddie's death: "A man tentatively identified as Fred Herko, a 29-year-old choreographer and dancer, jumped or fell to his death yesterday afternoon from a fifth-floor apartment at 5 Cornelia Street in Greenwich Village. The police said the apartment belonged to John Dodd, a lighting designer. Mr. Herko's address was unknown."[28]

* * * * *

"He did it himself," I breathed again into the phone that foggy Friday in June, though Robin's sister was no longer there. We had already hung up, and I remained on the floor, repeating those words over and over, each repetition a kind of keening. I do not know how long I sat there. I only know that when I turned back to the window of the patio doors and looked into my garden, the sun was peeking out from the clouds, much higher in the sky. There were shadows that barely stretched out from the bases of their primary objects, the places where those objects touched ground; it was likely nearly noon. My cat Izzy, ever sensitive to the sounds of my moods, had lain down next to me. I pulled myself up from the floor, thinking of my father's story, how the night before the fateful shot, his father collapsed into his arms and then was righted again. "Why must I suffer?" my grandfather had asked, a pleading worthy of Job. I walked to the linen closet and gathered old bedsheets, which I draped across the mirrors in my house. When I caught myself performing this ritual as if by rote, I wondered: What was I doing? Where had I learned this elaborate enactment of mourning? And on whose behalf was I doing it? I thought of that old Auden poem, the one that always made both Robin and me cry. But modern clocks cannot be stopped—no gears to jam, no hands to still, no key to stop winding.

"I should eat something," I told myself. I did, though I can't remember what, and I don't think I could possibly have tasted anything. And then I remembered that two friends—both of whom had also known and loved Robin—were coming for dinner that evening, and had likely not yet heard the news. I had promised to make a pot of cioppino; there were fresh cuts of fish and bags of mussels and shrimp in the kitchen, waiting for their slow simmer. There was a bowl of tomatoes that needed crushing, herbs that needed trimming, dishes that needed washing. These things I did before phoning my friends, partly because I needed to summon the nerve, partly because I wanted to say the dinner was already in process and we shouldn't cancel. I eventually called them, and I heard my own even keel as the shock rolled over and through them. I was witnessing my own catastrophe in the sounds of others. In the end we agreed: our dinner would be an ad hoc memorial for Robin, the cioppino a minor offering.

Later that evening, as I cleaned the kitchen, I thought about the false proximities of telephones. For that, too, was how I had learned of the deaths of Lana and Alec, from phone calls to Chicago in 1994 and to Chapel Hill in 1997. Each time, I remembered, I sat on the floor, phone still in hand. Each time, the world fell away as an echo played through the handset pressed to my ear. Later still, I lay in bed remembering the last time I saw Robin. That spring, I had been back in Oakland. Robin picked me up in his perennially shambolic car—papers and books everywhere, an empty drink can, detritus from this or that performance piece—and we drove to a favorite breakfast place to eat. He had lost weight, thinner than I'd ever seen him, his clothing draped like billowing sails across his frame. He was alert but dampened, still burbling with his trademark giggles, but these were somehow more clipped than usual, not as infectious, quick to come and quick to go. I asked him about this, and he said yes, it was true, I wasn't wrong. As we ate, he drifted through the full range of emotional projections: flaming joy at an anecdotal memory, fast tears when reciting a beautiful phrase, sharp indignation at a retold affront. *He is himself*, I thought, *just viewed through darkened glass.*

After breakfast, we went for one of our long, rambling walks through the tree-lined Oakland streets. We talked as we always had, flitting across subjects and sometimes digging in. Occasionally Robin would stop, as he always did, to speak with a stranger. He talked about giving up alcohol. He talked about the difficult breakup with his ex-partner and selling the house where they had lived. He talked about his newest job at a children's theater in Marin. He talked about his theatrical adaption of a book and an invitation to stage it in China. But most of all—he had warned me about this over breakfast—he wanted to apologize to me; he thought he owed me amends. Over many years, Robin and I had had only two major arguments, one of which had wrenched us apart and nearly ruined our friendship. As we walked that day, Robin told me that he couldn't remember what those arguments were about, but that he thought forgiveness was mine to give, not his. I remembered them, and this moment should have been a clue: Robin always held his ground. But it wasn't, and as we walked I listened without objection to his apologies for things that he could not remember doing.

When I finally fell asleep the night of that foggy day in late June, cioppino still warm in my belly, I dreamed of Robin and me together at our favorite bar in San Francisco. As we entered, we saw the bartender who was always there, the one who knew the perfect way to pour and shake my drink, the one whose smile beamed forth like a flashlight in a cave. "Oh look, the Twink and the Bear are back," he said in the dream, the same way he always had when we saw him in waking life. The dream replayed our entrance again and again: the Twink and the Bear were back over and over and over, with minor changes every time. In the final repetition, Robin lags behind and I cannot see him. I open the door and look inside. With a heavy stare, the bartender says, "The Bear is gone." I enter the bar, which is now noisy with people who no longer remember him. I stand alone.

When I woke from the dream the following morning, I found that for the first time in fifteen years, I had been overtaken by night sweats so prolific that my bedsheets and nightshirt were drenched. As I began to strip the bed, I realized that Robin had died on the summer solstice, and that for the rest of my life, the longest day of every year would be defined by his sudden and gutting departure.

* * * * *

Immediately before their deaths, Reggie Beaton, Hart Crane, and Freddie Herko all left the ground and soared, if only for a moment, into the air. They became weightless as they arced up and over a platform edge, a bulwark, a window's apron, and hovered there fleetingly before their momentum turned and their bodies fell. At that point, in that infinitesimal moment at the peak of their final arcs, they must have known with glaring certainty that they would spend the rest of their now-brief lives clenched by gravity in the rush of descent. But for a fraction of a moment on each of their respective final days—from a platform at Piccadilly Station, over the railing of the *Orizaba* ocean liner, through a window overlooking Cornelia Street—Reggie, Hart, and Freddie took flight.

III
Kyrie Eleison

She loved deeply, far more deeply than many a one who could fearlessly proclaim himself a lover. Since this is a hard and sad truth for the telling; those whom nature has sacrificed to her ends—her mysterious ends that often lie hidden—are sometimes endowed with a vast will to loving, with an endless capacity for suffering also, which must go hand in hand with their love.
  RADCLYFFE HALL, THE WELL OF LONELINESS (1928)

a longing, half pain and half rapture
    EUGENE COWLES AND MARY KAVANAGH,
      "FORGOTTEN" (1894)

i. Sorrowful is my soul

Tristis est anima mea

On Sunday, November 28, 1926, in Salt Lake City, Utah, Ruth Drake picked up her girlfriend Sarah Lundstedt in a roadster she had borrowed from her friend Alfred Burrell. Sarah had announced several months earlier that she was moving to Los Angeles to live with her family, who had relocated there from Salt Lake City the previous year. This was to be their last day together, and Sarah brought two pieces of sheet music with her so that they could sing together while they drove.[1] The music was for Irving Berlin's 1925 ballad "Remember"— *remember we found a lonely spot / and after I learned to care a lot / you promised that you'd forget me not / but you forgot / to remember*[2] —and for an 1894 song by Eugene Cowles and Mary Kavanagh called "Forgotten":

> Well, if forgetting
> be yearning with all my heart,
> With a longing, half pain and half rapture,
> For the time when we never shall part,
> If the wild wish to see you and hear you,
> To be held in your arms again,
> If this be forgetting, you're right, dear,
> And I have forgotten you then.[3]

Ruth was driving the car. She left her home and met Sarah outside a house owned by the Corliss family, where Sarah had been living for the last month. Previously, Sarah had lived in the Hillcrest Apartments in Salt Lake City, where she had moved after a bitter divorce; and at some point during her year there, Ruth had lived with her for a short time. As Alfred told reporters the following day, "One was working while the other went to school and kept house,"[4] though he did not specify who did what.

They drove north on the state highway to Ogden, ate lunch with Ruth's uncle, and then visited her grandfather. After these visits, they went to see a motion picture at a theater where Ruth's cousin worked. The cousin, named Edna, "was second prize winner in a beauty contest held in Salt Lake last summer, an honor of which Ruth was very proud."[5] When the film was over, they began driving back to Salt Lake City. Sometime around nine o'clock that evening, a police officer who was driving a "heavily laden truck" saw the two women standing outside the automobile on the side of the road, but did not stop. A short time later, Edward Jacobsen, who was also driving to Salt Lake City, saw the stalled roadster, but now the women were lying together on the ground nearby. "Ruth . . . was lying stretched out on her back, while Sarah's head rested on Ruth's arm."[6] Neither was conscious, but Sarah's body showed signs of life. Another passing motorist, Ted Mauser, stopped and helped load the women into his car, which he then drove to the hospital. By the time they arrived, both women were dead.

In the following day's issue of the *Salt Lake Telegram*, a series of sensational stories about the deaths dominated the front page. A reporter from the newspaper who had traveled to the scene discovered a Thermos near the roadster. Investigators found small crystals inside the Thermos, which were later determined to be cyanide. Further investigation revealed that Ruth had obtained the compound from Daynes Jewelry Store, where she was employed. Interviews with friends and acquaintances of both women deepened the mystery: Alfred recalled Ruth telling him that Sarah "told her to be careful, should they part, what kind of liquor she drank when they parted if she felt despondent, as it might contain poison."[7] Police detectives Lester Wire and M. D. McGinness devised three theories: first, that Ruth had poisoned herself and Sarah in a murder-suicide; second, that they had developed a "suicide pact"; and third—a twist on *Romeo and Juliet*—that after

Ruth killed herself, Sarah "became so grief stricken that she decided to follow her friend in death."[8] Over the course of the following week, and throughout the formal inquest, numerous commentators offered their varied opinions in the pages of several newspapers.

Alongside the journalists' obsession with this question of intent was their fascination with the women's letters, which had been discovered in their homes shortly after their deaths. Several newspapers printed examples of the letters verbatim, using their texts to construct a narrative for how the relationship had developed and evolved. The November 29 edition of the Provo *Evening Herald* relied on interviews with neighbors of Ruth's mother:

> An unusual and deep-rooted love is said to have been shown by Ruth towards her chum. It is said that these deep feelings have considerably worried Mrs. Drake, who feared that it was not well for her daughter to allow her feelings to run in that direction. Mrs. Drake is said to have told neighbors here that Ruth's love for Sarah was such that she would do anything for her.[9]

Mrs. Drake herself reported that Ruth had purchased a ring for Sarah, which she intended to give her before Sarah departed for Los Angeles. Ruth's friend Alfred suggested instead that Sarah had given Ruth the ring, which Ruth now intended to return. Either way, "The ring was later found on Miss Drake's body."[10]

Ruth and Sarah had first met several years earlier while their families were on a camping trip in Provo Canyon. Ruth traveled to Salt Lake City to enroll in college shortly thereafter, and was invited to stay with the Lundstedt family during her studies. Near the end of her time as a student and before returning home from Salt Lake City, Ruth wrote in a diary,

Last times at school today. Leave for home tomorrow.
Not supposed to make love to Sarah any more. Sarah
can come back any time. When she does, she can
have me—until then, I am to leave anyone else alone.
. . . Sarah says she has always loved me, but I don't
believe her. She will have to prove it. Time will tell. I
want everything or nothing.[11]

In letters, Sarah was equally passionate about Ruth. Several months later, while Ruth was visiting California, Sarah wrote,

If only you were here. I just want to get you, hold you
tight and give you one long kiss and then more and
more. . . . I love and adore you, darling mine. I want
you and some day I'm going to have you and no one
will matter. Just we two. And we'll be ideally happy.
Please come back to me soon, sweetheart mine. I
want you. I adore you, darling. I can't think of anything but you.[12]

Over the course of the following year, their relationship would experience intense periods of intimacy and similarly intense periods of turbulence. By the October before their deaths, after Sarah had announced her move to California, Ruth was sending letters like this:

I can never be happy without you. It is awful hard to
give you up entirely when I have loved you so and I
am so used to you. Everywhere I go and everything
I do hurts me because I can see you and the things
we did together. . . . Without the one you love, life is
worthless. What is there to live for without love?[13]

The letters are filled with this kind of florid prose, and equally with apologies from each about unnamed offenses. They wrote about each other's families, and whether each could love the other's as their own. They wrote about their arguments, and about their consternation over the impossibility of living openly as a couple. But mostly, they wrote of their love, their devotion, and their passion for one another. Alongside its reprint of the letters, the *Telegram* also printed an image of the two in hiking clothes, their arms around one another. In contradistinction to the floridly affectionate tone of these letters, for a decidedly less enthusiastic missive to a man in California whom her parents hoped would be her "sweetheart," Sarah wrote, "Clarence dear, if my fountain pen continues to function you may receive an answer to your letter."[14] This letter was never completed and never sent.

On December 1, the first day of the coroner's inquest, Leona Bennef read from a letter Sarah had sent to her two months earlier, in which Sarah related that Ruth had threatened to kill herself. This letter would be used by the jury to justify their verdict that Ruth's death was intentional. At the same inquest, medical examiner J. J. Galligan testified about his examination of the women's bodies: "Dr. Galligan gave it as his opinion that Sarah had taken the larger dose of the poison, and was further of the opinion that Sarah had not taken the poison until after Ruth had swallowed it, and that her action was prompted by hysteria." Concurring with this opinion, state chemist Herman Harms testified

> that a dose of two to five grams of cyanide of potassium would cause almost instant death. There were forty to sixty grams of the poison remaining in the stomachs of the girls not absorbed by the system. . . . According to the witness, one dose of the poison was taken slowly and deliberately and the other impulsively and in large quantity. . . . Mr. Harms testified that the poison had not been disguised by liquor or any other beverage and that it could not possibly have

been administered to any person . . . without its
nature being known.[15]

Despite the conclusions drawn by Galligan and Harms, and their implication that both deaths had been intentional, the inquest did not provide closure on the story: "The jury took more than an hour to find that Ruth came to her death through drinking a poisonous solution with premeditation. The jury was unable to determine whether Sarah's death was the result of suicide or otherwise."[16] Perhaps they had been swayed by Sarah's family's insistence that she was incapable of suicide, or perhaps they interpreted the medical examiner's use of "hysteria" to suggest that Sarah was acting against her own will. Whatever the case, newspapers seized upon the open mystery and continued publishing excerpts from the women's letters for several more days.

The tone of these press stories and the many negative allusions to Ruth and Sarah's relationship give some sense of the climate in which their love had bloomed. The *Salt Lake Telegram* coverage on November 29 included numerous gestures to their "strange friendship": they had an "unusual attachment," an "anomaly which has been in existence as long as the human race." The *Salt Lake Tribune* described a "psychopathic abnormality . . . so strange that psychologists the world over have sought furtively for concrete proof of theories."[17] Ruth's friend Alfred had been interviewed extensively in the papers; asked if Ruth had ever expressed romantic interest in him, he replied "'hardly.' He declared that he knew that she cared for someone else, but had never been able to determine who it was."[18] When asked if she knew of the women's relationship, Ruth's landlord Mrs. Daugherty commented that "we all have our peculiarities. . . . Ruth was a cheerful sort of person, but I think any girl who has a mad infatuation for another girl is peculiar. But if Ruth was infatuated with Sarah, Sarah was just as much taken with Ruth."[19] And Sarah's former landlord, a Mrs. DeVries, said of Ruth, "She struck me as being a peculiar kind of girl. She was pretty, dark, and of medium build, but I didn't like her voice. I can't explain just why or what there was about it that I didn't like."[20]

The November 29 issue of the *Telegram* seems to have reveled in "the strange friendship which apparently drew the girls apart into a weird land of their own—which established a closer understanding than that existing between usual friends—which plunged them to a sudden death."[21] The *Tribune* for that day pored over the salacious details disclosed by the letters, the interviews with friends and acquaintances, and comments from witnesses and investigators, sensationalizing the lives and the deaths of the "sister adventurer[s] in the fields of morbid romance."[22] To their credit, both newspapers called upon sympathetic psychologists for comment, and received varying replies as to those who "seek to fill their want by association with someone of their own sex."[23] For the *Telegram*, this was the first issue in its long history in which the word *homosexual* (or its close companion, *homosexuality*) had ever appeared; the *Tribune* declined to use either word. But for both papers, the expansive coverage of the story of Ruth Drake and Sarah Lindstedt comprised their first explicit considerations of love between women—all in the context of suicide.

ii. What am I, miserable, then to say?

Quid sum miser tunc dicturus?

Two months before Ruth and Sarah drove that borrowed roadster from Salt Lake City to Ogden, Édouard Bourdet's play *La Prisonniére* (*The Captive*) opened on Broadway. The play had previously been produced in Paris, Berlin, Vienna, and Budapest, where audiences raved about it. In the United Kingdom, censors prevented its staging on claims of obscenity; but in New York, a resourceful producer successfully opened its North American premier at the Empire Theatre on September 29, 1926. In three acts, *The Captive* tells the story of Irène De Montcel, who convinces her longtime friend Jacques Virieu to help her stay in Paris after her father moves to Rome. Irène has told her father that her reason for staying behind is that she is in love with Jacques, but although Jacques is genuinely smitten with her, Irène is embroiled in a passionate romance with another woman. Jacques initially suspects that she is carrying on an affair with a Monsieur D'Aiguines; he confronts the man and learns that in fact it is Madame D'Aiguines who has captivated Irène's heart.

Monsieur D'Aiguines urges Jacques to abandon Irène, knowing that she is unavailable to him. When Jacques presses him, he eventually declares, "Hers is quite another kind of bondage. . . . It is not only a *man* who may be dangerous to a woman. . . . In some cases it can be another woman."[24] Jacques, perplexed, asks "What kind of story is this?" to which Monsieur D'Aiguines responds,

> The kind of story that often happens—regardless of what men think. The kind of story that people don't believe for the most part, or which makes them smile, half amused and half indulgent. . . . Don't wait! There's no use. She'll never return—and if ever your paths should cross again, fly from her, fly from her. . . . Do you hear? Otherwise you are lost! Otherwise you'll spend your existence pursuing a phantom which you can never overtake. One can never overtake them! They are shadows. They must be left to dwell alone among themselves in the kingdom of

shadows.... Can you imagine the existence of a man if he has the misfortune to love, to adore, a shadow near whom he lives?... Take my word for it, old man, it's a rotten life![25]

Monsieur D'Aiguines's soliloquy builds as he is finally able to speak openly about his relationship with his wife:

Understand this: they are not for us.... Don't say, as I said in a situation almost like yours, don't say: "Oh, it's nothing but a sort of ardent friendship—an affectionate intimacy, nothing very serious.... We know all about that sort of thing!" No! We don't know anything about it! We can't begin to know what it is. It's mysterious—terrible! Friendship, yes—that's the mask. Under cover of friendship a woman can enter any household, whenever and however she pleases—at any hour of the day, she can poison and pillage everything before the man whose home she destroys is even aware of what's happening to him. When finally he realizes things it's too late—he is alone! Alone in the face of a secret alliance of two beings who understand one another because they're alike, because they're of the same sex, because they're of a different planet than he, the stranger, the enemy![26]

Near the end of this scene, just before Irène arrives to speak with Jacques, Monsieur D'Aiguines offers something like empathy for her:

There's only one way to love, you see, and one way to suffer. It's the same formula for everybody—and in that respect she and I have been in the same boat for some time. Only she hasn't got used to it yet—and I have.[27]

Madame D'Aiguines herself never appears on stage, but nonetheless drives the entire plot. Jacques confronts Irène, and she agrees to end the relationship and marry him. But a year later, after returning home from a long honeymoon journey, Jacques has realized that Monsieur D'Aiguines was right: Irène will not reciprocate his passion, and so he rekindles an affair with another woman. In the final moments of the play, Irène returns from a gallery where she confesses to having seen Madame D'Aiguines, who left her husband after learning of his conversation with Jacques. Enraged, Jacques tells Irène, "I've had enough. I resign from a useless and ungrateful task."[28] He leaves the house, at which point their maid arrives with a delivery from a florist: a bouquet of violets, sent without a note. Irène "turns and looks at the violets. She walks toward them, lifts them from the box, caresses them." And then she rushes out of the house, presumably to return to the arms of Madame D'Aiguines. Rich with exuberant pathos, *The Captive* only once gestures to suicide: during their confrontation before their marriage, Irène discloses that "there are times I wish I was dead." But when Jacques presses her on this she responds, "Oh! I'm not thinking of killing myself. It takes courage to die like that. And I haven't even any courage left. . . . I have nothing left."[29] By the end of the play, her courage seems to have been restored: Jacques and Irène have both determined to abandon the marriage and return to their former lovers.

Audiences in New York adored the play, and some of the most respected theatre critics of the time raved about it. In an October 10, 1926, issue of the *New York Times*, for example, Brooks Atkinson, whose reviews were enormously influential on Broadway, wrote that "the quality of performance and the treatment of the theme have cleared the air like a northwestern breeze." Of the lesbian relationship at the heart of the play's narrative, he wrote,

> Certainly the facts of the subject discussed in this tragedy are disquieting.... The preoccupation of the current stage with diverse phases of eroticism seemed to indicate another salacious flourish in the direction of prurient theatregoers.... The theatrical news from Paris, where this play began its career as "La Prisonniére," stressed the audacity of the theme, with a general tintinnabulation about censorship and the decadence of the stage.... After the fashion of classical tragedy, M. Bourdet accepts the fact of abnormality and treats of its consequences with austerity. Before he defines this aberration in the second act, holding it aloof as a malignant threat, an indefinite horror, he reveals all its consequences.[30]

Atkinson's review was later revised and expanded into an introduction for the published version of *The Captive*'s script. There he elaborated by describing the play as "a restrained though uncompromising tragedy, rather than a malodorous trucking to low curiosity."[31] For the student newspaper at Barnard College, Dorothy Frankfeld wrote that the lesbian story at the heart of the play was "unpleasant and yet it is thoroughly enjoyable as a work of art. Our curiosity, our thirst for experience sweetens the bitter taste in our mouths." She continued,

> Homo-sexualism is an abnormality which is taboo by society because it is abnormal, yet because it is human, it attracts our curiosity, it appeals to our instinctive gregariousness. As the basis of a stirring, emotional drama in which human beings suffer, it loses its aspect of shocking strangeness and painful ugliness.... Let us hope that the Censorship Committee has some aesthetic sensibility.[32]

Despite the generally positive responses to the production and its popularity—the flamboyant newly elected New York City mayor Jimmy Walker was present on opening night, along with other luminaries[33]—censors eventually descended upon it: on February 9, 1927, police officers appeared at the Empire Theatre with a warrant for the arrests of the manager and cast of the show. According to a story in the *New York Times* the following day, shortly after the curtain rose for the previous evening's performance, Lieutenant James Coy said to the manager of the show, George Kondolf Jr., "I am sorry that I have to inform you that I have a warrant for your arrest, and for the arrest of [the director] and the cast. . . . However, we are not going to interfere with the performance. The arrests will be made afterward." That same evening, the police arrested the casts of Mae West's wildly popular show *Sex* at Daly's Sixty-Third Street Theatre and the poorly reviewed *The Virgin Man* at the Princess Theatre. Most of those who had been arrested were released later that evening; but the arrests had a chilling effect on Broadway's willingness to stage productions that included explicit depictions of homosexuality. Most concerning was the backstory of these arrests: the district attorney had pledged to accept the judgment of the Citizens' Play Jury, which had acquitted *The Captive* of obscenity and immorality charges. Despite this promise, officers were sent with warrants citing Section 1140A of the New York Criminal Code, which forbade "indecent performances."[34]

It was in this context, this "tintinnabulation about censorship" of queer narratives, that Lillian Hellman wrote *The Children's Hour*, which was first produced on Broadway in 1934.[35] Hellman's play tells the story of two women, Karen Wright and Martha Dobie, who run a girls' boarding school. One of the students at the school, the disagreeable Mary Tilford, starts and spreads a rumor that Karen and Martha are lovers. Mary's grandmother ensures that all of the girls' parents have heard this rumor, at which point they withdraw their daughters, ruining the teachers' reputations and destroying the school's chances of survival. Although we learn that the two women had not been involved in a romantic relationship, Martha eventually realizes her romantic feelings for Karen, and proclaims them to her near the end of the play; Karen doubts and denies them, and leaves Martha's room. In the play's climactic scene, Karen hears a gunshot, and we learn that Martha has killed herself.

Hellman's idea for *The Children's Hour* had come from the 1931 anthology of true crime stories *Bad Companions*, written by Scottish lawyer and criminologist William Roughead. The chapter "Closed Doors; or, The Great Drumsheugh Case" details an extended libel case in Scotland brought by two women, Marianne Woods and Jane Pirie, against Lady Helen Cumming Gordon in 1811. Marianne and Jane had opened a boarding school for girls in Drumsheugh Gardens, Edinburgh, in 1809. One of their pupils—Lady Cumming Gordon's granddaughter, whose mother was Indian and father was English—told her grandmother that she and other girls had witnessed the two women engaged in sexual activity in their beds at night. Lady Cumming Gordon spread this rumor to parents of the other pupils, who were withdrawn from the school within forty-eight hours. The school was forced to close in November 1810, and Marianne and Jane filed libel charges on March 15, 1811. Although they eventually won their case, the damage to their reputations had already been done, and the school never reopened.

In his narration of these events, Roughead focuses primarily on his distrust of the young girl's account; his prose is littered with racist allusions to her background and lineage, leading him to hold the testimonies of the two white governesses as being above reproach. He embarks on a full exploration of the school, including its architecture, room layout, and geography, noting that "the priestesses of this scholastic temple, twin tenders of the virgin flames of which it was the shrine, were two gentlewomen of high endowments and fair repute."[36] He describes the young girl's story about their late-night encounters as being "at once so monstrous and extravagant as to baffle belief."[37] He nonetheless summarizes it "briefly, and with as little offense as may be, . . . that these two gentlewomen had conceived for one another an inordinate affection, which they did not scruple wantonly to display in the very presence of their pupils."[38] The rumor itself, he claims, is not his primary interest; and here he gestures to differences between attitudes in 1810, when the story unfolded, and 1931, when his book was published:

> I fully realise that I am between two fires: belated Victorians will account me overbold; resolute psychologists will deem me not bold enough. But, in fact, had the accusation been well founded, nothing would have induced me to deal with it. I make no claim to the license granted to Professor Krafft-Ebing, Mr. Havelock Ellis, and other scientific exponents of such problems. No, my interest in the case resides in the fact that *the charge was false*.[39]

This disclaimer notwithstanding, Roughead describes the women's "midnight conferences by one another's bedside" as witnessed by the young student: "on four several nights she was awakened by the coming of Miss Woods to Miss Pirie's bed, and had apprised them by her action at the time that their wickedness was discovered."[40]

In 1983, the historian Lillian Faderman published *Scotch Verdict*, a lightly fictionalized narration of her search for the transcripts from the *Misses Woods and Pirie v. Lady Cumming Gordon* suit and her attempts to re-create the trial. The book opens with the narrator describing herself at the age of twelve, developing a crush on the wife of the man who taught her acting classes. The classes consisted of five girls around her age, and for one rehearsal, they were given a scene from *The Children's Hour*. Assigned the role of Mary Tilford but knowing no other context for the scene, the narrator describes finding a copy of the play in the adult section of a local library. She remembers gleaning that her character had "fabricated a tale, claiming that her two women teachers, who operated a girls' boarding school, were doing things they were not supposed to be doing"; but it took several rereadings of the play for her to realize that "the two teachers were ruined because Mary Tilford had accused them to her grandmother of being 'in love with each other.'"[41] She finally understood, and saw herself in their passions.

A decade later, while in graduate school, the narrator recalls that while conducting research for her dissertation, she came across a copy of Roughead's *Bad Companions*, and recognized it as the source material for Hellman's play. Entranced with Marianne Woods and Jane Pirie, she obtained from the Secretary of the House of Lords Office "some incomplete pages of the appeal transcript."[42] Years later, having completed her degree, she had moved on to other projects, but had never forgotten the story. She decided to spend a summer researching it in Edinburgh:

> I wanted to know whether they were really guilty of what they had been accused, what words were used to make such accusations in their day, how they defended themselves, how their judges responded, what happened to women like them after such an experience in the early nineteenth century, what might have happened to me had I, with my temperament, lived then instead of now.[43]

The rest of *Scotch Verdict* consists of an exhaustive re-creation of the accusation, the trial and appeals, and an imaginative reconstruction of what happened to Marianne and Jane after the conclusion of the conflict—it is not a pretty picture.

Faderman reveals from the actual transcripts of the trial that the judges and attorneys were nearly apoplectic at the thought that two women could have the kind of sexual relationship with one another that was described in great detail in the young girl's allegation. In one particularly explicit excerpt, the transcript reads:

> One night during the said period, Miss Cumming was awakened by Miss Pirie speaking to Miss Woods. Miss Pirie said, "Oh, do it, darling!" Miss Woods answered, "Not tonight, it would awaken Miss Cumming," or they respectively used words to that effect. In a little Miss Woods came into bed; upon which Miss Pirie put down her hand and lifted up her shift. Miss Woods then lay above Miss Pirie, and when in that situation said, "I would like to have someone above me," or words to that effect. Miss Woods then put down her hand, and they made a noise described to the defendant as a wet kind of noise, attended with motions of the body, quick and high breathing, and a shaking of the bed.[44]

Beds were shaking throughout the detailed descriptions of what, as it turned out, several girls and one nurse claimed to have witnessed. But the men of the House of Lords found the charges impossible to believe. For his part, Lord Meadowbank, who had referred the case to the Inner House of the Court of Session, made the following testimony about lesbian sexuality:

> The crime in question, when imputed to women of the ordinary conformation of this country, for the purpose of gratification of the venereal appetite by

means of copulation with each other, was equally imaginary with witchcraft, sorcery, or carnal copulation with the devil. Their private parts were not so formed as to penetrate each other, and without penetration the venereal orgasm could not possibly follow.

Throughout the transcripts, the Lords reveal themselves to be both naïve and unimaginative in their unquestioned supposition that specific body parts (which they associated only with men) were required for any and all experiences of sexual pleasure. Lesbianism—in the homeland territories of the British Empire at least—simply could not exist.

Hellman made several changes to the story in *The Children's Hour*: it was set in the United States instead of Scotland and in the twentieth century rather than the nineteenth. The accusing girl was white rather than mixed race, and she was written as a more vindictive personality than evidence suggests the original Miss Cumming may have been. In Hellman's version, the women lose their libel suit, sealing the finality of their destitution. And finally, in Hellman's version, Martha realizes her love for Karen, and this knowledge (along with Karen's seeming lack of reciprocation) compels her to suicide. Hellman's relationship to this change—and to Martha's realization of her own lesbianism—evolved throughout the play's long production history. She was very clear on her intent, that *The Children's Hour* was primarily a morality play about the consequences of a socially embraced lie; but over time, she deepened the complexities within that theme presented in the final act, when Martha comes to terms with the fact that on *some* level, the lie was rooted in truth.

In advance of the 1934 production, Hellman's producers remembered the then-recent censorship that had plagued *The Captive* and worried that *The Children's Hour* would meet a similar fate. These fears were not unjustified: performances of the play were banned on moral grounds in Boston, Chicago, and London. But at the Maxine Elliot Theatre on Broadway the show went on, and was a critical and financial success. The play was adapted to film first in 1936 under the title *These Three*, for which the writers converted the lesbian storyline into a heterosexual love triangle; the Hays Code, which applied to Hollywood but not Broadway, forbade the overt representation of queer narratives.[45] In post-Code 1961, a more faithful version was released with Audrey Hepburn and Shirley MacLaine in the leading roles.[46] This version was widely acclaimed, receiving five Academy Award nominations. But while the film represented one of the very few explicit depictions of lesbian desire in Hollywood, its ending—in this version, Martha chooses a noose rather than a gun—reinforced that narrative archetype in which queerness and suicide are inextricably interwound.

In a 2004 essay published in *Modern Drama*, theatre historian Jenny Spencer meticulously tracks Hellman's thinking about the play across several decades and numerous production. One thing remained true for Hellman throughout the long life of *The Children's Hour*. In notes written before the 1934 staging, she explicitly considered Martha's epiphany:

> The idea of an unrealized yearning, a sublimation that would never have appeared if let alone, is in one way unsound. However, I think it's right and recognizable and should be used. The confession [is] the last straw: the difference between having been injured unjustly—some comfort in that—and being injured with some possible justice. Could the kid have been right. Could she, because of her own and different abnormality, have seen what they couldn't see themselves, have sensed it and unconsciously known about it. Suicide is part of that and not

separate. If it's separate it will be phony melodrama, instead of cause and result.[47]

In other words, for Hellman the suicide at the end of play was unquestionably the result of Martha's epiphany that she is in love with Karen. Linking suicide to lesbianism protected the play, in Hellman's view, from becoming the "phony melodrama" of a death attributable to the social ruination caused by a young girl's lie, the story at the heart of her morality play. In Spencer's chilling words, "If the audience senses that the play is about lesbianism (Is she or isn't she?), then the 'truth' of Martha's sexual orientation is the question that her suicide resolves."[48]

iii. My soul is weary with my life

Taedet animam meam vitae meae

In 1977, married sexologists Vern and Bonnie Bullough published an essay in the journal *Signs* about lesbian life in Salt Lake City in the 1920s and 1930s. Bonnie's mother's partner, who had died several years earlier, had given them a draft manuscript she had written about interviews conducted with other lesbian women she had known decades earlier. Several dozen women's lives were represented in the material, along with "data on some eight male homosexuals who were on the fringe of this particular community or active in a bohemian literary club with which many of the homosexuals in the city, male or female, had some affiliation."[49] The author was forty years old when she completed the draft in 1938; she "had been gathering data for twenty years," first as a college student working on her honors thesis. Dissuaded by her adviser from continuing the project, she had persisted, though she never completed it.[50] None of the women lived openly as a lesbian, and all of them were terrified of exposure: when Radclyffe Hall's *The Well of Loneliness* was released in 1928, "instead of applauding the fact that lesbianism was being brought out in the open and discussed publicly, almost to a woman they decried its publication."[51] The author was familiar with the work of sexologists including Magnus Hirschfeld, Havelock Ellis, and Richard von Krafft-Ebing.

Vern and Bonnie explained that while the transcripts themselves had not survived, the manuscript included summaries of every interview its author had conducted. The women's ages ranged from nineteen to fifty-six, and they worked in diverse occupations, including as teachers, nurses, engineers, and farmers. Three of the women were married to men, and most were members of the Church of Latter-Day Saints. The author had written meticulous descriptions of the women's physical appearances, suspecting that "masculine" builds were more common among lesbian communities; this suspicion was not confirmed by her data. In the interviews, she asked questions about the women's lives and relationships, about their first awareness of their sexual identities, about childhood trauma, and about their experiences with people outside of this closed community. The women "consistently denied that they were sick, pathological, or disturbed, although they were very much aware that a society tended to regard all homosexuals in this light."[52] On the whole, despite the profound stigmatization that would have awaited them had their sexualities been publicized, the tightness of their community made them "remarkably well-adjusted to society."[53]

In the newspaper articles covering the story of their deaths, there is no indication that Ruth Drake and Sarah Lundstedt were aware of the existence of this apparently thriving underground community. In the reprinted letters they sent back and forth, there is no mention of any queer friends or former lovers in Salt Lake City, no description of meeting in a place they knew to be safe, no hint that they'd heard of the "bohemian literary club" where queers would gather to talk, no nostalgia for nights when they could dance surrounded by "remarkably well-adjusted" queer kin. The letters and the news stories cast them as utterly alone in their turmoil, isolated from anyone who might have given them a glimpse of something other than homosexuality as perversion or deviance or criminality, from anyone who might have framed the question of homosexuality so that suicide was not its only and inevitable resolution.

Or perhaps none of that would have altered their story as it transpired. In the years between the Broadway premier of *The Children's Hour* and its filmic re-creation with Audrey Hepburn and Shirley MacLaine, Tennessee Williams wrote *A Streetcar Named Desire*, another play later adapted into a classic film with queer suicide at its core. It slowly unfolds in the fractured stories told to Stanley and Mitch: Blanche DuBois's young husband, Allan Grey, had killed himself after Blanche had discovered him in the arms of another man, and she had since been unable to shake her sense of guilt. She never would: by the end of the play and film, she is forcibly carried away by a psychiatrist, the man to whom she delivers her most famous line about depending on the kindness of strangers. Allan Grey haunts *Streetcar*, a disembodied ghost of queerness driven to its own destruction by a painfully antiqueer world.

Robin and I shared a love of *Streetcar*, especially its film version: the Southern Gothic writing, thick as sweet tea; the campy tragedy of Vivien Leigh's portrayal of Blanche; the sultry atmosphere of balconies and balustrades in New Orleans; and the tongue-numbing beauty of young Marlon Brando. We once watched a screening of it together at the

Castro Theatre, surrounded by drag queens done up in diamonds and lace and other queers reciting lines with the actors on screen. We both knew the film well, and could quote our favorite bits; but Robin knew it better than I, and he loved to show off. One night, during a particularly warm summer in San Francisco, we met at his apartment before going out to dance. I had been at Black Sands Beach for most of the day, and I still smelled like the coastal sagebrush that covers the Marin headlands. He buzzed me in; and as I pushed through the front door of his building, he emerged on the landing at the top of the stairs wearing a gray silk kimono robe. Looking down at me as he toweled his head dry, he called, "I just got out of the shower. I feel fresh as a daisy."

"One that's been picked a few days," I said.[54]

Robin gasped with his most theatrical mock offense, then doubled over as he cackled. When he caught his breath he asked, "How long have you been waiting for me to say something that would set you up for that line?"

"Feels like my whole life," I told him.

"There was something different about the boy," he recited in a soft drawl as I climbed the stairs, "a nervousness, a softness and tenderness which wasn't like a man's, although he wasn't the least bit effeminate looking." Robin was famous for this, able to jump into character at the drop of a hat. "He came to me for help," he said, wrapping me in a hug.[55]

"Have you memorized the entire script?" I asked, rolling my eyes.

He giggled and released me, shifting back out of the role. "Pour yourself a drink while I get dressed," he said. "I think I'm going to meet an angel tonight."

And we went out dancing, as we had on countless nights before, as we would on countless nights after, throwing ourselves into the crowds, drenched with our own and others' sweat, embraced in the welcome that only a queer dance floor can offer. Robin knew the queer friends and former lovers, knew the places where we were safe, knew the bohemian literary clubs, knew the best places to go out dancing, and he reveled in them all. He was loved there; he was cherished; he was adored. And none of this—none of it—would save him.

IV
Lacrimosa

From the corner of his eye he watched his friend, who held him with such power; and felt, for that moment, such a depth of love, such nameless and terrible joy and pain, that he might have fallen, in the face of that company, weeping at David's feet.
     JAMES BALDWIN, "THE OUTING" (1965)

Hungry is his sorrow and catastrophe is ready at his side.
     JOB 18:12

A group of people—two dozen or so—stand together in a nondescript space. They appear to come from all walks of life, and although they are in close physical proximity, as if waiting for a subway train or city bus, they seem to maintain a stubborn psychological distance from one another. One man is reading. One woman turns to greet someone standing behind her, grasping her hand. There are other small interactions—a glance, a nod—but aside from the two women smiling at one another, each person is isolated from the others. Suddenly and with great force, torrential waters begin to press in from either side of the image, as if shot from firehoses at left and right. The water overwhelms the crowd: a man is shoved violently by the spray, and the group is compressed like dominoes. Some raise their arms in defense, trying to hold back the onslaught, while others turn their backs to shield its relentless force. An older woman, knocked off-balance, falls to the ground. She does not rise while the deluge persists. As the video ends, others are kneeling at her side, helping to revive her.

This is Bill Viola's 2004 installation, called *The Raft*.[1] Screened in extreme slow-motion and lasting for ten-and-a-half minutes, the video permits viewers access to an evolution of micro-expressions and gestures as the calamitous event unfolds. We see the slow emergence of shock, which transitions to panic and pain as the torrent increases. Watching the video in an otherwise darkened gallery space, we can feel the press of the water, the fear for ourselves and others, the determination to survive. We are immersed in the shock of catastrophe.

This is what raw, guttural grief feels like when it catches you unawares.

* * * * *

In the days after Robin died, I would find myself immersed without warning in imagining the scene of his death. I would see the cats running amok and the door slightly ajar. I would see the mess of the room where it happened, papers and clothes and mugs everywhere, all untidy. I would see strange shadows on an unfamiliar wall. I would shake myself out of these terrible fantasies, but they would later appear again no matter where I was or what I was doing, like uninvited guests who cannot take a hint. It did not matter that I had not been present when his death occurred or that I had not witnessed the scene afterward. I would hear the huffs of his most anxious breathing, like caged beasts hungry for release, and see him sobbing alone. It did not matter that I did not want to watch this scene. It would replay over and over, like a syndicated sitcom on daytime TV. There he was again the night it happened, huddled over his phone in horrible resolve as he typed out what I would only later understand to be his final message to me. There he was again as he stood from the chair, climbed atop it, and reached for the beam overhead. I would shake myself out of it, desperate to dissemble the scene. And hours or days later, having forgotten to remain vigilant against its reappearance, I would watch it replay as if on a film screen in a private cinema. There he was again. There he was again. There he was again.

As the weeks unfurled into what felt like a time-stunted future, these images began to intermingle with scenes from the last moments of Bud's life, of Alec's life, and of Lana's life, all conjured from the stories I had been told. Bud on the porch, Alec in his living room, Lana in her car. I saw these scenes from various angles, heard their soundscapes from near and far, watched as their durations flexed and expanded with every repetition. In some variations, impossible conjunctions emerged: Robin and Alec sitting separately in the same darkened room, or Lana driving the car that Alec had used, or Bud on the porch of Robin's house, or Lana at the wheel as Bud sang through the car's stereo. In some of these patchwork visions, each figure was weeping in profound isolation, frothy and unmoored. In others, the figures had long since stopped sobbing and were staring resolutely ahead, numb as novocaine. In every case, I would seize with shock at the scene's rude interruption and then shore up a dike to restrain the tears that had begun to leak. These I would store up until late at night when, home alone, I would let the dike crumble and fall. My almost-nightly sobbing was cathartic, but it was also work; and when I would finally climb into bed, I could feel the toil of it, the ache in my shoulders and chest and back, the soreness in my cheeks and mouth, the exhaustion in my lungs from having gasped and gulped as I wept. And then I would fall into a dreamless sleep, heavy as rain in a summer monsoon.

* * * * *

On March 6, 1965, five months after Freddie Herko danced out a window and fell to Cornelia Street, his friend Andy Warhol shot a Technicolor film called *Suicide*.[2] Warhol had long been intrigued by suicide. In 1962, he had completed his well-known silkscreen "Suicide (Fallen Body)," which used as its source image a photograph printed on the cover of the May 12, 1947, issue of *Life* magazine. That photograph, taken by Robert Wiles, shows a well-dressed women lying in apparent peace in a cavity made by the crumpled steel of an automobile's roof. The caption, printed in bold white font in the lower right-hand corner, reads, "At the bottom of Empire State Building the body of Evelyn McHale reposes calmly in grotesque bier, her fallen body punched into the top of a car." This was *Life*'s "Picture of the Week" for that issue. It has often been described with the title "The Most Beautiful Suicide."[3] Details that later emerged included that the woman in the photograph had leaped from the observatory on the eighty-sixth floor of the Empire State Building after leaving her fiancé's home, that she had landed on a limousine used by someone at the United Nations, and that she left the following note:

> I don't want anyone in or out of my family to see any part of me. Could you destroy my body by cremation? I beg of you and my family—don't have any service for me or remembrance for me. My fiancé asked me to marry him in June. I don't think I would make a good wife for anybody. He is much better off without me. Tell my father, I have too many of my mother's tendencies.[4]

The sentences beginning "My fiancé asked me . . ." and "I don't think I would make . . ." were crossed out in the note but were still visible beneath the lines of their intended deletion.

In Warhol's silkscreen, the image is printed sixteen times in columns and rows, and is infused with a dark teal hue. It is part of what Warhol called his "Death and Disaster" series, which also includes a silkscreen based on a second suicide: "Suicide (Purple Jumping Man)," completed in 1963, is based on two photographs of the same tragic event. In the first image, we see a man falling after he has leaped from a building. In the second, shot from above, we see the site of his body's impact. In Warhol's silkscreen, the images are arranged in repetitions—the first image doubled at the top, the second appearing six times in columns at the bottom—and are tinted in a purple hue. "Fallen Body" and "Purple Jumping Man" are mournful and vertiginous but simultaneously banal. As with much of Warhol's work, they extract and contemplate beauty from the ordinary. But in their formal and aesthetic dependence on reproduction, they refuse and refute any primacy in the value of the extraordinary, the original, or the exceptional. In the frame of these images and the series of which they are a part, "death and disaster" are wholly mundane, constituent parts of the everyday.

Throughout his career, Warhol—never reluctant to shock—had expressed an interest in filming an actual suicide as it occurred. In an October 10, 1965, article in the *Sydney Morning Herald*, for example, correspondent Margaret Jones describes Warhol's intention to shift away from silkscreens and focus on his films: "he wants to film real things, including a suicide." Warhol wryly tells Jones, "One of my friends committed suicide recently but he didn't phone me," indicating that he wished he could have filmed Freddie Herko's death.[5] In his biography of Warhol, Blake Gopnik writes,

> Stories have always circulated that Warhol said he was sorry not to have been there to film the fall. If that's true, it may tell us as much about his desire to shock an unshockable underground as about his cold-fish voyeurism. Within a few weeks of the suicide, he had dedicated that white Flower painting to Herko.[6]

Warhol never got his wish. But in shooting *Suicide* in March 1965, he indulged his spectatorial fascination by filming a young gay man named Rock Bradett narrating his many previous attempts to kill himself. Ronald Tavel had been asked to interview Rock and to write a script for the film, which he and Rock would then perform. In his notes on the film, Ron described Rock as

> a *Gentleman's Quarterly*-chic and trim, classically small-featured, French film actor who jet set his time in a kind of frenzy between expensive hotels on either side of the Atlantic.. . . It was in his guise of a multiply wrist-slashing, would-be suicide that he interested Andy, and I thought should be rendered representative.[7]

The setting was spare: Rock and Ron sat facing one another, with Rock's wrists bared and turned up to reveal the multiple overlapping scars. With each recitation of one of his suicide attempts, Ron would pour water from a pitcher over his wrists and into a basin between his feet on the floor.

The script consisted of conversations between Rock and numerous lovers, transcribed from Ron's interviews with him; Rock played himself, and Ron played the lovers. After Ron had completed the script but before the camera started rolling, Rock changed the names of his lovers—all men—to suggest they were women, "to conceal his homosexuality and on occasion the identity of certain celebrities peripherally involved in his misfortunes. How crucial some felt it was to cover their minority sexuality in those days could not be more graphic than the living record this movie makes of that."[8] With each story, Rock crushed a flower from a bouquet Warhol had purchased that morning: "I picked, per vignette of suicide-try, a sunflower, tuberose, or Bird of Paradise from the bouquet for Rock to grind between his shaking fingers."[9]

The scenarios in the script are morbid and explicit, and several begin or end with Rock's plaintive words, "I open my arms," "I open my arms again," "I open my arms with the razor." He grows more and more agitated with each scene, made worse by the crowd that had gathered to watch. "They amounted to an unexpected, public confessional for him," Ron remembers, "which added to the agony of our reliving his life's most unhappy—and self-absorbed—moments. At last, he reached down to the nearly full basin, lifted it up and poured its contents completely over me."[10] Rock rushed out, threatening to sue if the film was ever screened publicly. Reflecting years later on his experience with making *Suicide*, Ron remained haunted by the film: "this portrait of bewildered, groundless aristocracy in his World War II-hungover generation remains vivid in its zeitgeist plea, as unforgiving as it is unforgivable."[11]

* * * * *

Several months after Robin's death, I received a box of his possessions from the friend who had cleaned out his Oakland home. I could not initially bring myself to look through the box, so I cleared some space in a closet and put it there, quiet beneath the coats. But I began to dream of it, and when I would walk past that closet's door, the box would call to me, pleading with me to open it. And so, the following week, I dragged it out and began to excavate its contents. I found Robin's silk kimono robe, the one he wore after his long baths. I found the spandex shorts and tops he wore for his AIDS Lifecycle ride from San Francisco to Los Angeles. I found the framed cork board on which he had taped old photographs of his friend Kevin, who had died of AIDS in the 1990s; this shrine had been given pride of place in the bedroom of his apartment in San Francisco and later his home in Oakland. I found a bundle of notebooks for the theatre productions he directed, filled with his notes and sketches, and a DVD of our mutually favorite film, *Nights of Cabiria*.[12] Among a stack of books, I found copies of two James Baldwin books: *Giovanni's Room*, which was creased and torn, and *Going to Meet the Man*. The latter of these had several dog-eared pages midway through "The Outing," Baldwin's parable of two boys, Johnnie and David, who slip away for discrete moments alone during their church congregation's day-trip. The first of the notched pages describes a moment when David and Johnnie share a secret embrace; David asks, "Who do you love? . . . Who's your boy?" and Johnnie replies "You . . . I love you."[13] On the second notched page, Johnnie watches David from across a room, overcome with longing: he feels "such a depth of love, such nameless and terrible joy and pain," that he feels himself falling and "weeping at David's feet."[14] And on the last page, when David and Johnnie have again found one another for a secret embrace, Robin underscored the story's final line, which describes Johnnie's realization that this love for David, which had felt like a source of peace, was also inscribed with risk: "where there had been safety, danger, like a flower, opened."[15]

Also packed in the box, I found another book that Robin had first read when we were in graduate school and that he had often tried to persuade me to read: psychologist Alice Miller's 1981 classic *The Drama of the Gifted Child*. To his constant frustration, I resisted his entreaties and never read the book. So on this day, his archives now spread out on my floor, I took it to the couch, turned on a lamp, and sat down to read. Opening the front cover, I found Robin's round, playful handwriting on the first page. In itself, this was no surprise: Robin was an enthusiastic inscriber and note-taker in his books, scrawling his reactions to phrases and paragraphs in the margins throughout. But when I read this particular inscription, I was stunned to realize that I had read it before. Suddenly struck with an old memory of holding this very book, I recalled that Robin had given it to me years earlier, two decades before he died. He had asked me again to read it, telling me that I would find something of myself in it. And he had written this inscription to entice me: "This is a book about sensitive, intelligent people, people who have for so long pleased others, that they have forgotten how to please themselves." I tried to recollect what had happened with the book, faintly remembering that he had found it on my shelves much later and asked me what I thought of it. When I confessed that I still hadn't read it, he'd responded angrily, "Then I'm taking it back." Sitting on the couch and looking down at the artifacts from the box splayed out on the floor, I felt a rush of guilt and blushed, sorry but unable to make amends.

I flipped through the book, looking for more of Robin's writing. He'd left a blue note card as a bookmark on page twelve; there he'd drawn several lines alongside the following: "the 'as-if' personality (Winnicott has described it as the 'false self'). This person develops in such a way that he reveals only what is expected of him, and fuses so completely with what he reveals that—until he comes to analysis—one could scarcely have guessed how much more there is to him, behind this 'masked view of himself.'"[16] I continued skimming through the pages, finding only two other marks from Robin. Two-thirds of the way through the book, he pressed his pen deeply into the margin, scribbling many vertical lines to highlight this:

> He himself indeed is surprised when he realizes how long this repressed feeling of shame has survived, and how it has found a place alongside his tolerant and advanced views of sexuality. These experiences first show the patient that his early adaptation by means of splitting was not an expression of cowardice, but that it was really his only chance to escape this sense of impending destruction.[17]

I shuddered as I read these sentences, wondering how old those vertical lines were. Had he drawn them years ago, before he had given me this book? Would that mean he had intended for me to see them? Or had he reread it more recently, seeking himself again in its harrowing diagnoses?

I kept looking for more evidence of him in the book. Stuffed between pages near the end, I found the tag from a birthday gift I must have given him many years before. I could not remember what gift this note accompanied; but I recognized a younger version of my own handwriting, sharp and wild: "For Robin, in praise of friendship - happy birthday and love, Patrick xoxo." I do not know why he had kept this tag, or why was it stored in this particular book. But it marked the page on which the final inscription had been made in his childlike scrawl: "I always confess before discovery."

* * * * *

On March 3, 1975, *The New Yorker* published a poem by Maxine Kumin called "How It Is." The prior year, on October 4, 1974, Kumin had lunch with her close friend, the poet Anne Sexton, to copyedit the manuscript for *The Awful Rowing toward God*, a collection of poems Anne had written while experiencing overwhelming depression. After lunch, Anne returned home, where she took off her rings, put on her mother's fur coat, and closed herself in the garage. There, she started the car she had purchased seven years earlier and turned on its radio. She sat, drinking a glass of vodka, until she succumbed to carbon monoxide poisoning from the fumes of the car's exhaust.[18]

Maxine lived for forty more years, during which time she grieved by writing numerous poems and essays about her friend's death. "How It Is" is the first that was published. The poem begins with Maxine wearing one of Anne's blue blazers, whose scent her dog still recognizes. In the second stanza, Maxine dwells on imagining the day of Anne's death, and "how [she] would unwind it, paste / it together in a different collage . . . / running the home movie backward." In the third and final stanza, Maxine presages what in fact later occurs: "I will be years gathering up our words, / fishing out letters, snapshots, stains."[19] The following year, on February 2, 1976, *The New Yorker* published a second poem by Maxine. "You are four months dead," she thinks while chopping wood, likening the shared mortality of trees and humans. She closes the poem with what reads like the rage of grief: "See you tomorrow, you said. / You lied."[20]

In "Itinerary of an Obsession," published in a 1979 issue of *The American Poetry Review*, Maxine begins by quoting a line from an unspecified "time-zone chart": "Just remember that everything east of you has already happened." She narrates her travels to Paris, Rome, and the Red Sea, imagining Anne among the various people she sees. "I put my hands in your death," she writes, "as into the carcass of a stripped turkey." She considers the time that has passed, and that will pass, since Anne's death. "It is true that I dream of you less. / Still, when the phone rings in my sleep / and I answer, dream cigarette in my hand. . . . / You haven't changed. / I, on the other hand, am forced to grow older."[21] Maxine is describing the strange, changed momentum of time after a loved one's suicide: forward into a future defined by absence, but simultaneously unable to depart—and tethered to—the day of Anne's death. "I, who alone survived, move through / my old age like a camera / in the hands of a hard-core realist," she writes in a 2002 poem; "We had planned to age elegantly."[22]

In the 1982 poem "Aprostrophe to a Dead Friend," Maxine describes herself as "remaindered in the conspiracy," marking that "how it was with you now / hardly more vivid than how / it is without you" but conceding still "the sheer weight of the telling."[23] In 1992 she remembers that "my world . . . threatened / to stop the day you stopped, faltered, / and then resumed, unutterably altered." But she also warns: "Annie, there will be no more / elegies, no more direct-address songs / conferring the tang of loss, its bitter flavor / as palpable as alum on the tongue."[24] And yet she is immersed in remembering again in 1996, reconstructing a 1959 New Year's Eve party when Anne was still alive: "I alone am saved to tell you / how they could jive."[25] Several years later, in 2000, she published "Oblivion," a poem that explicitly envisions suicide—the act—itself. "The dozen ways they did it," she begins, "off a bridge, . . . / pills, head in an oven . . . / wrapped in her mother's old mink coat / in the garage, a brick on the accelerator." It is here, in this poem, where she engages most directly with "Wanting to Die," which Anne had written in 1964, ten years before her death:

> But suicides have a special language.
> Like carpenters they want to know *which tools.*
> They never ask *why build.*[26]

In "Oblivion," Maxine is still trying to run "the home movie backward," fantasizing about unwinding the day of Anne's death, just as she was in the immediate aftermath of its occurrence in 1974. The poem ends gravely with a nod to the unending repetitions of that original event: "for us it is never over / who raced to the scene. . . . / We are trapped in the plot, every one. / Left behind, there is no oblivion."[27]

* * * * *

"I always confess before discovery": this was true of him. Robin could not keep a secret, especially when the secret was about him. He was a font of confessions, relishing the narratives of his betrayals and indiscretions, and loved to elaborate them with story-telling that grew in its theatricality with every iteration. Confessions were rarely sad affairs, offering as they did an opportunity for him to perform, to act out the various roles of those involved in or implicated by his misdeeds. He loved most of all to perform the scene of confession itself, telling and retelling the moments when, with cathartic exuberance, he had previously come clean. "She was shocked," he would say with barely bridled glee, or "and then he confessed to me, too." For Robin, fessing up was a *mise en abyme* of dramatic enactments, a story within a story within a story about whatever original sin had occasioned the advent of shame. This he guarded deep within himself. For him the point of confession was not to absolve or repent, but to construct stages upon stages, accruing impersonations and audiences with the greed of the famished, which paradoxically prevented the evaporation of his guilt. He used his theatrical brilliance, his fluency with performance, to embalm his shame—casting it again and again in crystalline amber— rather than to release it.

Robin rarely wept when confessing. As gifted an audience member as he was a performer, he most often cried when watching a play or film that moved him. But with these, he was as likely to be stirred by the craft of the performance as by the narrative thread of the story itself. He would watch, sitting up on the edge of his seat, as a particularly nuanced performer contoured the lines of a character's arc with subtle grace, and gasp with delight as he threw himself into the depths of that character's life. In moments like this, when an actor's performance approached his definition of genius, he would sigh and laugh as his eyes brimmed and spilled. This was Robin's concept of beauty: a performance so deeply inhabited, so deftly drawn, so capaciously embodied, that one couldn't help but be overcome with empathic response, as if acting itself was a kind of whirlpool dragging us, oarless passengers on a flimsy skiff, into its gravity.

When he wept for himself, he was shambolic: his eyes casting about for purchase on any object, any thing; his body small and hollowed; his arms and hands frantically winding around, then rubbing his thighs, then shooting out this way and that. He was never consolable when he sobbed like this, impatient both with the crying itself and with anyone who happened to witness it. In the first section of the 1962 book *Historias de Cronopios y de Famas*, the Argentinian writer Julio Cortázar offers a series of poetic but sober meditations on a number of mundane activities. These are his "Instructions on How to Cry":

> Average, everyday weeping consists of a general contraction of the face and a spasmodic sound accompanied by tears and mucus, this last toward the end, since the cry ends at the point when one energetically blows one's nose.

As if he had read this script, Robin always ended this kind of sob with a fistful of tissues and a noisy bleat as he cleared his nose. He would shake himself out of it—and needing immediately to move, he would stand and walk aimlessly but speedily around whatever room he was in, as if searching for a long-lost key.

Cortázar's instructions do not end with the gestural choreography of crying. He also gives suggestions on how to trigger the sobbing to begin: "in order to cry, steer the imagination toward yourself, and if this proves impossible . . . think of a duck covered with ants or of those gulfs in the Straits of Magellan into which *no one sails ever.*"[28] I picture those gulfs, the pull of their currents, the gust of their winds, their rocky shores. Is their air balmy or cold? What do they sound like? What underwater colonies do they harbor? Do they know loneliness, or are they at peace in their unvisited complacencies? What desperate fatalities do their waves dream of occasioning, so that no one sails into them *ever*?

* * * * *

In 1970 and 1971, the Dutch artist Bas Jan Ader created a series of conceptual works called *I'm Too Sad to Tell You*. The works included two films with the same title and postcards mailed to friends around the world. Only a segment of the first film, shot in 1970 in front of his house in California, remains. But the second film, shot in Amsterdam in 1971, is still intact. It consists of Aden's face, framed as a head shot by the camera, contorting through various states of anguish while he is weeping. There is no script, no voice, no text to elucidate his grief. As the title of the project makes plain, Ader's sorrow has overwhelmed his ability to explain. The photograph used on the front of the postcards sent to friends is a still from the 1970 version of the film. It shows Ader—whose hair is much shorter than in the later film—leaning at a slight slant into his left hand, his face frozen in despair.

In 1973, Ader began what was originally conceived to be a triptych of works, collectively called *In Search of the Miraculous*. The first part of the triptych was a series of photographs, which show a solitary figure carrying a flashlight as he wanders through a variety of scenes in Los Angeles at night. The intended third part of the triptych would have entailed taking a similar set of photographs in the Netherlands, Ader's native land. But the intermediary work, a solo trip across the Atlantic on a small boat called the *Ocean Wave*, ended with Ader's mysterious disappearance: he never arrived, and his vessel was eventually discovered floating captainless off the coast of Ireland.

In his analysis of Ader's work, art historian Alexander Dumbadze writes that "every image in which he is present, like every thing that may allude to his absence, has been charged with a significance that creates an aura surrounding [him]."[29] This is especially true with *I'm Too Sad to Tell You*, as we watch him sobbing, giant tears streaming down the crevasses of his wrenched face and sometimes dangling from his nose or chin. "Ader's larger-than-life head shows suffering literally magnified," Dumbadze writes; "It is hard not to be affected by the film, not to feel some empathy, some sense that it really is Ader who offers such raw passion to anyone willing to watch."[30] In *The Crying Book*, Heather Christie

LACRIMOSA

writes of Ader's film that "I do not know why he is crying, but when I watch I feel myself nodding with him, affirming his great sorrow."[31] She also writes of his fateful *In Search of the Miraculous* journey: "A particular cruelty to losing someone to disappearance at sea is the uncertainty of knowing when the tears ought to begin. Today? Long ago? There is a mist."[32]

After Rock Bradett left Warhol's Factory on the day *Suicide* was filmed he effectively disappeared, leaving no trace of his later life in the historical record. But there are some hints of him from earlier. For example, in an entry for the Whitney Museum's catalog of Warhol's films, Tom Kalin describes viewing "a photographic postcard of [Rock], printed in Paris, [that] reveals a brooding young man with a thatch of dark hair, strong brows, and a cleft chin; handsome in a midcentury way, he vaguely resembles Alain Delon."[33] All other references to him refer mainly to his scars, which Warhol described in this way: "I found this person, my star, who has 13 scars on one wrist and 15 scars on the other wrist from suicide attempts. He has marvelous wrists. The scars are all different shades of purple."[34] But in a small museum in Péribonka, Québec, there is an ink drawing by Jean Cocteau called *Hommage à Rock Bradett* (*Homage to Rock Bradett*).[35] Sketched on paper mounted in a modest gilded frame, the drawing consists of an outline and contours of a beautiful face with large, clear eyes; wildly tousled hair; a pert nose and full lips; and the edges of a chin, neck, and raised shoulder. It is signed and dated 1962, three years before *Suicide* was shot. Inscribed vertically on the left side of the paper canvas in Cocteau's florid script are the following lines:

D'un voile noir couvert
tel que toi-même enfin
sur ton visage l'ange
De la beauté court

Plus vite que le talent
La mort est vivante.
>Covered with a black veil
>True to yourself at last
>On your face, the angel
>Of beauty runs
>Faster than talent
>Death is alive.

V
Offertorium

It's very difficult to keep the line between the past and the present.
　　　　　　　　EDIE BEALE, GREY GARDENS (1975)

This fabulous shadow only the sea keeps.
　　　　　　　　HART CRANE, "AT MELVILLE'S TOMB" (1926)

i. Through the tombs

Per sepulcra

In a quiet, shaded grove at the edge of the school where I met Alec and Lana, there is a little graveyard surrounded by a stout wall. Small tombstones mark the places where four people are buried. Anne Parthenia Miller, who died in 1920, was the most recent burial. Her husband, Thomas, died in 1905. One of their children, Charlie, died in 1871 at seven months old, and their grandson Frank died in 1903 at three years old. Charlie was buried first, having experienced birth and death within the first decade after the Civil War; Anne was buried last, having lived as a widow for fifteen years. The wall, now covered in moss, surrounds an area much larger than these four graves cover, as if it was built in anticipation of further deaths, or of larger memorials, or of visits from many mourners. The wall is surrounded by longleaf pines, red maples, and willow oaks. Through the trees, one can just make out an old state highway that cuts across the forest, the road from which one turns and passes a guard-house to enter the campus. Aside from Charlie, Anne and Thomas had four daughters and one other son. That son, also named Frank, had a long, storied career as mayor of a nearby town. It is his son, named after him, who died before his fourth birthday and who is buried here with his grandparents and infant-uncle. The elder Frank and his sisters were buried elsewhere, in statelier cemeteries with fewer trees.

In this space carved out for Anne, Thomas, Charlie, and grandson Frank, we students used to sit on the old stone wall, watching and waiting for ghosts. Sometimes we came alone, seeking a quiet place to read or to write. Sometimes we came in couples, up for a tryst far away from the faculty's watchful eyes. Sometimes we came in groups, one of us having stashed some gin or pot in a nook nearby. Sometimes we came to hide from someone else; sometimes we came to sing without listeners; sometimes we came to sketch or photograph ourselves among the ancient grave markers. But always, no matter why we had come, we stepped carefully around those giant trees as we approached the wall, hushed in reverence, peering expectantly at the gravestones, half-wishing to be haunted by their erstwhile owners.

Bud's body rests in a grave in Fort Denaud, Florida, thirty miles east of the porch where he died. Lana's ashes were buried in an unmarked grove of trees on a campground that, when plotted on a map with our school and the place where she was born, forms a roughly equilateral triangle. Alec's body is buried at a large and beautiful cemetery less than a mile from the school. Robin's ashes are interred alongside his father's at a military cemetery in California. If one were to drive from Bud's grave to Robin's urn, stopping along the way to visit the places where Alec and Lana are buried, it would take 41 hours and cover 2,731 miles. If one were to walk this route at an average pace, it would take 881 hours, or 37 days, but only if one walked without ceasing. This is roughly the same amount of time it takes to walk the Camino de Santiago pilgrimage via the French Way through the Pyrenees, with nightly stops to sleep.

Some graves are unremarkable, camouflaged among the daily routes and ways of unknowing passers-by. Some graves reek of ostentation, compelling hushed acknowledgment from those who dare to approach. Some graves inspire pilgrimages that require long, arduous treks through spectacularly dangerous mountain paths. Some graves shimmer and throb with baroque, arcane hauntings. Some graves are wholly invisible, buried artifacts of the terrors of brutal pasts. And some graves—for me, the graves of Bud, Robin, Alec, and Lana—vibrate with such intensely private significance that, in the urgency of their summons, they bear witness to us instead.

ii. Seeking me, you sat down wearily

Quaerens me sedisti lassus

In the autumn of 1960, on the campus of the school with the small family graveyard, a physics teacher named Mr. Jones enlisted his students in a project: to build a small house that would appear to defy the physical laws of the universe. He developed plans for this house with Mr. Moore, who taught carpentry and general science. Once built, this structure, which was called the Truth House, seemed from the front to be oddly askew. There were a few stairs leading up to a front door, but the slant of the roof seemed off, as if it had slipped from its central fulcrum so that it was now oriented along an entirely different axis than everything else. Upon entering the house, one found that the roof's precarious tilt foreshadowed vertiginous conditions inside: the floors were built at an angle so that one's sense of vertical rightness was thrown off-kilter. Furniture was nailed to the floor, forcing unnatural perspectives and making the room feel simultaneously too deep and too shallow. A spigot on one of the walls appeared to drip water into a sink that was horizontal to it rather than below it. On a different wall were fixed two nearly parallel railings that served as tracks for a ball that appeared to defy gravity by rolling upward rather than down. Interviewed by a reporter for the *Florence Times* shortly before the Truth House was built, Mr. Jones commented that "you [will] feel that *down* is somewhere other than it has been before."[1]

The purpose of the project, Mr. Jones continued, was to demonstrate the relativity of one's "frame of reference" and to destabilize one's sense of the inviolability of rightness and wrongness. "Not only will it be valuable in science and physics. It will be an important tool in the teaching of social science as well."[2] When I arrived at the school and first encountered the Truth House, surfaces inside had been inscribed with lines of poetry, various slogans, and the names of students who had come before. The murals on the walls, originally designed to contribute to the sense of fluctuating perspective, had faded and were only barely discernible in that dark space. But the floor, which had been painted with a large black-and-white spiral, was still nauseating in its impact.

Two years before the Truth House had been built, Alfred Hitchcock's *Vertigo*—whose promotional poster may have been the inspiration for the spiral on the floor—was released to mixed reviews.[3] By the time I first encountered that slanted floor in the 1980s, *Vertigo* had been reassessed as a classic, and was regularly included on lists of the most important and influential films in Hollywood history. I had first watched the film as a teenager one night when everyone else was asleep sometime after its re-release in the middle 1980s. I had always been afraid of heights, not because of the dizzying perspective they force, but because of the inevitable proposition they occasion: step back from the edge, or fly and fall. I remember understanding James Stewart's character's psychosomatic acrophobia and wondering if this film might teach me something about my own. I remember loving the high camp of Kim Novak in those two glorious roles, and becoming distracted by the intricacies of makeup. But I also remember realizing while watching *Vertigo* that it was not, in the end, a film about vertigo. It was instead a film about the narrative power—the mythological power—of suicide.

Much of *Vertigo*'s action centers on a suicide later revealed not to be a suicide at all, but rather the cover for a brutal murder: Kim Novak as Judy Barton pretending to be Madeleine Elster, who is presumed to be the great-granddaughter of a woman named Carlotta Valdes.[4] James Stewart's character Scottie Ferguson, a former police officer suffering from acrophobia after a colleague's fatal fall, encounters Judy-as-Madeleine sitting in a gallery at San Francisco's Legion of Honor, staring intently at a portrait on the wall. As Scottie watches her, he notices that she carries a bouquet of flowers similar to those held in the portrait, and that her hairdo, tied into a coil resembling a vortex, is mirrored by the hair of the woman whose image appears on the canvas. He learns that the woman in the portrait, Carlotta, killed herself after her lover abandoned her and absconded with their child. As the film proceeds, Scottie learns that Madeleine is haunted by Carlotta; in a fateful scene, he watches, horrified but unable to follow her because of his fear of heights, as she climbs the stairs of a bell tower and leaps to her death.

Of course, it is later revealed that this was all a ruse. Madeleine's husband, Gavin, enlisted Judy to play the role of Madeleine in order to seduce Scottie into following her to the tower for the staged suicide, knowing that he would not be able to climb to its roof to intervene. There, out of sight, Gavin is waiting with the real Madeleine's body; he has slain her, and he intends to use Judy's performance to mask the killing. We never learn whether Madeleine's presumed connection to Carlotta Valdes was concocted to support the deception or was real; it is never revealed whether the real Madeleine even knew of this portrait at the Legion of Honor, or knew the tragic story of its subject. But none of this matters in the end: the very existence of Carlotta Valdes's suicide was sufficient to drive the plot and the suspense of *Vertigo*. "I have to go back into the past once more, just once more, for the last time," Scottie says as he and the unmasked Judy return to the bell tower near the end of the film; "I want to stop being haunted." Seemingly cured of his acrophobia, Scottie climbs to the roof of the tower with Judy. And then, spooked by a shadow that rises from the dark, Judy trips and falls from the great height. Scottie never knew Carlotta Valdes, but he will now forever be haunted by the narrative legacy of her self-inflicted death.

And so when I, a teenage boy who had been entranced by *Vertigo*, stepped into the Truth House for the very first time, I did not look around in physics-trained wonder at the optical illusions surrounding me. I stared at the painted floor instead, transfixed by that spiral, infused with the dizziness of nonexistent heights, and stilled by the memory of a nun ringing a bell atop a tall mission tower. I told this story to Lana one afternoon when we had snuck into the Truth House and were both feeling nauseated by its kinky slant. She had never seen *Vertigo*, and she asked, "Why do the women always have to die in stories like that? Scottie sounds like an asshole."

"You know," I said, "since this is the Truth House, I should probably tell you something." She looked at me with her velvet eyes, glasses fogged and smudgy. "I'm gay." She was not the first person I'd ever told, but there hadn't been many before her, and I knew the risks: Lana was rarely discreet with other people's secrets. She stared at me for what felt like an hour, then smirked and started laughing. "Well I'm bi," she said in her profoundly bulbous Alabama accent. I stared back at her, then asked of her then-current boyfriend, "Does he know?" She smirked again and looked across the room at the spigot on the wall. "Nobody knows everything about me," she said. "*Nobody.*"

When Diane di Prima received that phone call telling her Freddie Herko had leaped from a window and died, she described feeling the "finality" of it, as if "the end of the film [had been] cut off and burned so [she'd] never see it."[5] She also described being struck with the realization that "no one will ever see me like he did": she had lost not only her beloved friend but also the otherwise unknowable truth of herself through his idiosyncratic gaze. In other words, she lost his knowledge of her, which was now utterly and completely irretrievable, gone for good. This is an aspect of loss whose strange, profane sensation is difficult to describe: a film cut off and burned, and the film is partly about you, shot from an angle you can never see again.

I had known Alec in middle school, though he was a year below me. I remember sometimes seeing him in the hallway, or talking to him on the math team, and sensing the secret we shared. Lost to me now is his sense of me in those fleeting encounters, his shared suspicion that our secrets rhymed. "Some pig," Robin used to say to and about me, the Charlotte to my Wilbur. Lost to me now is what he saw in me when he said it—along with all of the nights in all of the years when we would be out prowling and he would know the vicissitudes of how I flirt, watching for cues that he should intervene. Lost to me now is the thinking behind Lana's long look as I told her what she must have already guessed, and the reasons for her laugh, and the secrets behind her smirk, and the simple truth of our presence together there on the slanted floor of an experimental shack that, like Lana herself, would soon disappear.

Two months after Lana died, on Palm Sunday in 1994, a swarm of violent tornados swept through the South. That afternoon, one cut through the hills and forests of the land south of Birmingham, including our school's campus. Among the many felled trees, one large pine was knocked to the ground, where it crashed into and crushed the Truth House. I heard about the storms several days after they occurred, though I do not remember who called to tell me. Whoever it was, they told me there was no loss of life at the school, but many trees had fallen. After those headline facts, they told me almost as an afterthought that one tree in particular, a tall stately pine, had splintered and collapsed that tiny house built in 1960 to play with the laws of perception—where *up* became *down*, *deep* became *shallow*, *after* became *before*.

Lana's death was still fresh, so I thought of that one particular day when she and I were there together, and shivered at the fragility—the mortality—of places thick with personal gravity. I thought of all the places on campus where Lana and I had gone, wondering if one by one they would all disappear. There was the little arched bridge where everyone went to smoke, and the nearby grove with its softly boiling springs. Farther back, across the lake, there was the old family graveyard with its mossy stones and deeply unfamiliar dates. Farther back still, there was the place where vines had hardened into almost-trees, rounding and cupping like tents an odd assortment of spaces defined by their shadows. Closer in, there was the old building filled with kilns and easels and looms and, back in the dankest corner, the darkroom with its chemical haze. Each of these recollections seemed a kind of film strip, a gathering of images that threatened to burn away as I thought of them into nothingness, no longer shared and forever gone.

iii. Let not the abyss swallow them, lest they fall into obscurity

Ne absorbeat eas tartarus, ne cadant in obscurum

Forty-one days after Freddie Herko performed his grand jeté out of that window at 5 Cornelia Street, Andy Warhol screened an excerpt from *The Thirteen Most Beautiful Boys* at the New Yorker Theatre: the *Screen Test* he had shot of Freddie. Against a black background and lit in red and purple hues from the side, Freddie shifts and fidgets throughout the five-minute film, sometimes smoking, sometimes chewing gum. The camera is close, so that we only see his face and occasionally a forearm and hand. More rarely, we catch a brief glance of his torso as he seems to lurch and stand. When Freddie appears in the first few frames, he is looking straight at the camera. He blinks several times and works his jaw, then turns to his left and lights a cigarette. From this point forward, he will hold various positions for fluctuating periods of time, occasionally shifting so dramatically that he nearly disappears. Halfway through the film, he has slumped so that we can see only half of his face in the bottom right-hand corner of the screen. At certain moments, he slips out of the frame entirely before returning to a different pose. At one point, his head is propped on his hand, slightly tilted as he stares back at us. Several times he seems to smirk at us, aware that we are watching. In the final frames, he has turned so that his eyes are unlit, revealing only the sharp contours of his cheek and jaw, before a strange burst of the tinted light reveals his full face again, staring at someone off-screen.[6]

Many commentators have written about the haunted feeling of this brief film, its demonstration of Freddie's twitchy love for amphetamines and its strange anticipation of Freddie's suicide later that year. I sense these things too. But the first time I watched the film and every time since, my most immediate feeling was that I was being cruised— aggressively, bawdily, insistently cruised. Perhaps it is the lighting and dark background, a mise en scène that most closely resembles a backroom, bathhouse, or bar. Or perhaps it is that unrelenting stare and intelligent smirk, both infused with recognition, conveying that the seduction has worked and pivoting to what comes next. In his discussion of Freddie's *Screen Test*, José Estéban Muñoz provides a reading similar to my own:

> Herko cruises the camera and the spectator; he flirts with it, not able to sit, wanting to display himself

> beyond the limits of Warhol's portraiture. Herko wants us, his future—a future he will choose not to meet—to see him as a desiring subject, in all his uneasy embodiment. . . . [It is] a dark, drug-tinged cruise, purposely brooding and deliberately conveying a certain intensity that probably served Herko well in countless bars and shadowy public spaces.[7]

There are other filmic artifacts of Freddie alive, but this *Screen Test* is the one that accosts most directly, drawing in and seducing those who never knew him, living as we are in a time from which he willfully chose to absent himself. There are also textual artifacts, especially in the memoirs of those who knew and loved him: writing about Freddie and another boy, Diane di Prima gushed over "the high cheekbones, incredible angular faces. Pale skin with its own light, incandescent: Nicky, Freddie, almost caricatures of themselves. The bodies a bit *too* lean, we loved them for it, the asses *too* tight."[8] He "looked like a downtown demigod. He was lithe, dark, intense, and mercurial."[9] And there are contemporaneous reactions to Freddie performing, including this review from the *New York Times* nine months before he died:

> Another intermission; then Fred Herko, a dancer, crept into the room on his haunches, wrapped in a long fur coat and playing a flute. Ritually arranging the coat on the floor, he spreadeagled on it. A violin twanged, people tittered. The baby cried some more. Herko got up and began a barefoot balletic dance. "You have to be in a state of grace to dance," he said. "I'm getting winded," he announced after a very long time. The violins twanged nervously. "This is the noisiest gallery in town," Herko said, still pirouetting. Finally the violins ran down. So did Herko. "Well, I meant this dance to be monotonous," he said.[10]

More hauntingly, a mutual friend of Freddie and Andy Warhol named Stanley Amos once described one of Freddie's impromptu performances in this way:

> One night, I was walking with Billy Name and Freddy on the Lower East Side. There was no wind, but it was very cold, it was winter. We came to a group of buildings that were being razed. One of them was a church. There was a sort of an altar place you could just make out in the rubble. Freddy rushed across the street into a store that was still open and bought a penny candle, came back and took all his clothes off, lit the candle, and danced through the set for the life of the candle.[11]

With all of these relics, one gets the sense of a Freddie who is vibrantly, eccentrically, twitchingly alive. This is especially true in the *Screen Test*, and equally—though perhaps paradoxically—so in a photograph taken by George Herms in the spring of 1964, in which an almost-nude Freddie lies splayed out across a stone wall on the roof of the Opulent Tower on Ridge Street, as if he had fallen there from a great height. Writing about Alexander Gardner's 1865 photograph of the twenty-year-old Confederate conspirator Lewis Payne, Roland Barthes describes the acute intensity of the image with the phrase "He is dead and he is going to die," summoning both the historical fact of Payne's execution and the photograph's capture of this moment after he had been condemned but before he was finally hanged.[12] *He is dead and he is going to die* is true of Freddie in Herms's photograph too, as he lays splayed out in the present tense of the dance he performed on that roof, and simultaneously in the future-perfect tense of his later fall onto Cornelia Street. And there on the screen every time the cruisy *Screen Test* is replayed, the tension between *dead* and *going to die* becomes thick with desire, seduction, and the infinitely suspended promise of a sweaty future.

Barthes distinguished between the "facts" of a photograph—which he called the *studium*—and the affective pull that a photograph can have on us. This he called the *punctum*, which he described as the "element which rises from the scene, shoots out of it like an *arrow*, and pierces me . . . the accident which pricks me (but also *bruises* me, is poignant to me)."[13] In my favorite photograph of my grandfather, Bud is a young man sitting with a young woman, Verlou, who will later become my grandmother. They are in a photographic studio with a nondescript background, and they are both wearing hats. My grandfather is dressed in a dark shirt unbuttoned at the neck and a thin sweater. He does not smile, and his gaze is strangely both shrouded and direct. His head tilts back and away from Verlou, who is positioned at an angle to the camera. She looks through the photograph with slightly wary eyes and smiles faintly. They look to be in their late teens or early twenties, and they are beautiful. I do not know what occasioned this photograph, or why they decided to sit for it. I do know that alongside the facts of the photograph's *studium*—their presence, their postures, their hats—are the *arrow* of a single button on my grandfather's shirt, closing its gape at the base of his neck, and the *bruise* of his pleading gaze, his eyes the same shape and slant as my father's eyes and also my own. He seems to be looking both inward and out. He seems to know, even so young, that this photograph will make its way to kin that he will never meet. He seems to suspect that one day, when he has long departed, someone like me will seek him here in this image. He looks sorry not to be (or have been) found.

In a second studio photograph, handed down from a distant cousin I do not know, the two are slightly older. Bud wears a dark suit jacket, white tie and shirt, and a jaunty hat with a slimmer brim. Verlou wears a dress that drapes like silk topped with a double collar. Their heads lean toward one another, not quite touching. They are looking directly at the camera's lens, neither smiling nor frowning, and Bud's eyes again seem haunted, again seem to gaze both inward and out. I am moved by the perfectly casual knot of his tie, the tilt of his hat at an angle, and the pride I sense he took in this vestmental ensemble, almost a dandy. But it is again the cast of his eyes that absorb me; he looks not only as if he sees me across the stretch of time between the flash of the camera's bulb and my long stare at his image, but also as if he is *listening* to me—present, empathic, attentive. It is almost a look of doleful recognition. The complexity of this gaze—the depth of it, the texture of its focus, its intermingled clarity and shroudedness—invites speculation on whether he already knew, at that young age, about his eventual leave-taking, even as it stubbornly declines to resolve whatever queries we make of it.

Here is a photograph of another man in another time: he is wrapped in a plush mink coat, and he is wearing a green Mardi Gras mask adorned with sequins and ostrich feathers that stretch two feet above his head. His voluminous beard, thick with silver and brown, escapes from beneath the mask and covers his neck like an ornate, unruly collar. He smirks at the absurd opulence of it all, ogling the photographer with a brash, playful stare. And here, another photograph: she lies on her back on a patch of sod, her long hair fanned out above her. Her right leg is cocked up, bent at the knee, its foot tucked under the other thigh. One hand is draped at the waist, fingers unfurled. Her head stretches back and away from the camera, a lazy, secret smile caught between shadow and sun. Eyes closed, spectacles askew, chin barely grazing her shoulder, she seems half-awake and dreaming. And here, another: he stares challengingly ahead, his hair tied back away from his face, eyebrows arched and alert. One shoulder is higher than the other, as if he has only just lowered himself into a chair. His mouth, slightly ajar, is frozen in the most hesitant of grins. This is the last photograph I took of him, three years before he died, when we had both briefly returned to the city of our childhoods and met for lunch.

And here, where he leans against a wall, eyes fixed on an unknown man, while a younger me stands five feet away, startled by the camera's insistent click. And here, where she sits on a New Orleans staircase late one night, body hunched and shivering as she stares bitterly forward. And here, when he was younger, body ambered in perfect posture, arms at the side, neck alert, chin tucked in at the just-right angle, with a smile designed by Olan Mills. Let not these photographs fade. Keep them whole in the tint of their chemistries. Protect them from corrosion and decay, unwarped by rains or floods, unbleached and untorn. Let the times of their creation unfurl within them, preserved in the vertiginous complexities of their happening, bounded only by the demands of their own constraints. These are their bodies now, handsome, illumined, unravaged by what was to come. Let them thrive in photography's bardo, alive as they ever were and will have been.

VI
Sanctus

Congeries of bodies; the slow, blind tread on sloped steps; the faces floating up like thoughts out of ink, then trailing away like thoughts out of memory; entrances and exits; the dignified advance and retreat as an approaching car on the highway outside casts a headlight through the window and plants a faint square on the wall.

EDMUND WHITE,
NOCTURNES FOR THE KING OF NAPLES (1978)

He had a word, too. Love, he called it. But I had been used to words for a long time. I knew that that word was like the others: just a shape to fill a lack.

WILLIAM FAULKNER, AS I LAY DYING (1930)

Are your wonders known in darkness,
Or your saving help in the land of forgetfulness?

PSALM 88:12

i. I kneel with submissive heart

Oro supplex et acclinis

On November 18, 1930, several years before Reggie Beaton dove in front of an underground train and Hart Crane leaped from the promenade deck of an ocean liner, a man named Harvey Woodward died in Portland, Maine. Harvey had inherited a fortune from his family's ironworks, which included mining operations, large furnaces, and an independent service railroad in and around Birmingham. While alive, Harvey had been something of an eccentric: he eschewed religion, avoided social gatherings, and spent his time wandering around Birmingham polishing brass fixtures and tooling with various pieces of machinery. Shortly before his death, he commented bitterly that "wealth was thrust upon me," and wrote an exceedingly detailed will that bequeathed the vast majority of his estate to the creation of progressive, independent schools across the South. He deplored "the evils of mass education," believing that the strict formalism of standard curricula destroyed children's spirit of curiosity and interest in self-education. His schools would forbid religious instruction, and would be focused on holistic experience—"all shall be taught as a complete and correlated whole and not as separate courses"[1]—and critical thinking: they "would train the mind and body of the pupil so that he may apply his own faculties to facts which come to his knowledge throughout life."[2]

But at the time Harvey died, one year after the Wall Street crash of 1929, the Great Depression was deepening its disastrous effects, leading to widespread desperation to gather and protect all available resources. Several interested parties and powerful institutions, including the First National Bank of Birmingham, contested the will, asking the courts to invalidate the bequest and redistribute the funds. The case played out over the next two decades and was finally resolved by the Alabama Supreme Court in the late 1940s: the bequest was upheld, but would be used for the creation of only one school in the Birmingham area. A Board of Governors was convened to plan the campus and hire faculty and staff. They found and purchased a parcel of land for seventy-five thousand dollars and hired a professor from Peabody College as the school's director.[3] The site chosen for the school was seventeen miles south of Birmingham, bordering a large and lush state park. It originally included six hundred acres of forests, pastures, orchards, and farmland; an eleven-acre tree-lined lake; fourteen natural springs; and the mossy stone wall surrounding the graves of Anne, Thomas, Charlie, and Frank Miller. The Board of Governors hired the Olmsted Brothers firm — led by the sons of Frederick Law Olmsted Jr., who had designed Central Park in New York — to develop the land and design a layout for the school. In 1952, the first cohort of fifty-nine students and ten faculty members inaugurated the school's first year of boarding and instruction. Today, the school includes five grades with roughly sixty students each.

These are the sacred places on the grounds of this school: the site of a Japanese bridge that once crossed a small stream of water branching between the lake and nearby springs, and the springs themselves; a little shaded cove beneath another bridge, just above another stream; a photography darkroom, heavy with layers of decades-old chemicals; a small plot of soil, heavily tilled, in the trees behind the soccer field; a strange little house with a slanted roof, since destroyed by a tree blown down in a storm; the lawn on which modern sculptures were installed on the far side of the lake; The Hut, a building whose roof stretches down to the ground and whose cavernous interiors bear the inscriptions of students now long-dead; the central lawn in the dorm circle and the grass behind the dorms; a small, cool grove carved out by thick, woody vines that block most of the light from above; one particular row in the library where elsewhere-forbidden books were shelved; and the wall that surrounds those four old graves. Just off-campus, in the adjacent state park, there is another site thick with a history of happenings: the wooden deck surrounding an aviary for injured birds, water-stained but sturdy, unpatrolled after dark.

And these are the sacred places in sites far away: the long back patio of a bar in San Francisco and a smoky room with a pool table across the bay in Oakland; the west-facing bedroom of a hundred-year-old house in Forest Park; a pond, orchard, and farm near Tampa Bay; the base of a tree in Tilden; the front bedroom, with bay windows facing Castro, on the top floor of an old Victorian; a small patch of soil on the edge of a canyon; the far corner of a porch in front of an unremarkable white house; a hospital room with sterile floors and quarantine barriers; a tiny room with a view of a power plant that steams and roars at night; a small diner, open late, on a busy city street; a dirty dance floor, thick with sweat, under an elevated track; a ten-foot-square patch beneath an old magnolia tree; a lakeside park in Chicago with wide, open skies; a cedar shack, now demolished, perched beside a babbling brook; and another room in a forgotten town with whitewashed floors and a window that doesn't quite close.

These are the sacred places that have the silent power to set me whirling with longing or shame, all of them haunted.

ii. Great trembling there will be

Quantus tremor est futurus

On May 26, 1974, the *Wichita Eagle and Beacon* published a story that began this way:

It's not a large tavern. The square-shaped bar stretches onto a dance floor on one side. Tables and booths are arranged neatly elsewhere. It has a pool table and a juke box. Psychedelic lights are connected to the music machine and vibe with the sounds. The floors are well-swept. The bartender clears away tables immediately and keeps the bar immaculate. On the surface it's just like any other bar. But it caters to a specific clientele.

And then, with a hint of melodrama, the climax of this opening sketch: "Most of its customers are homosexuals." The story, "Gay Social Life Centers on the Traditional Bars," appeared on the front page of the newspaper and was the first of a six-article series "exploring Wichita's gay lifestyle and homosexual citizens." Written by staff writers Betty Wells and Don Wall, the story offers a sympathetic, almost anthropological description of what must have shocked many Kansans in the 1970s: a thriving gay bar in Wichita. Wells and Wall note that "a few customers in the tavern often come 'in drag,'" that "the bartender would often pick up the ringing telephone and answer 'queer bar,'" and that "the women come dressed in jeans and masculine shirts [and] shoot a good game of pool." They also describe—perhaps in preparatory caution to a curious readership—that "it is not unusual in the tavern to see two persons of the same sex greet each other with a kiss and a hug. And they dance with one another. The boys or men think nothing of a close dance or of gyrating their bodies seductively to the music."[4]

Throughout the 1970s, stories like this one appeared in newspapers in small and large cities across the United States. On February 19, 1973, the *Journal-News* in Rockland County, New York, published an article about several gay bars that had opened in the local area. The author, John Dalmas, notes that the "lighting and setting ... provide an ambiance that helps protect the anonymity important to many patrons." He describes seeing "a lot more closed relationships in progress. ... There seems to be much more billing and cooing, hand-holding, and lingering embraces than one sees in a straight bar." He postulates,

> Gay bars may serve as "public places" for normal expressions of affection that are permitted heterosexual couples almost anywhere. ... Gay bars seem to allow for other normally public freedoms generally denied homosexuals. For instance, it would not be out of place ... for a woman seated at the bar to stare hard into the eyes of another woman, a complete stranger, and to telegraph a sexual desire. A woman might do this in public to a passing man, but she risks censure if she tries it on a woman she does not know. The same, of course, applies to homosexual men, with the added risk of physical injury.[5]

Two months later, for the Binghamton, New York, *Evening Press*, journalist Leo Griffin wrote a story about "Broome County's only exclusively homosexual bar," noting that weeknights were "quiet and relaxed," with "songs like Barbra Streisand's 'People' or Diana Ross' 'Good Morning Heartache' [playing on] the juke box near the small dance floor in the back." But on weekends, "homosexuality is popping out of the walls, men will be dancing with men and women with women on the crowded dance floor." He interviews a bartender who characterizes the clientele as "people from all walks of life, truck drivers, construction workers, hairdressers, college professors, clergymen," and who notes that "most customers use the back door, which exits onto an alley, so no one will see them coming into the bar."[6] "Among the patrons," wrote Ken Wells for the *Miami Herald* in 1979, "are wolves and wallflowers, gulpers and sippers, dancers and sitters, the pensive and the pushy, fighters and passivists [sic], the good, bad, beautiful, ugly."[7]

In a series of interviews for a 1978 story in the *Daily Tar Heel*, the student newspaper at the University of North Carolina at Chapel Hill, Chris Fuller spoke with a student who said that "the gay bar is a sort of mecca for the gay community . . . a place a lot of gay people go to get away from straights. . . . There are no other social-type places for gays to meet."[8] Seven years earlier and fifty miles away, Ken Irons and Mike Forte wrote an article for the *Greensboro Record* about the Renaissance, a gay bar with "a dance floor in a rear room decorated in a psychedelic style" and "an ultra violet (black) light sweep[ing] across signs: 'Gay Power,' 'Gay Lib,' 'It Don't Make a Damn.'" They interview a "handsome, dark-haired young man who . . . freely admits he is a homosexual"; the man recalls that "when my parents found I was a homosexual they got the shotgun out and went after me." The authors note other horrific events, including forced outings, harassment from neighbors, and "round-ups" from the police, though they optimistically suggest that "times are changing." For the queer people interviewed by Irons and Forte, the Renaissance was a haven.[9]

All of these stories were printed in the decade after the years when the Black Nite brawl in Milwaukee, Compton's Cafeteria riot in San Francisco, the Black Cat Tavern and Patch Bar protests in Los Angeles, and the Stonewall riot in New York had drawn public attention to the harassment faced by proprietors and patrons of queer bars—from hostile passers-by, rageful bigots, and the police. In the previous decade, for example, on June 7, 1960, the *San Francisco Examiner* reported the indictment of seven San Francisco Police Department officers for demanding "graft payments by operators of bars frequented by homosexuals." Several of these officers, who controlled liquor licenses in the city, threatened to deny the bars' applications. Several others threatened to "hound [them] to death" with regular raids, searches, and arrests of their patrons. Called before the grand jury, one of the indicted officers, Sgt. John McFarland, denied the bribes but added, "I am aware of what happens in these places if you don't watch them very closely. . . . They kiss, they dance and they rub their knees together. I explained to one of the accusers [Edward G. Bauman of Jack's Waterfront Hangout] that I wasn't going to have any of that and that we would be in often to check him."[10]

We kiss, we dance, and we rub our knees together—all apparently threats to public order. On March 9, 1967, two years before the Stonewall riot, George Waas reported "Deviates Difficult to Ferret Out" in the *Fort Lauderdale News*. Waas describes gay bars as places where "they make their social contacts for the evening, exchange pornography and set up their dates." He quotes Duane Barker, an investigator for the Broward County school system, who testified before a grand jury on the "problem" of homosexuals being "difficult [to] discover" in everyday life: "It is at the homosexual bar that they learn who the local doctors are who'll treat them for their various bouts—and repeated bouts—with venereal disease." In a charge that will sound all-too-familiar to contemporary readers, Barker explains that his intention was to stop homosexuals from "going after the kids."[11] The previous day, Waas had published another story, "Homosexual Problem Growing in County" with the subtitle "Youngsters Are Prime Targets." The article opened with panic: "homosexuality has spread alarmingly in Broward County." Waas railed against "the homosexual's avowed intentions to infiltrate the young," and "the effects a single homosexual can have upon children—especially adolescent boys ranging in ages of 11 to 13."[12] These rationales drove police harassment in particular. Gay bars were demonized as purported sites of pestilence, pornography, promiscuity, and (especially) pederasty.

In this context, the appearance of newspaper articles across the United States portraying queer bars in a relatively sympathetic light in the 1970s seems remarkable, if not transformative. It was during this decade that more robust spaces were carved out and defended as places where queerness could blossom and thrive in the halcyon days before AIDS struck and decimated our people. And still, the bars continued to be targets of extortion, harassment, and violence: interviewed by a reporter for the *Charlotte Observer* in 1978, twenty-nine-year-old Fred Kistler said what many nonqueer people felt: "this club just came out of the depths of hell. . . . We just don't want that kind of thing going on around here."[13] On June 15, 1976, an article in the *Tucson Citizen* detailed multiple gay bashings in and around the town's gay bars, some of which had then closed. The previous week, twenty-one-year-old Richard Heakin was leaving one such bar when he was jumped, beaten, and killed by a group of young men. The reporter for this story, Sam Negri, heard stories from other gay men and lesbians who had been similarly attacked, but who refused to abandon their bar, which had been named after Stonewall. It was "a liberated zone," one said, where "men can dance with men, women can dance with women, and affection can be openly expressed and demonstrated."[14]

Descriptions of queer spaces as meccas and liberated zones have persisted in the decades since the 1970s, especially in response to violent threats. In an article about the June 12, 2016, shooting rampage at the Pulse nightclub in Orlando, Florida, Michael Barbaro writes that gay bars "are refuges and havens, places where, the moment you cross the threshold, there is an unspoken understanding: You will feel accepted and safe. . . . These spaces exist to shelter their inhabitants from the slights and sallies of the world." Barbaro interviewed an activist named David Drake outside the Stonewall in New York one week after the Pulse shooting:

> He described the outrage he felt about the Orlando gunman's decision to carry out his massacre at a gay nightclub. His frame of reference was telling. "It's like when the gunman goes into a church and shoots people. . . . It's sacred," he said of the bar behind him, draped in rainbow-colored flags. "These spaces, even though they are quote-unquote 'bars or clubs,' are those spaces for people in the L.G.B.T.Q. community. Those are the spaces we come to."[15]

In the days after that 2016 shooting that wounded fifty-three and killed forty-nine, numb with sorrow, I was entranced in a state of strange nostalgia, thinking about all of the nights I had spent sweaty, uninhibited, and alive in the queer bars and clubs of countless cities and towns. I thought about the space in those places, the cavernous rooms made for dancing with anyone who happened to sidle up next to you, because dancing like that is a radical act of uncategorized love. I thought about the smell of sweat and the feel of it dripping down your front and back, because dancing is work. I thought about all of the people who gathered in those spaces, because there are still so few places where gathering is safe. I thought about all the queer blood—a source of our power, a fixation of their fear—spilled at Pulse and at so many other sacred queer places. I remembered the touches from so many others on those crowded dance floors, and I remembered the sense of unthinking being-with as we twisted and shook in ecstatic community. These are our sanctuaries.

I remembered one in particular: beneath the El station at Belmont, a dark, crowded space dominated the weekly rotations of 1990s Chicago queer nightlife. In earlier decades, the space had been occupied by businesses including a shoe repair shop, but by 1983 it had been converted into a nightclub for queers. It was originally opened by Tim Sullivan and Shirley Mooney, two friends who wanted to develop a club open to the many constituencies of Chicago's queer community: gay men and lesbians, trans people and drag queens, and everyone else who did not have a bar of their own. Their club was called Berlin, invoking the vibrant, epicurean queer nightlife scene in that city before the rise of the Nazi Party, the era of *Different from the Others* and Magnus Hirschfeld's Institute for Sexual Science. As later owners Jo Webster and Jim Schuman remembered at the bar's thirtieth anniversary party,

> "Tim loved [the city of] Berlin. Think of the Weimar Republic, which was pre-Hitler, and characterized by innovations in art and culture that were later dubbed degenerate and socially disruptive by fascists," Webster said. "Think of 'Cabaret,'" added Schuman, referring to the musical and film set in Berlin during the Weimar Republic.[16]

I had moved to Chicago from Birmingham in the early 1990s to attend Northwestern University. I took with me a small collection of books by queer authors that I had been covertly collecting during my high school years. Among them, a thin volume by Edmund White, *Nocturnes for the King of Naples*, was both my compass and my guide. I could recite from memory the elusive ways in which White describes the complex nuances of queer spaces—the passing glances of public cruising, the electricity of queer erotics—but I hungered to experience them in fuller ways than I had before. For White, all of these elements of queer life are threaded with both longing and loss: "the answer to the riddle—what's preserved but moves? what existed only in the past but rustles, flickers brilliantly into sunlight, then soars?—is you, your presence, thoughts of you."[17] I carried this line like a chant that could take me back to the old wooden deck of a canopied grove in the lush state park that bordered our school's campus in Birmingham, and to the boy who had summoned me there to teach me what my body could do.

But most fervently compelling to me was White's description of queer spaces: the "congeries of bodies," the "faces floating up . . . then trailing away," the "dignified advance and retreat" of cruising. I longed for these places and the sultry choreographies they invoked. And so almost immediately after arriving in Chicago, I began to explore the queer parts of town, those havens and sanctuaries and "liberated zones" that were so elusive in Birmingham. Sometimes I would explore alone; other times I tagged along with friends who'd come from less-hostile backgrounds and already knew how to enter and move through these places. We would set out long past nightfall, taking the El from Evanston down to Lakeview and mapping our way through a weekly rotation of bars and clubs. Most nights we ended up at Berlin. Returning home in the wee hours, and before letting myself fall asleep, I would sit at my desk and write about what I had learned, what I had seen, what I had done. I was teaching myself how to be queer alongside other queers. And though it was so long ago that I can only barely remember what it felt like to be in my body then, reading these entries now immediately takes me back to that dark, sweaty dance floor underneath the Belmont El station, where longing and loss pulsed and thrived. Initially, I focused on describing the rich sensorium of the place. I wrote about the overwhelming impact of smell while we danced:

> *There is a department store-quantity of scents—*
> *colognes, perfumes, aftershaves, deodorants, soaps,*
> *shampoos. And it is surprising, despite the confluence*

> *of odors, how specific aromas recall a previous waft—from immediately behind at the bar, or pressed together while dancing, or even from afar while staring. Each fragrance is a picture-book, a photo album, with a family tree of the men we have smelled or tasted or just wanted before, and their culmination is the unmistakable tag of these places. When we leave, we all smell the same: pieced-together quilts of the family of scents that live here. There is also smoke, which makes its musk visible, floating from mouth and dissipating through the lights that highlight its ever-shifting terrain in the air we all breathe. There is in this smoke a community: smoke gathers and joins other smoke. By the time we leave, the space is roofed by the aggregate of everyone's exhale.*

I wrote about touch, and the significance of skin's sense of the world:

> *The feel of clothes against your skin will increase in importance as the heat and sweat accumulates, clings to you more and more as the night passes. Tops are generally tighter (better for dancing and accentuation of one's arms, chest, abdomen) and trousers usually looser (liberation of the legs). There are variations: those who are particularly proud of their thighs or hips or bulge and wear latex, leather or rubber to identify them; or those who tear off their tops and dance and drink half-clothed. At any point, you may feel the massage of someone's grasp. It is as if there are lines and hooks connected to the inches of your body, any of which may snag a passing hand—hungry, floating free but firm, ready to be snared. Sometimes, if the line is too short, you may drag someone with you and either reel him in or find some way to cut the cord. You have*

options: keep walking; turn and smile or smirk; pry the grabbers off you; or simply stop, wait for their release, then move along.

And then, as I gradually settled into my sense of myself in these places, I began to nurture and elaborate variations on the theme of my erotic subjectivity. Here, for instance, is someone whom I knew only during the time of this encounter, but who still lives, alive as anyone, on my skin and in my memory:

Scene: Berlin. A dark, relatively small club with three bars, a dance floor, and a coat check.

I see out of the corner of my eye a tall man dancing behind me. He is staring at me. My quick glances seem to satisfy his attention, and he dances closer. My back is to him. I let go, relax backwards, let him get closer. He smells like old wood, dark but sweet, and his body is strong, tight. We begin to move together—waves at low tide, winds from a tornado, seagulls diving. Our rhythms embrace, and he gets closer. I can feel him pressing into my back. I keep dancing.

We are interrupted when my ride home says she's ready to leave. I start to turn, smile and shrug, walk to the coat check. The line there is still long, and I give my ticket to my friend, tell her stop for me on her way out. I return to the floor.

Within seconds he is back, this time moving into place not slowly as before, but picking up almost immediately: his arms are around my waist, I can feel his breath in my ear, his chest and stomach against my back. This is no slow wooing. I let my hands explore the tops of his legs, the small of his back, his pockets.

That smell is maddening. We continue to move together, my back to his front, for hours. Time has evaporated, my watch has stopped working. His palms are following the thumping of the spinner's techno-mix along my sides, my stomach, my chest, legs. He reaches down and takes my hand, interrupting this purely carnal interaction with connection—his fingers are woven into mine. I lean back into him, relax my head against his chest and shoulder, feel his quick breaths in my left ear. The people around me do not disappear but become part of me, extensions of my arms and legs, fetal fluid surrounding all of me, keeping me safe.

Eternity passes, and my ride again interrupts with her smile, her loud, sharp actor's voice: "I have to take him home now."

I told her to do this.

I turn and smile, say this is my ride, introduce myself. I can't hear his name. He points to the bar, finds a pen, some paper. I write my number, put it in his hand. We leave, and finally I get a good look at him.

The ride home: laughing, staring out the window and reliving the dance. I can smell him on my shirt. I've forgotten what he looks like, but I remember the feel of his wallet, stuffed deep in the pocket behind him. His taste is stuck in my mouth, on my tongue; there is an imprint of his hand on the back of my neck. I can feel its contours, trace its edge from the top of my spine to the graph of my hair; its dips and mounds are obvious. Is it visible from the outside too?

"From these random glimpses of identity," Frank Browning wrote in 1993, "a window can open between the souls of unconnected people, a window framed only by intuitive readiness and undimmed by a lifetime's accumulated judgments."[18] Over time, my writing became more evocative than descriptive as nights blended together, wrapping themselves around one another, into a great ocean of night. Sometimes, after a succession of nights when I had fallen asleep before writing an entry, I struggled to keep track of which was which and when was when:

> *Some of these nights are interchangeable;*
> *they bleed, and blood mixes, rolling*
> *into other blood, guzzling space like hounds*
> *still hungry from the kill.*

And sometimes the entries were poems, especially when I had encountered someone who inscribed themselves into my elaborate fantasies, where countless versions of entwining—a night together, or three weeks, or the rest of our lives—took root and replayed with unending variations, as with this one:

> *On the screen*
> *there's a physical: doctor*
> *reading patient's curves,*
> *double-checking weight,*
> *ordering positions unusual,*
> *bent. He's older; the younger,*
> *athletic. Everyone watches—*
> *dancing slows—*
> *as he begins to sketch,*
> *following the contours of*
> *cheek and nose, the eyes,*
> *hair aloof, intermittent smiles.*
>
> *He's standing next to me,*
> *this young one, grinning,*
> *pupils ahead. I asked him about*
> *a snake once—is it a real snake?—*

*as the drag queen on stage
moved a thick boa in and
out of her legs, thighs,
around her neck.
He smiled and said
he thought that it was.
I think it is too.*

*Ordering a drink,
giving your number,
standing in my way as
I walk to the loo;
I am recording your grin.
I remember your quick wave,
the way you turned from me,
said something to the man standing next to you,
turned back,
the invitation to move
away from my group, toward yours.
I knew you could leave them.*

*You remind me of me:
too shy to talk first,
or maybe too proud,
and the almighty touch,
the brush of skin, hand to back
(waist if you're bold),
then pretending you were just moving past
and checking to make sure I follow you.
I do this too. You are an actor.*

*I thought your friends were leaving.
I didn't expect to see you hail that cab;
I would have spoken otherwise,
this time. I would have stepped forward.*

I was ready. I was drinking. I was rehearsed.
My smile is crooked,
I can be coy, I can be distant,
I can make you wonder too.
I know how to flatter—
comment on your admirers.
I like your shirt,
that haircut suits you,
I've seen you here before.

I've mythologized you: you're a
minor deity. I have stories,
poems, written about your birth,
the way nature folded you into herself,
made you a day, a sunset, some trees.
I've used you to explain the way
things are calm after a deluge,
there are rings around the moon some nights,
the sun gets bigger as it sets.
I've built you an idol, a temple:
these words. You have hymns.

I can see the road his shoes have stamped
from here, this window, to the car waiting.
I can smell him closing the door—that
first inhale:
the residue of someone else who was smoking,
the cologne clawing its way up the vinyl,
the sweat of some other dancer.
Someone else has used this car before,
told the driver where to go,
the quickest route,
drive fast for a tip.
His legs are not the first to journey
from seat into floor,

other hands have opened this window,
his eyes are seeing nothing new.
This originality is feigned.
I've seen you here before;
you've left, but
I can see you here now.

And this one, from months earlier:

Holding your head at an angle, leaning
against the square that rises to join floor and roof,
grasping at a drink, a smoke,
you hold gazes hard. Fast with seduction,
the coy turnaround,
watching someone else until you know I've
noticed. And then: desperation, the return,
maybe to dance nearby, maybe to leave.
Try to touch me, feel the way I bend,
tireless.
Hands in pockets are giveaways: stuffed discomfort
with scene or self, or boredom.
Take your pick of the art and bid.
This is rodeo, a selling of free jump
for lasso. Your hat falls as you turn,
your shirt creases open: I can see flesh outlined
becoming mountains, foothills, a plain.
You can show your courage,
the strength of your cord to rope me
and the swiftness of your tug,
your reeling me in,
pruned of the traits you can't stand.
Now find my interests,
put me to work in your fields, wear me
like the sweater knitted from scratch
by a mother, a grandmother, an aunt

already distanced, made foreign,
sold. You take compliments well.

Near the end of my last summer in Chicago, we all went out to Berlin to dance again, saying farewell to the bar that had been our oasis for those years, saying goodbye to each other and to the many others with whom we had lingered on one or many of those late nights. Returning home early the next morning, still damp with sweat, I found a folded piece of paper that someone had slipped into my pocket. This is what it said:

This love is a bruise
Discovered in the shower.

The day I met you I knew
What I was going to do:

Wear green to dramatize my eyes,
Combine silence and wit

In measures calculated
To make you suffer a bit,

Maybe even become
Your 'secret sorrow.'

I thought I could handle it.
Ten thousand proverbs

Couldn't have kept me
From digging this pit and falling in.

Serves me right that you're leaving,
Now let the pain I planned begin.

"How many times," Robin asked me one night when I was reading him some of these late-night diary entries, "did you have your heart broken in that Chicago club?" I looked up at him and saw that his eyes were wet.

"I don't know," I said, "probably a couple times a week at first, when I was still new to the bars."

"And then?"

"And then I learned that hearts should not be broken in these places. That's not what they're for."

He sighed the breathiest of his laughs, the one that indicated recognition. "That's a hard lesson to learn."

"Where did you learn it?" I asked.

"Same as you, a bar somewhere. I don't remember. But I remember that I learned it."

"I don't know," I said, "maybe it's not something we learn once. Maybe we never stop learning it. We just learn how to learn it, and that's the hard part, learning that it's something to learn."

He laughed again, this time conspiratorially. "Let's go learn again tonight."

So we gathered ourselves together and walked from his apartment on the top floor of the old Victorian down Castro Street and turned left onto Market. A few blocks later, we were back at the Pils, our favorite haunt. We walked inside and heard from the bar that welcome refrain, "Oh look, the Twink and the Bear are back!" And we learned again, as we had so many nights before and would again so many nights after, that although these are not venues for the breaking of hearts, our hearts would be broken anyway—because these were our sacred places, our havens, our sanctuaries, where we allowed our greatest and most supple vulnerabilities to roam, safe at last.

iii. Hail, true body

Ave verum corpus

In another story my father sometimes tells, his grandfather Lum was near to dying. He lay prostrate on a bed, a swift

Mississippi breeze pushing through to blanket him in the only air he'd ever known. Two years prior, Lum had died, a doctor glancing over at the family to say it was over: he was gone. But minutes later he had returned. He had been sixty-eight then, and he prayed to live to seventy, longer than he had thought he could live, though not long enough to work through the deep treads of an aching, throbbing loneliness carved deep within him in childhood. Now, at seventy, he heaved a great sigh, opened his eyes for a moment, and reached down to grab the sheet. He pulled it up and over his face, doing the final job that someone else ought to have done, and sighed off into oblivion, dead for good this time.

William Faulkner told this story, too, but for him the name was not Lum: Addie lay heaving, barely there, while sounds of work—human hands and wood, making things together—came drifting through. Addie knew that "words are no good; that words don't ever fit even what they are trying to say at."[19] She knew, too, that *love* was "just a shape to fill a lack; that when the right time came, you wouldn't need a word for that anymore than for pride or fear."[20] These are the things that Addie thought as she drifted between the past that haunted her and the present that waited for her departure. Death in the South is slow, even if it's sudden. Death takes time, and makes time go.

I think of his body, Lum's, as it held then released what he so desperately wanted. It seems so oddly smooth the way my father tells it, the movement of *what will happen* back into *desire*: did he really want to live to 70 before he'd lived that long? Did he die at 70 only after he'd longed for that age? Or was it my father's later telling—the chronicles set forth by a grandson Lum would never really know—that retroactively kept him alive? It's a story my father loves to tell: Lum was near to dying, prostrate on some rickety slats, feeling the push of the breeze as if it were time itself, blowing back and forward and back again.

And then there is the other story my father tells: his own father, Lum's son, on the front porch of the family home. As I started to suspect at an early age, for my father the telling helps manage this story's unbounded flows, keeping his guttural grief at bay by performing it. I understand this impulse, this use of narrative not just as a salve but also as a veiled approach to the ends of our lives and the lives of others, a flirtation with finitude, a way to touch the void without risking falling in. Telling is recitation, but it is also high drama of the most productive kind.

My father is always clear on this point: when he and his sister heard the bang while hanging laundry behind the house, he *knew*. He as a boy knew what the sound meant. He stepped gingerly through the house: in the back door, tiptoeing through rooms, finally out to the front porch. There his father lay. For my father, then a boy of fifteen, time whirled like a too-familiar hurricane, pulsing forward and back, inward and out, like heartbeats when the blood pressure is too high. The world became a time-lapse replay of that walk through the house, that creep out to the porch, that first shuttering glance at the body in the corner. The replay was relentless, cushioned only by the story he began telling when I was a child myself, not even fifteen years old.

Later, when I was well into adulthood, he expanded beyond the standard narrative of this event, elaborating parts of the story he had never told before: the smell as he approached, the look of the body's slump, what happened next. These details, and more, would slip out of him like hiccups, bursting forth then falling back into regular rhythm. He would start again: "we were hanging laundry. Daddy had been drinking. Momma was away." And always, always, "it was hot," a reminder of when (the day summer becomes fall) and where (the very deep South) it had all occurred. With all of these elaborations, my father would find and refind his own body in the story: a body that could hear fine distinctions between sharp sudden sounds; a body that could creep through a shadowed house; a body that could smell the nuances of gunpowder, smoke, and blood; a body that could discern death in another figure; a body grown slick with sweat from the wet southern heat. A body that knew.

Some tellings are told as a way of seeking bodies lost to time, of trying to recover them. A telling like this: Alec had a rich bass voice whose depth and weight anchored the ethereal harmonies of Faure's *Requiem* as our school choir sang one spring, I with a baritone that I later learned had been inherited from my grandfather. And this: Lana often asked to be held and squeezed—not by just anyone, but by those who knew where and how to pull her in, by those who could wrap themselves around and envelop her. And this: Robin was an *event* on dance floors when the music was right, and no one could avoid his first sliding steps as he twisted himself like a wave, his wild leaps and jerky spins around others, and then, when finally entranced, his arms and hands flailing up and around like sails in a hurricane. The shock of Alec's piercing glare. The tidal foaminess of Lana's laugh. The gasps and wheezes and giggles of Robin listening to the gossip he loved to hear. Alec's mouth. Lana's hair. Robin's eyes. Spitting anger. Oceanic sobs. The feral tracks of a kiss left throbbing on my cheek. And echoing through all of these, told too many times for me to remember them all as I sat still, my body folded into itself, my silence gathering and deepening, my father beginning over and over and over again, "It was hot. We were hanging laundry out back. We heard a sound like a firecracker. I knew what it meant."

VII
Benedictus

Was this not the very tree—the tree to which the young saint was bound with his hands behind him, over the trunk of which his sacred blood trickled like driblets after a rain? that Roman tree on which he writhed, ablaze in a final agony of death, with the harsh scraping of his young flesh against the bark as his final evidence of all earthly pleasure and pain?

YUKIO MISHIMA, CONFESSIONS OF A MASK (1949)

How lonely lies the city, once so full of people. Once honored by the world, she has become like a widow. She who was a princess among the provinces is become tributary.

LAMENTATIONS 1:1

i. Death has struck

Mors stupebit

On September 30, 2010, the Gay, Lesbian and Straight Education Network (GLSEN) released a statement cowritten with Parents and Friends of Lesbians and Gays (PFLAG) and the Trevor Project. The statement advocated for swift passage of the Safe Schools Improvement Act by the US House of Representatives and the US Senate. Early the following year, the act was formally reintroduced as Senate Bill S.506 by Pennsylvania senator Robert Casey, and as House Resolution H.R.1648 by California representative Linda Sánchez. Among other requirements, the act would mandate local education boards and commissions to develop clear definitions and prohibitions of bullying and harassment, and would direct state education agencies to collect data on bullying incidents in schools and provide resources for education and prevention. Both the bill and the resolution failed to receive formal votes. In every successive Congress when they have been reintroduced, they have similarly stalled without passage.

The immediate impetus for GLSEN's advocacy in September 2010 was a series of widely reported suicides in the United States among "youth who were known to be bullied relentlessly because of their actual or perceived sexual orientation or gender identity."[1] The most publicized of these was the death of eighteen-year-old Tyler Clementi, a first-year undergraduate student at Rutgers University who jumped from the George Washington Bridge after learning that his roommate had surreptitiously live-streamed him having sex with another man.[2] Around the same time as Clementi's death, there were at least twenty other publicized suicides in this category, including Justin Aaberg in Minnesota (age 15), Cody Barker in Wisconsin (age 17), Jamarcus Bell in Indiana (age 14), Brandon Bitner in Pennsylvania (age 14), Asher Brown in Texas (age 13), Harrison Brown in Colorado (age 13), Raymond Chase in Rhode Island (age 19), Ty Field in Oklahoma (age 11), Zach Harrington in Oklahoma (age 19), Corey Jackson in Michigan (age 19), Samantha Jones in Minnesota (age 13), Montana Lance in Texas (age 9), Billy Lucas in Indiana (age 15), Caleb Nolt in Indiana (age 14), Felix Sacco in Massachusetts (age 17), Christian Taylor in Virginia (age 16), and Seth Walsh in California (age 13).

The previous month, in August 2010, a cluster of suicides among young gay men in their twenties was reported in Utah: David Standley, Todd Ransom, and Tim Tilley. And the following year, in 2011, a "suicide contagion area" was identified in a single Minnesota school district, where two of the adolescents listed above had killed themselves because of relentless bullying. Tom Prichard of the Minnesota Family Council argued that "homosexual indoctrination" was to blame for the suicides, while his colleague Barb Anderson asked, "Why aren't we outraged that [Gay-Straight Alliance groups] affirm sexual disorders?"[3] Prichard and Anderson were responding to students and teachers developing a group for LGBTQ students (and their allies) in the Anoka-Hennepin School District, where at least seven students had died by suicide in the preceding two years. Interviewed in December 2011, the faculty adviser of a Gay-Straight Alliance in a local middle school said that seven of his students "had to be hospitalized for suicide attempts in the first five months of 2011," and that his "phone rang nearly continually with reports of students who were hurting themselves or engaging in unsafe activities." He described keeping crisis center contact information near every phone and computer in his house and office. Meanwhile, in response to one of the suicides a local right-wing group, the Parents Action League, "organized an event called the Day of Truth, created by the 'ex-gay' ministry Exodus International."[4]

In the same year that GSLEN's press release was issued, an article published in the *Journal of the American Academy of Child & Adolescent Psychiatry* indicated that "for GLB [gay, lesbian, and bisexual] adolescents the lifetime rate of suicide attempt is between 20% and 40%, approximately two to six times that of non-GLB adolescents."[5] The statistics underlying that claim relied on several previous studies of the relationship between sexuality, gender identity, and suicide. The vast majority of these and similar studies established much higher rates of suicidal ideation and suicide attempts among gay, lesbian, bisexual, and transgender people. The first cluster of formal scientific studies had been conducted in the 1970s, following decades of anecdotal evidence in popular, clinical, and other literatures. As Samuel Huneke asserted in his 2019 essay about the literary and filmic mythology of queer suicide in the late nineteenth and early twentieth centuries, suicide among queer people "continues to outpace [suicide] among the general population," marking a "tragic and unintended legacy of the gay rights movements of Imperial and Weimar Germany, the bequest of an identity marred by a death wish."[6]

In other words, by the mid-twentieth century, the archetype of queer suicide had expanded well beyond its geographical distribution in Weimer literature and film, and well beyond the neo-Romantic portrayals of the "morbid eroticism" in the aesthetic works that Huneke considered.[7] In his 1983 book *I Thought People Like That Killed Themselves*, activist and author Eric Rofes noted,

> It is not difficult for anyone familiar with gay literature to name dozens of novels and stories that climax with the suicide of a homosexual. . . . In addition to novels with specifically gay themes, popular books that include a gay character who ends up killing herself or himself continue to flood the market [and]

movies that need to find motivation for a character's unhappiness or suicide [often] throw in a gay incident.[8]

What I have been calling the *archetype* of queer suicide, Rofes describes as a "pernicious trick played on lesbians and gay men" in the history of these kinds of narratives: a mythology that asserts "that lesbians and gay men not only commit suicide at a rate considerably higher than society-at-large, but that somehow a person's homosexuality is itself the source of self-destructiveness."[9] Rofes tracks the development of this mythology through the history of medical and legal writing on homosexuality as pathological and criminal, dangerous not only to the person themselves but also to the very fabric of society. But the "most dangerous assertions" in these literatures, Rofes writes, are those that view "homosexuality as inherently self-destructive," which is to say homosexuality as suicidal *by definition*.[10] This pernicious assertion is exemplified by this line from the 1962 book *Suicide and Mass Suicide* by Dutch psychiatrist Joost Merlot:

> The homosexual act in itself may already represent a suicidal tendency, an inner fury against prolonging the race, or an unconscious need to merge with the stronger person of the same sex.[11]

Before the 1970s, gay and lesbian authors often resisted the correlation of homosexuality and suicide, insisting that despite that widespread mythology, gay and lesbian people were not more likely to consider or attempt suicide. Rofes is sympathetic to these writers, who were motivated to resist psychological and criminological assertions of the self-destructive nature of homosexuality. But he also notes that these "denial[s] took place in the same context in which the myths were created: without statistics, without a view of the entire lesbian and male homosexual population, and with little awareness of the difficulties in defining or verifying suicides."[12]

As late as 1968, psychiatrist Martin Hoffman wrote in his landmark exposé *The Gay World,*

> There are, regrettably, no quantitative data on the matter, but it is my distinct impression that the homosexual world produces clinical depressions at a far higher rate than the heterosexual world, and though I cannot substantiate my opinion, I would venture to say that the suicide rate among male homosexuals is higher than among heterosexuals.[13]

Fortunately, by the time Rofes was writing his book, social scientists had begun performing extensive statistical surveys of gay and lesbian communities, surveys that explicitly asked about individuals' experiences with suicide. The first of these, a 1970 study conducted by Alan Bell and Martin Weinberg of the Institute for Sex Research at Indiana University, found the following:

> 37% of the white homosexual men had either seriously considered or attempted suicide, compared to 13% of the white heterosexual men; of the black homosexual men 24% had seriously considered or attempted suicide, compared to 2% of the black heterosexual men. Of the white lesbians 41% had similar experiences, compared to 26% of the white heterosexual women; and 25% of the black lesbians had seriously considered or attempted suicide, compared with 19% of the black heterosexual women.[14]

A 1973 comparative survey of people in Chicago, San Francisco, and St. Louis, conducted by Marcel Saghir and Eli Robins for a book titled *Male and Female Homosexuality: A Comprehensive Investigation,* found that "7% of the homosexual men had attempted suicide while none of their heterosexual male sample had; 12% of the lesbians had attempted suicide while only 5% of the heterosexual women had."[15] Finally, a much more extensive, nationwide survey of gay and lesbian people conducted by Karla Jay and Allen Young in 1977 found that 40 percent of gay men and 39 percent of lesbian women had attempted or seriously contemplated suicide.[16]

In his review of this cluster of studies, Rofes is careful to clarify what they can and cannot tell us. Generally speaking, the surveys confirm that lesbians and gay men in the 1970s reported suicidal ideation and suicide attempts at much higher rates than did heterosexual people. However,

> We cannot adequately estimate how much greater the risk of suicide is for gay people. We cannot conclude that homosexuality or lesbianism causes suicide or that suicidal people are "vulnerable" to homosexuality. And, because we only have recent statistics, we cannot determine if the suicide rate for lesbians and gay men is currently increasing or decreasing.[17]

Further, rather than confirming the notion of an inherently pathological and self-destructive nature to homosexuality, survey respondents who had attempted suicide generally indicated that the widespread and longstanding traditions of pathologizing and criminalizing gay and lesbian people were *themselves* primary motivators for their previous suicide attempts. As Jay and Young remarked on the 1977 survey's results,

> Suicide and attempted suicide are frequent responses of gay people to the difficulties of the gay experience in a hostile society. It has been suggested that psychiatrists, clergy, and others who insist on characterizing gays as sick and sinful are responsible for driving

many gay people to suicide. It is a form of violent oppression resulting from isolation, discrimination, and the problems of suicide.[18]

Since the 1970s, numerous studies have validated and expanded on the findings of these early surveys. A 1987 essay in the journal *Death Studies* reviewed five large studies on the incidence of suicide attempts among gay and lesbian people, including the three described above and two additional large-scale studies. Authors Judith Saunders and S. M. Valente evaluate the empirical results and ultimately establish that

> Gay men and lesbians reported 2.5 to 7 times more suicide attempts than heterosexual controls. These studies support the findings that suicide attempts are significantly higher in gay men and women than in heterosexual controls. Moreover, both the impressive sample size in four of the studies and the careful sampling procedures provide basis for confidence in the findings.[19]

A 2002 article published in the *American Journal of Public Health* reviewed numerous additional surveys conducted in the late 1980s and throughout the 1990s and conducted an additional large-scale survey of men who have sex with men (MSM). In addition to confirming earlier researchers' findings on the increased prevalence of suicide attempts among lesbian and gay people, the authors found in their own survey the following:

> The most immediately compelling findings were the high rates of suicidal ideation and attempts in this cohort. More than 1 in 5 men reported having made a suicide plan. Twelve percent of the sample reported suicide attempts (with 70% of this subgroup reporting suicide attempts before age 25). Furthermore, 45% of

those who had attempted suicide had done so more than once.[20]

More recent surveys have found similar results for bisexual people, transgender people, and queer people more broadly, with special attention to the particular intensity of risk for youth and adolescent populations. In all of these studies, researchers have emphasized the limitations inherent to the topic. Most notable, of course, is the problem of sampling: because they must identify themselves as queer in order to be counted, survey respondents must, by definition, be *out*, at least to some degree. In addition, successful suicides are inherently difficult to ascertain, except in the limited number of cases in which a person has made a clear, explicit communication that they are willingly choosing to die (for example, by leaving a suicide note). Finally, the studies are limited by the difficulty in providing a commonly acceptable definition of suicidal "ideation" and suicide "attempt": for example, should "chronic self-destructive behavior," as Eric Rofes put it, count as a long-term suicide attempt, or should it be excluded "because the death is not immediate and not violent"?[21] Nonetheless, even with these limitations in mind, the researchers described here and many others have confirmed again and again that queer people experience significantly higher rates of suicidal ideation and suicide attempts than nonqueer populations.

When Eric Rofes published his book in 1983, his was the first extended treatment of suicide among lesbians and gay men. Four years earlier, he had published an article in the August 9, 1979, issue of *The Advocate* entreating lesbian and gay communities to take the issue seriously:

> While some activists see suicide as a vestige of the pre-Stonewall gay sensibility that will decrease with the growth of gay pride, lesbians and gay men have not stopped taking their lives. Suicide remains a part

of the contemporary gay experience, and it will not go away simply by being ignored. Only by bringing the subject of suicide out into the open and confronting the fact that many gay people *do* kill themselves, will we as a community continue to develop resources and techniques for coping with it.[22]

This article became the basis for the 1983 book, in which he describes what he terms "the myth and the fact of gay suicide." In both the article and the book, he pleads for the development of community-based resources and structures of support, connecting the prevalence of suicide to other large-scale problems faced by queer people. Rofes ends the book with this stirring indictment and call to action:

Ending gay suicide requires an end to the discrimination, hatred, violence and trivialization used against lesbians and gay men; ultimately, it requires a strategy for social and political change that will transform our society radically for all of us.[23]

But in the four years between the publication of Rofes's article in *The Advocate* and the release of *I Thought People Like That Killed Themselves*, another threat had emerged, one that would profoundly alter the context and the significance of queer suicide. By 1983, two newspaper stories briefly describing "Outbreaks of Pneumonia among Gay Males"[24] and a "Rare Cancer Seen in 41 Homosexuals"[25] had been in circulation for two years, and panic had swept through queer communities as the number of dying young queers began to rise with unrelenting acceleration. In those early days—before the virus was known or named, before the arsenal of drugs had been invented, before "fatal" became "chronic"—queerness was locked in another dance with death, one that would upstage and overshadow all the others that had come before.

ii. May the martyrs greet you at your arrival

Adventu suscipiant te martyres

On December 23, 1982, the San Francisco *Bay Area Reporter* published a front-page story by Paul Lorch about the death of gay twenty-nine-year-old Richard Brian Herbaugh. The article, titled "KS Diagnosis, Takes Life," begins, "A 20-year-old Haight-Ashbury man exercised a grim option on learning he was a KS victim. He hanged himself in Golden Gate Park Thursday, December 16 at 1:30 am."[26] Two days before his suicide, Richard had learned from his doctor that a lesion inside his mouth was Kaposi's sarcoma (KS), a rare, malignant skin cancer. The following evening, he met his friend Allen Young and told him about the diagnosis. Allen was worried but not surprised: by late 1982, queer communities in San Francisco, Los Angeles, New York, and other cities had been facing mysterious outbreaks of KS for several years, as well as an inexplicable rise in cases of pneumocystis carinii pneumonia (PCP), an opportunistic infection that was affecting otherwise healthy gay men. Case reports later revealed that many patients presenting with one of these conditions also tested positive for the other. The previous year, in June and July 1981, two stories had appeared in the *Los Angeles Times* and the *New York Times* reporting on bulletins about these unexplained outbreaks issued by the Centers for Disease Control (CDC). Since that time, scientists had attributed the illnesses to weakened immune systems, though they did not yet know why the patients had become immunocompromised. They initially suspected that poppers (amyl nitrate) or popular lubricants, including Vaseline and Crisco, might be to blame. Three months before Richard died, on September 24, 1982, the CDC gave the condition a name: Acquired Immune Deficiency Syndrome, or AIDS.[27]

Richard had been experiencing bouts of inexplicable symptoms for some time, including recurring staph infections on various parts of his body. In an interview for the newspaper article, Allen recalled that Richard had been "avoiding physical contact with him for weeks," denying him even the most casual forms of affection. At the time, Allen interpreted his friend's withdrawal as emotional distance, a sign that he might be ending their friendship. But in the interview, he wondered if Richard was just trying to protect him from contagion. He described Richard's recent life, "spending four to five nights a week at the 8th and Howard baths, . . . living in the fast side of the fast lane." He had many lovers, but had not found what he wanted most: someone to love. He worried about his health, but even then, when KS was the primary fear and AIDS was unknown, he already felt overwhelmed by the prospect of endless doctor's visits. "I don't know what is worse," he had said to Allen, "facing the medical tests or facing death."[28]

Just after midnight on December 16, Richard wrote a note to his friends and family. This is how it began:

> Act 2, Scene IV: the curtain closes. Thank-you, everyone, thank you. I feel like I am in a giant stadium on the 20 yard line. No lights, no sounds and no one to touch. I have longed to love and be loved but I never saw it, heard it or felt the wonderful things love brings. But folks please don't disappear for I love you all and be assured that I am at rest. I can no longer stand the pain. My head constantly hurts, my gut is never still and I can not stand the pressure. I am weak and no one to touch, to hold, to cry on. Oh my loneliness. The void. I sigh. Offer my body to science for KS study only. Maybe they can conquer this evil soon.

He coiled a rope in his pocket and walked the half-dozen blocks to Golden Gate Park. There, in a quiet grove lush with greenery, he found a sturdy branch and tied his noose. He had carefully selected this venue: Richard had majored in horticulture at college, and had been disappointed when the best job he could find in San Francisco was as a flower arranger at a florist. His body was discovered the following afternoon, at which point it was no longer viable for scientific donation. Still, said Allen, "there's a sort of poetry in the ending. He lived his life alone, he died alone." The article closes with a dramatic crescendo of sorrowful indictment:

> Richard Herbaugh had had enough. He had found more sex and action in San Francisco than fills the lives of a dozen men. However, he never found the love that only he saw himself capable of. Untapped. Worn out. The alabaster skin of his face turning red and puffy, he had had enough . . . of a life too full and not full enough.[29]

Three years later, on October 30, 1985, a thirty-five-year-old man used a cane to break a window in his seventeenth-floor hospital room in New York. Once the window was clear, he climbed out and jumped to his death. He had been admitted the day before, when he had been diagnosed with AIDS.[30] The prior week and across town, on October 24, Gilbert Rodriguez and Charles Villalonga leaped from the window of their thirty-fifth-floor apartment. Before jumping, the men had carefully decorated a bedroom in the apartment with fresh-cut flowers and shared a bottle of wine. They tied a white silk sash around both of their waists and climbed onto the window sill. As they embraced, they stepped sideways into the void. Investigators later confirmed that they had both been diagnosed with AIDS.[31] The men were unknown to local support agencies like the Gay Men's Health Crisis. But the story of their deaths was not a surprise; a spokesperson for the National Gay Task Force commented that "there have been cases of suicides of AIDS patients in various places around the country. I know there have been some in San Francisco." Stephen Caiazza, a local physician working with many people diagnosed with AIDS, noted that the story "was not unusual except in the sense of the drama with which it happened. But in terms of suicide *per se* and AIDS, it's not [unusual]." As an Associated Press reporter sympathetically wrote, in jumping from the window, they were "choosing instant death over the slower ravages of AIDS."[32] Charles was forty-three years old and Gilbert was forty-four.

On March 4, 1988, Gina Kolata published a story in the *New York Times* reporting on the research of Peter Marzuk, a psychiatrist at the Cornell University Medical College in New York. Marzuk and his colleagues had analyzed death records from New York's chief medical examiner for the year 1985. Isolating records that indicated suicide as the manner of death, they found that people diagnosed with AIDS were sixty-six times as likely to die by suicide as those in the general population. This significantly exceeded the suicide rates for people living with other chronic and terminal illnesses, including kidney disease (ten to fifty times as likely), Huntington's disease (three to twenty-three times as likely), and cancer (only slightly more likely). Most of these suicides took the form of jumping from a great height, often a hospital room. All of them took place "within nine months of receiving the diagnosis of AIDS, most within six months of diagnosis." In addition to the suicides by people diagnosed with AIDS, there were several additional cases in which "the recent death of a homosexual lover with AIDS was a precipitant for the suicide, [or] an AIDS victim and his companion, not known to have AIDS, jointly committed suicide."[33] Marzuk notes that the elevated rates of suicide cited in his study likely *underestimate* "the true AIDS-related suicide rate": first, because AIDS itself was underreported to the medical examiner, and second, because a significant number of deaths that may have been intentional were not definitively ascertainable (and recordable) as suicides.

The study proposes a number of factors specific to AIDS diagnoses that contribute to a person choosing to end their life:

> The social stigma of the illness, the withdrawal of family support, diminished or lost occupational functioning, long-term dependency, the loss of friends or lovers of the victim (often to AIDS), and the specter of an inexorable, terminal illness that may lead to pain, disfigurement, and emaciation.[34]

In 1985, the year for which these death records were analyzed, the epidemic was expanding at an accelerating rate. In its first weekly update in January 1986, the CDC reported that 16,458 people had been diagnosed with AIDS since 1981, and that 8,361 people had died, a mortality rate of 51 percent at that time. These numbers also showed that there was an 84 percent increase in incidence for 1985 from the preceding year.[35] One new antiviral medication, AZT, had been approved by the Food and Drug Administration (FDA) in March 1987, but its ultimate effectiveness was unknown, it was unaffordable for many people, and its side effects were brutal. A test for detecting HIV antibodies in blood had been released in 1985, but it was approved for use by private blood banks, not for individuals—in other words, to assuage the fears of the general public, not to provide resources for the communities most affected. When Marzuk's study was published in 1988, an AIDS diagnosis still implied a slow and painful death. Nonetheless, in her story on the suicide rate among AIDS patients, Kolata interviewed the coordinator of crisis intervention services at the Gay Men's Health Crisis, who said that the majority of their clients were now "living with, rather than dying of, AIDS."[36]

But at the same time that social structures had been developed within queer communities to respond to the lack of public health support at the federal, state, and municipal levels, AIDS remained a terminal diagnosis for most people. Disease progression, once it began, was unrelenting in its painful prognosis. Shortly after Dr. Marzuk's research was published, on March 31, 1988, the *Nightline* news program on ABC broadcast a segment called "AIDS and Suicide." The broadcast was hosted by ABC News medical editor Dr. Timothy Johnson, who began with this brief introduction:

> AIDS is the kind of disease that highlights and intensifies all kinds of social and legal issues that often go beyond the disease itself: job discrimination, school restrictions, insurance coverage, just to name a few. Tonight we are going to look at another issue that involves both medical practice and social ethics: whether or not doctors should be allowed to help people without medical hope to die before the time of natural death. And once again, AIDS patients are the focus of a debate which could affect us all.[37]

The program transitions to an interview with thirty-nine year-old David Cadieux, who "is wasting away under a death sentence from AIDS" in his hospital room. David describes his inability to eat solid foods, the pain of his many symptoms, and his prognosis of having six months to live. The reporter asks him, "Would you consider suicide?" Before he has completed the question, David's eyes widen as he responds through shallow breaths:

"Yes. Yes."

"At what point," the reporter inquires.

"Right now."

In voiceover, the interviewer notes that "suicide is an idea so common among AIDS patients, doctors say, that nearly all consider it during their illness." He explains that "one of every ten calls to San Francisco's suicide hotline is from someone with AIDS," and quotes San Francisco medical examiner Stephen Boyd, who describes suicide as a "deadly companion to the epidemic."

The program then transitions to its primary focus: a Los Angeles-based man named Marty James. Marty describes his friend Keith, a twenty-eight-year-old "high-flying skydiver" who had enlisted his help in ending his life after he had fallen gravely ill with AIDS. "He had lived a very good life, and he wanted a very good death," Marty says before describing the method that had been developed by an underground network of queer people who stockpiled medications for this purpose. Marty emptied thirty barbiturates into a cup of grape juice, which Keith then drank. "There were no convulsions, no discomfort that I could see. It was quiet. It was peaceful." The voiceover adds, "It was also illegal," noting that assisted suicide is a felony. The program briefly transitions back to David Cadieux, who says, "I've talked to my nurse, I've talked to my doctor outright about suicide, asking *will this work, will that work, will this work.* They won't give me an answer." He is almost panting, as if speaking each word requires herculean effort.

The image shifts to a page from the most recent issue of *The Advocate*; the voiceover continues, "AIDS patients find their answers elsewhere. Now appearing in gay newspapers are ads for the Hemlock Society," the euthanasia advocacy group founded by Derek Humphrey after he had assisted his wife in ending her life peacefully while suffering the painful and debilitating symptoms of a terminal cancer diagnosis. In the years since her death, Humphrey had begun publishing guides that included drug dosage formulas for a quick and painless death. According to Humphrey, Hemlock was originally an "elderly ladies' organization" advocating for changes to laws banning euthanasia. "I would speak at meetings and it would be a sea of gray heads," he recalled in a *Los Angeles*

Times story a few years later. The group radically transformed with the advent of AIDS, which had "shown young people that they can die of a terminal illness as well as elderly people."[38] The story notes that when Hemlock was founded in 1980, it had only two members. By 1990, when this story was published, it had grown to "33,500 members, . . . about a dozen employees, and . . . a budget of $700,000," largely due to the massive escalation of the AIDS epidemic.

The *Nightline* segment proceeds with a live discussion between medical ethicist Daniel Callahan, California Medical Association representative Richard Corlin, and Marty James. Marty remains steadfast in his insistence that people facing painful terminal AIDS diagnoses should be supported in ending their lives, and that medical professionals should be at the forefront of providing that support. But both other guests—the doctor and the ethicist—reject his position, repeatedly using the phrase "morally wrong" to justify those refusals. This appeal to morality would circulate throughout a number of news articles that followed the broadcast, and again in an episode of *60 Minutes* the following year. On April 16, 1989, the CBS program aired "A Question of Mercy," a segment featuring Marty, a mother whose son Marty had assisted and her two surviving sons, and a UCLA doctor opposed to euthanasia.[39] Near the end of the segment, the host, Ed Bradley, poses an observation to Marty: "There's a ritual that's involved. I mean, you prepare the room, prepare the tray, and. . . ."

"Wash the body. Console the family," Marty adds.

"But you're not trained to do that. You're not licensed to do it. What gives you the right?"

"I don't think I have any right. I don't see it as a right. I'm just a caring person, you know? I'm somebody who cares, and I'm somebody who's willing to step in there and assist when nobody else is willing to take that risk."

The image shifts to a group of four men, members of a group called Safe Passage, sitting in a living room. Bradley muses, "I don't have to tell the four of you, but this isn't the kind of country that accepts your viewpoint readily. I mean, just the opposite. We are a nation that would say bite the bullet and suffer. This is what you have been given. This is your burden. Bear it."

"That works great philosophically," one of the men replies. "That works great theoretically. But when it's your sister or your lover, and you get to see firsthand the suffering, the screaming in the next room, that tortured person out there, that's not Joe Middle America somewhere, that's me. I'm connected to it. I feel that same pain."

The image shifts again to Marty standing alone on a beach. In voiceover, Bradley describes that the previous year, Marty had helped his own lover, who had been diagnosed with AIDS, end his life. The segment ends with Bradley asking about Marty's ultimate goal:

> You know what my ultimate goal is right now? A cure for AIDS. That's what I'd like to see. I mean, it is not so strange that I have assisted eight people. I have lost over eighty friends. *Eighty.* I have seen more people die in six years than my grandparents in their entire lifetime combined saw loved ones die. It is devastating. I don't want to have to do what I'm doing. I don't want to have to hand a cup to another friend. You were saying people would say "what gives you the right, Marty James, to assist?" But what gives us the right in this country, as a people, to deny the terminally ill the right not only to choose their own healthcare, but the right to choose their own manner of death? . . . I hope I never am asked to assist at another euthanasia. But if someone should ever call me again . . . I would say yes.

In a brief commentary on Marzuk's study of suicide among AIDS patients published in the same March 1988 issue of the

Journal of the American Medical Association, Dr. Richard Glass acknowledges that "some individuals and groups have proposed that suicide can be a rational choice for patients with a terminal illness such as AIDS and that assisted suicide and active euthanasia (now prohibited by law in most countries) should be options for such patients and their physicians."[40] However, he argues against this position: "from the clinical point of view, careful evaluations of suicides, even in terminally ill patients, almost invariably reveal evidence that the suicide occurred as a manifestation of a psychiatric disorder rather than as a rational choice."[41] AIDS in particular, he explains, often results in late-stage neurological effects including delirium and dementia, making it difficult for caregivers to determine a person's capacity for rational decision-making. This leads Glass to "urge that physicians continue to consider suicide, in AIDS patients as in others, as an untoward illness outcome to be diagnosed, treated, and prevented."[42] He identifies an additional concern about people who have not yet developed AIDS but have been diagnosed with HIV in blood tests. These diagnostic tests had only recently become available, but had already been used by virulently homophobic politicians to propose "mass screening programs" to weed out and isolate HIV-positive people. Glass writes,

> Serological testing can certainly play an important role in AIDS prevention, but a number of anecdotal reports have indicated that suicides have occurred as part of the psychological devastation that can result from the news of a positive test result. Thus, the potential for severe, even fatal, emotional consequences should heighten concerns about inappropriate HIV antibody testing without proper indications, informed consent, or counseling. The risk of suicide is one more reason that such tests should never be considered as "routine."[43]

Glass's concern seems genuine, a forceful and direct rebuttal to the systemic neglect of public health and demonization of queer communities that had defined the Reagan administration's response to the emergence of AIDS in the first eight years of the epidemic. He urges a new approach to treatment, one focused on "open discussion of emotional reactions to the illness and the prospect of dying of it," empathic listening and active response to "suicidal thoughts, intentions, and plans," and the embrace and enhancement of every patient's "social support system," including their partners, lovers, and friends. In other words, Glass is proposing precisely what queer communities had built and sustained on their own in the context of a widespread, governmental failure to respond to the early signs of an epidemic primarily affecting queer people. And though the scale of public health responses to HIV and AIDS has increased significantly since the 1980s, the elevated risks first identified in Marzuk's 1988 study persist: in an article published in the journal *General Psychiatry* in 2021, researchers analyzed forty studies of nearly two hundred thousand people since the epidemic began. They found a risk of suicide "100-fold higher in people living with HIV than in the general population."[44]

The criticisms lodged against Marty James (and other supporters of assisted suicide) by journalists, public health officers, elected officials, and many physicians centered on three complaints: that the practice is criminal ("Marty, it's against the law," repeated Ed Bradley several times), psychologically pathological (Kolata's report spoke of "patients who became mentally unbalanced"), and—in multiple venues, again and again—"morally wrong." In all of the critiques, opponents of assisted suicide seemed genuinely invested in "caring for patients whose illnesses bring them to the painful extremes of human experience," as Richard Glass wrote in his commentary. But the irony of that particular trio of concerns—criminality, pathology, moral perversity—is that we have heard those very words in stories told about us before, echoed throughout the long history of legal, medical, and political repugnance at queer people's very existence. We have heard *this* story before: when that story "Rare Cancer Seen in 41 Homosexuals" appeared on July 3, 1981, in the *New York Times*, it was buried on page twenty, printed in a slender column to the far left.[45] The rest of the page—five-sixths of its total area—consists of the sheet music for "The Star Spangled Banner," complete with lyrics for all three verses, an advertisement for Independence Savings Bank. Visually, the page is striking, subtly conveying that queer death is simultaneously marginalized by and coextensive with patriotic celebration. We have heard *this* story before: when a cluster of suicides by queer youth was reported in 2011, some community leaders blamed "homosexual indoctrination" and organized a day for dangerous, so-called conversion therapy. We have heard *this* story before: there was a period of time in the 1980s, long before protease inhibitors and preexposure prophylaxes had been invented, when we were told that being gay and having sex was essentially a form of suicide. And though AIDS was the vocabulary in which this warning was posed, it wasn't always clear that they were talking about AIDS at all; queerness itself was the threat.

On December 25, 1991, Marty James died by suicide. He had been diagnosed with AIDS-related complex two weeks before his first appearance on television in the March 1988 *Nightline* episode. By the time he appeared on *60 Minutes* the following year, he had assisted with his lover's death. In the years since, as his own symptoms expanded and worsened, he had found another partner, Steven Kanengiser, and the two were living in West Hollywood. In an obituary published in the *Los Angeles Times* the week after Marty's death, Steven describes his last days: "he wanted to just fall asleep, but in the end the pain became unmanageable.... The doctor said he would only have lasted another week, and that it would have been agony." The obituary also describes Marty's early life, before his television appearances brought him national notoriety. As a young man, he had lived with his mother throughout her painful and protracted death from Hodgkin's disease, after which he "became a drifter and heroin [user]." He moved to Hollywood, where he sought addiction treatment and joined gay activist groups. With friends, he cofounded the Los Angeles branch of the Shanti Foundation, the San Francisco–based organization that provided holistic support for people diagnosed with AIDS. He had left Shanti after a dispute about assisted suicide, which the organization did not support. But a therapist who had worked alongside him then described him in this way: "Compassion was his main strength. He was one of the first voices to deal with how to live and die with AIDS." On Christmas day in 1991, it was seventy degrees and sunny in West Hollywood. Marty James was thirty-eight years old.[46]

VIII
Agnus Dei

O vanity of Sleep, Hope, Dream, Endless Desire,
The Horses of Disaster plunge in the heavy clay;
Beloved, let your eyes half close, and your heart beat
Over my heart, and your hair fall over my breast,
Drowning love's lonely hour in deep twilight of rest,
And hiding their tossing manes and their tumultuous feet.

WILLIAM BUTLER YEATS,
"HE BIDS HIS BELOVED BE AT PEACE" (1899)

And Jacob was left alone.

GENESIS 32:24

On New Year's Eve of 2019, halfway between the memorial we held for Robin and the first pandemic lockdowns, I went with two close friends—the friends who had come to my house for cioppino the day Robin's sister called me—to a screening of the film adaption of the Andrew Lloyd Webber musical *Cats*. By the time we went to see it, the film had already been widely panned and mocked to the point that it achieved that very rare status of a nearly universal joke, decorating news sites and social media feeds with what seemed to evolve into a widespread competition to write the most witty and withering screed condemning it. I had read numerous articles and had seen countless memes that lambasted its performances and the CGI technology used in its animations. But *Cats* had been the very first Broadway show that I had seen as a boy: in the early 1980s, the flamboyant oddness of the costumes, characters, story, and songs had entranced me and emboldened my love for theatre. So I convinced my friends to see the film version with me, critics be damned.

As soon as the film began, I was immediately transported back to that moment when, decades earlier, I had become aware that the Broadway cats were prowling down the aisles off-stage. The narrative of *Cats* opens with a kitten who's been thrown out, thrown away, left to rot. She's immediately adopted by a gloriously feral gang, like practical queer kinship of the most absurd kind. The film glories in this, flamboyant and unapologetic in its full embrace of walking *en pointe*, of leaps and kicks, of pirouettes and lunges, and, yes, of bizarre CGI. But this last felt to me like theatre taking a strange kind of revenge on the film industry: this screen will never let us do what we want to do, it seemed to say, but we'll take what you've got and run with it anyway. *Cats* is a film about cats made for people who love them. But it's also a film for kids who took tap and ballet and jazz; it's a film for sissies and tomboys; it's a film about feeling alone and finding solace in others who feel alone too; it's a film about theatre majors and early morning dance classes and trying Beckett for the first time and doing Shakespeare in period (and then Shakespeare "updated") and diaphragm breathing and *To sit in solemn silence on a dim dark dock*. It's a film that evokes learning how to shade when you do your own makeup before opening night, and then sweating it all off midway through the show but crying for real in that last scene anyway; it's a film that recalls adapting your own poetry for a one-person show. *Cats* is a film about queerness, a film about theatre, a film about the queer kids who find some respite in the weird world of theatre. And as I sat watching that night, absorbing it all, I realized that it was also a film about Robin. When Jennifer Hudson belted out the final refrain of "Memory" before being selected to ascend to the Heaviside Layer, I wanted nothing more than to reach over and grab his arm, knowing that he would have wept with glee at the unapologetically extravagant melodrama of it.

While the film's credits rolled, I thought about the strange greediness of grief, its tendency to wander and roam through the banalities and eccentricities of daily life like a scavenger, eager for any opportunity to feed. *Cats* truly was a disastrous film, fully deserving of every snide review it received. But it was a glorious mess; and for two hours on the last night of the year I lost him, that silly film about cats gave Robin back to me.

* * * * *

In her posthumously published novel *Last Words from Montmartre*, Qiu Miaojin documents the love affair and painful breakup between two women named Xu and Zoë. Shortly after completing this work and long before its publication or its translation into English, Qiu died by suicide. In the popular legend of her death, she pushed a kitchen knife into her chest and through her heart, though the veracity of this story is unclear. Qiu had received wide acclaim the previous year on the publication of her first novel, *Notes of a Crocodile*, which centered on a group of queer students at a prestigious university in Taiwan. The book's English translator described it as "a survival manual for teenagers, for a certain age when reading the right book can save your life."[1] In *Last Words from Montmartre*, which is structured as a series of letters, Zoë cycles through memories of her lost relationship, tormented both by her longing for Xu's return and by her desire for self-destruction. As Rhian Sasseen wrote in the *Los Angeles Review of Books*,

> [The novel] argues that both love and suicide require a certain self-annihilation, a willingness to abandon oneself in the face of something more overwhelming, and the end of a love affair can bring about an abject refusal to reconstitute one's individuality.[2]

Qiu's fans have speculated that her death was, in part, an homage to Yukio Mishima, the renowned Japanese novelist who died in a ritualized suicide in 1970. Mishima has been widely memorialized as a closeted gay writer despite the protestations of his wife and children. Long after his death, one of his former male lovers published a collection of their letters, but Mishima had also written about his sexuality in several books early in his career.[3] In the 1949 novel *Confessions of a Mask*, Mishima's narrator is a man who describes in florid detail his lifelong attraction to other men, a secret allegorized in the book's title. In one of the most tender and beautiful sections of the book, the narrator remembers staying home from school while ill one day and poring over the paintings reproduced in one of his father's art catalogues. He recalls coming across Guido Reni's seventeenth-century painting

St. Sebastian and feeling as if the image had been "lying in wait there for me, for my sake."[4] As he gazed at the nude young man tied to a tree, his "entire being trembled with some pagan joy."[5] Several years later, remembering the power that the image held over him, Mishima's narrator writes a short prose poem in which Sebastian and the tree to which he was bound continue to reemerge in his experience of the world around him: he describes a tree outside his schoolroom window and his fixation upon it, as if it were "the very tree— the tree to which the young saint was bound, . . . the harsh scraping of his young flesh against the bark [the] final evidence of all earthly pleasure and pain."[6]

Mishima's *Forbidden Colors*, published two years after *Confessions of a Mask*, tells the story of an aging writer who encounters an "amazingly beautiful young man [whose] body surpassed the sculptures of ancient Greece"[7] and urges him not to deny his homosexual inclinations. He sees in the young man "all the dreams of [his] young days—dreams he had hidden from the eyes of men. Not only that, he rebuked himself for them."[8] Mishima's work has been praised as being among the most important and experimental of postwar Japanese literature, especially for its lush aesthetics and its narrative focus on the thematic interrelationship of beauty, sex, and death. His political life and views were more controversial: he was a fierce nationalist opposed to the growing influence of US commercialism, and he famously participated in an attempted coup in 1970. When the coup failed, he staged his *seppuku*, slashing his belly with a traditional *tanto* blade.

Throughout Qiu's *Last Words from Montmartre*, Zoë mourns the death of the pet rabbit that she and Xu had adopted when they were together. Bunny was "tiny, maybe only fifteen centimeters long," and his fur was "pure white . . . flecked with grey."[9] Zoë explains in the first letter that Xu had left Bunny with her after leaving, but that within forty-five days Bunny had "departed this world suddenly," and that she had spent the entire night that he died "cry[ing] silently under the covers, holding [his] pure white corpse in [her] arms."[10] In a later letter to Xu, she describes burying his body with "the picture of father and mother, the pair of farewell letters that they wrote, the plant that had preceded Bunny in death, the big hairbrush, and a ball of toilet paper that Bunny liked to play with" in "that little triangular park near rue du Mont Cenis, just like you asked."[11] But before the novel begins, and foreshadowing the suicide that she has planned for when she completes her writing, Qiu includes this on the book's dedication page: "For dead little Bunny and Myself, soon dead." When she died in Paris on June 25, 1995, Qiu Miaojin was twenty-six years old.

* * * * *

In the long duration of my friendship with Robin, we had serious arguments only twice. The first of these arguments, which threatened to resurface eighteen months before his death, occurred in the early 2000s. The climax erupted during a rehearsal for the 2002 West Coast premier of Edward Albee's *The Play about the Baby*, which he was directing and for which I had been cast as The Boy. I will never speak of this argument's specific contents. It so radically buckled the intense but even keel of our friendship that I quit the show, and Robin and I did not talk for a month. The second argument pertained to a cat. It took place one year after the first, shortly after I awakened from a coma.[12] I had fallen suddenly and dramatically ill that autumn after several months of short-lived but, in retrospect, foreboding symptoms: fever and night sweats, mossy thrush on my tongue, a cough I couldn't shake, vision that clouded and blurred, and strange lesions that would appear and swell, throbbing painfully before they disappeared.

In the semiotics of gay embodiment, these symptoms were all too familiar, pointing toward what had always hovered at the edges of my consciousness like an inevitability: seroconversion and HIV. At the time they began cropping up, I was working as a volunteer medic in a free clinic near the campus of the University of California, Berkeley, where Robin and I were also in graduate school. I had worked with queer health organizations for many years, and had been trained in their methods of diagnosis—a focus on sex-positive harm reduction rather than judgy prohibition—and I feared these signs. One morning, when one of the first lesions appeared, I showed it to my friend Mazdak as we were preparing the clinic for a Sunday shift.

"It's really swollen," he said, touching it gingerly. "And it feels like there might be an abscess."

I sighed with relief. "That's what I thought, too. So it's not KS, right? But what is it?"

"It's not KS, but I don't know what it is. I just heard some gossip about gay men getting skin infections and doctors not knowing why."

We looked at each other, both thinking the same thing: this is how it begins, another plague. But the sore was gone within a few days, and I put it out of my mind. When, a few weeks later, I woke up with a white film in my mouth that wouldn't brush or rinse away, I went to the student clinic on campus to talk to a nurse. She pointed a small flashlight at my tongue, then glanced down at my chart. "You're gay," she said, and not as a question.

"Yes." I thought I knew where this was going.

"How long have you been HIV-positive?"

"I'm not HIV-positive," I said.

She looked back up into my eyes and tilted her head. "Have you ever been tested?"

"I've been gay my whole entire life. Of course I've been tested." I didn't like the sharp sound of my voice, but I didn't correct it either.

"When was the last time?"

"A few months ago."

"It's time for another test. This is thrush. Healthy people don't get thrush."

I gathered my things. I knew, even after the transformations of the 1990s, to keep my blood tests anonymous. "Please don't record this conversation in my chart," I said. She huffed as I left.

The thrush was gone within a few days with no explanation. When I returned to the free clinic in San Francisco where I had gone for a blood test, a small, butch woman called me back to a crowded room and asked what I would do if the test was positive. This was a common practice developed in the late 1980s, after Marzuk's study had shown heightened incidence of suicide among HIV-positive people, and after Glass's commentary on that study had urged sensitivity to the stress of test results. It had been developed not by epidemiologists at the CDC or by doctors in large hospitals, but by volunteers in queer clinics like this one. I had asked this question countless times, too, sitting in a small room in the Berkeley clinic with someone terrified of their results.

"First I'll call my friends. Then I'll find a specialist. Then I'll find a group."

She nodded and smiled, handing me a brochure. "Good," she said. "Your test came back negative." She read through the standard disclaimers about incubation periods and risk factors, then patted my arm as I stood to leave.

But the symptoms continued, scattered across the days and weeks of summer and into the fall. By early November they had escalated until, one day, my friend Monica found me winded and half-conscious in my apartment. She walked me to her car and drove me back to the student clinic on campus, where the nurses quickly realized I needed to be transported to the emergency room of a nearby hospital. "Well hello, boys," I crooned as the hunky paramedics lifted me onto a gurney and into an ambulance. This is one of the last things I remember saying before I sank into a strange, timeless void, deeper than sleep but lighter than death. When I finally emerged from this state, I was lying in a bed in an unfamiliar room, surrounded by tubes and blinking machines. Robin and my mother sat in chairs on either side of me. They explained what had happened: over the last several days, as I lay in the coma, doctors had struggled to find the cause of my collapse. They eventually found a systemic, drug-resistant bacterial infection, but not before it had damaged my eyes, organs, and bones. I would likely need to undergo a number of surgeries, and recovery would take a long time. I stared back at them from a morphine haze, taking it in stride.

"There's something else you should know," Robin said after a moment. "We can't find your cat."

Those five words triggered an avalanche of sorrow and rage, responses I should have had instead to the precarity of my health, to the bacteria that had already taken so much from me. "What do you mean you can't find Cabiria? He's in my apartment. Has no one checked on him? Has no one fed him?"

Robin glanced at my mother, then back at me. "No, no, I checked on him. I took him to my place. But when I let him out to explore yesterday, he didn't come back." I lived in a quiet building near Lake Merritt in Oakland. Robin lived in San Francisco on a busy street in the Castro.

My eyes turned to flames. "You let him out? He's an indoor cat. He didn't know where he was. How could you let him out?" I devolved into sobbing.

"I'm so sorry," Robin said, holding my arm. "We're still looking for him."

I yanked my arm away from him, weeping still. Robin stood and left the room, rubbing his head with his hands as he always did when anxiety or shame overwhelmed him.

Over the next few hours, I learned that Robin had come straight to the hospital when Monica called to tell him what had happened. He stayed there in the waiting room until my mother arrived from the East Coast, sharing with Monica the labor of managing all that they could. He had immediately thought of Cabiria, and went to gather him and his food and to take him to his apartment. But Robin had never lived with cats; he had a large, boisterous dog with a profound lack of boundaries. He hadn't known not to let Cabiria wander in a strange neighborhood far from home. It was an honest mistake, borne of a genuine desire to offer support: he was always above all a caretaker. But I couldn't stop thinking of my cat, scared and alone on unfamiliar streets, hungry and cold. As the days and weeks passed in that hospital room, Robin tried to apologize again and again, but I shut him down every time. "Look," I'd bark back at him, "I love you, and I'm really glad you're here with me. But I do not want to talk about Cabiria." After a year of halting, sometimes backsliding progress in my recovery from the illness that had almost killed me, I stabilized enough to live in the world again. Still missing Cabiria, I decided to mark the occasion by adopting another cat. I found Izzy, a tiny ball of fluff with piercing, intelligent eyes, at a rescue organization in Berkeley. It was only after I took him home—Izzy winding around my feet and purring loudly on my lap—that I finally felt healed.

Over the years, Robin would occasionally remember what happened with Cabiria. We might be having lunch somewhere, or hiking in Tilden, or playing pool at the Pils. We might be talking about something else entirely. Out of the

AGNUS DEI

blue he would lean over, grab my arm, and wait for me to look at him. "I really am so sorry about Cabiria," he would say, his eyes suddenly wet and pleading. And as the years passed, I would try to reassure him that it wasn't his fault, that he'd done the best he could, that all had been forgiven. But the last time I saw him, after the breakfast where he told me he needed to make amends, and as we walked through those Oakland streets, he begged forgiveness again for both of the fights we had had. He could no longer remember what either one was about, he said; he knew only that he was sorry. I listened to his apologies. "Those things happened so long ago, Robin," I said. "We dealt with them years ago. There aren't any more amends to be made between you and me."

He huffed out a long sigh, sputtering a few layabout tears. "Are you sure?"

"I'm absolutely sure," I said. "Really."

He seemed lost for a moment, as if seeking amends had anchored him somehow, so that now he wasn't sure where he was. But he shook himself out of it and chuckled. "Shame is a bitch," he said.

* * * * *

Cecil Beaton died in January 1980, still haunted by his brother Reggie's suicide forty-six years and three months earlier. For the last seventeen years of his life, Cecil lived in a country house with a white cat he called Timothy. One week before he died, having noticed that Timothy was "no longer enjoying life," he summoned a veterinarian to "come out and put Timothy to sleep." This proved to be a devastating loss for Cecil, who wrote in his diary:

> The life of Timothy was quickly at an end. Timothy who had been 17 years my friend was no longer. . . .

> He had his own ways, which would not be altered.
> He liked to sit on this or that chair. He liked the
> sunny side of the street. Now all was over and Timmy
> was alone, parted from us, while we were very much
> alone, parted from him. I took a long time coming to
> grip with ordinary life. I felt very lonely as I spent my
> time thinking back through the last 17 years.[13]

In this, the final entry of his diary, and like Maxine Kumin in her last poem about Anne Sexton's suicide ("Left behind, there is no oblivion"), Cecil wrote, "I was still alive, but Timmy had gone through to oblivion. He was perhaps lucky?" On the evening of January 17, Cecil was depressed. He had experienced a stroke several years earlier and was worried about the results of recent medical tests. Above his final entry about Timothy's death, the editorial notes in Cecil's last published diary read,

> It is not too fanciful to suggest that Timothy showed
> Cecil the way to escape. When he went up to bed, he
> had problems sleeping and asked Grant to summon
> the doctor. He was flustered. Dr. Brown came round
> and gave him something to help him sleep. His last
> words were "Thank you, Doctor" and he drifted into
> a deep sleep from which he did not wake up.[14]

* * * * *

Among our many common loves, Robin and I shared an especially strong passion for performance, and had spent much of our lives in the theatre. This is one reason why that first fight had been so traumatizing: *The Play about the Baby* was the first and only occasion in which we worked together professionally, and the fight had derailed the exhilarating opportunity to rehearse and launch a production together.

In the years after, we would always attend each other's shows, cheering from the front row with a bouquet of flowers for the afterparty. We would see countless other productions together, too, and we spent hours talking about them afterward. And we would often reflect on this: one of the most defining aspects of spending so much of one's life in the theatre is that you are constantly trained to imagine events that have never happened, that *will* never happen. And then, having imagined them, you are asked to give yourself over to the emotional task of living within those events. This is the labor of performance: to dream, to attend to the most intricate details of those dreams, and then to open yourself to everything it would mean to inhabit them fully, despite the fact that the world as it is offers no recognition, no nod of acknowledgment, no transferable currency to that which you have imagined. Never mind; you dream nonetheless, and work with others who dream in concert with you to make the dream manifest in one very specific room created only for the work of dreaming, to give it a name, and to invite others inside to watch.

The gift of this training—to trust the imagination, to give it attention and respect, to use it to work toward new realities— is profound. It structured my relationship to that life-threatening illness in the early 2000s: I knew already how to transform what Konstantin Stanislavski called the "Given Circumstances" (the limbo of illness) into a singular "Objective" (to survive).[15] It has contoured and nuanced my mode of undertaking major transformations in daily life: a move between cities or countries, a shift to a new piece of writing, meeting someone new. Over many years, it has facilitated my entries into the complex world of erotic and romantic connection, enlivening my heart and mind, and equally (or especially) my libido. This has not always been to the good: what happens when, with brute refusal, the world fails to unfold in the form you have imagined and rehearsed for it? This, I think, is the heart of all Theatre Kids' panic, anxiety, and alienation, when the world beyond the stage (and sometimes the world upon it) succeeds so expansively in disappointing us. But this faith in imagination also gives us an exceptionally powerful tool: to rehearse our lives in the world, to rehearse our responses to the obstacles that confront us, to prepare ourselves for—to gird ourselves against—the unrelenting repetition of heartbreak. Theatre is no wasteful dalliance. It is rehearsal for life itself.

And so when, two years after Robin's death and in the midst of a global pandemic that felt alarmingly reminiscent of the 1980s, Izzy—the cat I had adopted after my year of illness—developed a strange, persistent cough that his vet couldn't explain, my Theatre Kid reflexes kicked in, and I began imagining all the various ways this story could unfold. He had just turned seventeen years old, elderly for a cat. But he had been sick before; surely he would recover as he had then. More wet food might help, more quiet in the house, maybe a nice breeze. Or maybe he needs more attention: I'd been feeding a neighborhood stray for a while, and Izzy had sometimes been jealous. So I moved the outdoor food bowl around the corner where Izzy couldn't see it. Or maybe, I thought, this is the final illness, maybe this is the one that all pet lovers dread. So I began what the performance theorists call a rehearsal for loss,[16] noting all of his "ergotropic symptoms," his changes in behavior, his quieting, plaintive meows.[17] And as I had learned from the monks in Sri Lanka who trained me in Vipassana, I imagined his death, pictured it in vivid detail, sat with it as a possible version of Act III.

I spent time remembering the day I adopted Izzy at the end of that terrible year, two weeks after my final surgery. It felt like a precise form of victory: I had recovered enough to care for a cat. And so one bright day in early June, two friends drove me down to a Milo Foundation adoption event on Fourth Street in Berkeley. Izzy was one of three kittens found wandering the streets, and their pictures had been posted on the organization's website the day before; the Milo staff had temporarily named him Diamond. By the time we arrived at Fourth Street, all three kittens had all been claimed. But as we turned to leave, one of the volunteers came running over to me: "the people who claimed the one you were holding," she said, "changed their minds. He's yours if you want him." I was ecstatic. We drove him home with all the windows open, because one of the friends with me was severely allergic to cats and could barely breathe. At the time, still recuperating, I was alternating between crutches and a walker. Izzy first knew me as a sometimes-quadrupedal, sometimes-hexapedal giant. He would dart between all those legs, eager for attention but cautious not to trip me. From his first night with me, Izzy always slept in my bed, first near my arm, hungry for strokes, then at the foot keeping watch. I can't remember a single morning in those seventeen years when I didn't awaken to find him like that, curled up in the corner, face toward the nearest window.

I couldn't begin to compile a complete list of the entanglements that defined our seventeen years together. Finishing my dissertation, the academic job market, long-term relationships and painful breakups. He moved with me to San Diego and would make the long drives between there and San Francisco many times without a complaint. He rode in an airplane once, and he was so quiet and calm that a flight attendant asked me if he was real. He loved tuna and salmon, especially high-grade sashimi. He loved laser toys, and he would chase jump-and-grab-'ems: ferociously, sometimes leaping six feet in the air with an exquisite choreography. He had unbelievably soft fur, like eiderdown. He was kind with strangers, but cautious about interacting directly: he'd stand at the edge of the room watching me, waiting to see if I treated this visitor like a friend, and then slowly approach. He loved and was loved by my lovers. He had a hemispheric eccentricity: if I petted him on one side of his body, he would then turn around so that the opposite side would receive the same strokes. He loved sitting next to me. He became a lap cat later in life, draped across my legs as I sat in my desk chair. He loved patrolling the front windows, but he was never a bird-chirper. He was a merciless hunter of spiders, somehow knowing that I fear them. He knew when I was sad and would find me, wherever I was, to sit with me. He loved catnip cigars, and would leave them dripping with his drool. He had distinct moods, and he knew how to express them: his taxonomy of meows was extensive and meticulously organized.

Over those last two weeks, as I allowed myself to imagine and rehearse for his death, it seemed as if he was rehearsing with me. Eventually the cough disappeared; but by then he had started refusing to eat and, a few days later, refusing to drink any water. In those two weeks he utterly transformed from his lithe and elegant self into an unutterably frail being. Unable to walk more than a few steps, he would stop and rest, curling up wherever he was. I would sit with him, gently stroking his back and sides. And to the very end, despite whatever strength it sapped for him to do so, he would purr more loudly than he ever had before, a veritable engine of purrs, a minor earthquake.

The previous autumn, still in mourning from Robin's death and at the suggestion of another friend, I enrolled in an End-of-Life Doula certificate course offered by the University of Vermont. The course gave me a better way to think about and practice my grief then, but it also prepared me for what was coming. When, that final morning of Izzy's life, I began to understand the immanence of his death, I remembered the portions of the course that described what dying looks like from the outside with clinical but compassionate specificity. Something kicked in when I accepted what was happening in the immediate present—that is, what was no longer imaginary, no longer a rehearsal, but an actual event. Using what I had learned in the course, I became a doula for Izzy and treated my home as a hospice. I would leave his side for no more than fifteen minutes at a time. His final walk, which took him about an hour, was from a chair by the window in my office to a rug in one of my bathrooms, a journey of no more than thirty feet. I had scattered towels and rugs around so that he could rest anywhere. He chose the rug with a rainbow design, the one that probably smells the most like me. I sat with him as he experienced the final symptoms of his death, stroking his back, telling him how much he was loved, thanking him for his companionship and care. It was not the smoothest of transitions. But I sat with him through the full period of that final phase, remembering so many moments with him, seeing so many images of him peering up at me as I spoke to him, feeling so many nights when I would hear him climb up onto my bed and present himself for his nighttime snuggle. I saved my sobbing for later.

Izzy's final days forced me to set aside everything else and focus completely on him. They gave me a chance to witness and care for him as his health declined, to say goodbye to him slowly over several days. It was only later that I consciously realized that they had also given me a chance to do the very things that I had not been able to do for Robin. Robin had been with me through that year of illness in which it was not always clear that I would survive. He had faced that reality, and had had time to prepare for the very real prospect that I would die. His still-fresh suicide—the abrupt manner in which he was suddenly and unexpectedly no longer there—had foreclosed this possibility, this kind of rehearsal for loss, for those of us who loved him. This is true for all sudden deaths, of course, but is especially complex when a loved one has deliberately chosen to exit in this way. This is an uncomfortable quandary: how do we honor and dignify the agency of those loved ones who choose suicide, while also giving ourselves permission to feel everything—grief, anger, even indignation—that rises in wake of their death?

Auden knew grief in a way that resonates deeply with me—and that summons the elaborate rituals of mourning I inherited as a child in the South. When Izzy died, I thought of Auden's mournful demand to stop all the clocks and muffle the drums, to put out the stars and dismantle the sun. As I had on the day after Robin's death, I draped linen sheets across all the mirrors in my home. And with a solemn series of formalized offerings that I'd never thought would come so naturally to me, I also gave thanks for the gift of Izzy's companionship across so many years: *requiescat in pace*, I chanted that evening while I keened on the floor. The formality of that ritual—kneeling and bowing, incanting a liturgical prayer—was foreign to me, and yet I found myself unthinkingly performing it, as if it were an instinctual response to the gravity of such a gut-wrenching loss.

There were other seemingly instinctual rituals, too, more mundane but no less affecting. The following morning, before I drove his body to the crematorium, and as I was making my coffee, I prepared Izzy's food bowl, not realizing what I was doing until I saw myself, as if from a great height, placing it in the spot where he ate. *He's usually winding around my feet—where is he?* I felt myself think. And later that day, I washed and refilled his water bowl, only catching myself as I carried it back to his favorite drinking place. I stopped suddenly in the hall; the water sloshed over the bowl's edges and rained down onto a rug. *How do I unlearn these automatic behaviors, these unconscious choreographies?* I asked myself. And then I began to wonder, How do we speak about this most mundane aspect of loss: the rituals that suddenly become useless, superfluous, unneeded? What are we to do with them?

Can they really be unlearned, or would that unlearning amplify an absence so deeply engrained in our bodies and minds, so astute in its emphatic underlining of loss, that we'd be better off just performing them, day after day, week after week, year after year? Can such rituals ever truly be expunged from our unconscious remembering? What happens to us—who do we become—when they are?

IX
Libera Me

Be strong, saith my heart; I am a soldier;
I have seen worse sights than this.
        HOMER, THE ODYSSEY (C. EIGHTH CENTURY BCE)

we left, as we have left all of our lovers
as all lovers leave all lovers
much too soon to get the real loving done.
    JUDY GRAHN, "A WOMAN IS TALKING TO DEATH" (1974)

Tell me, what else should I have done?
Doesn't everything die at last, and too soon?
              MARY OLIVER, "THE SUMMER DAY" (1992)

i. A heart reduced to ashes

Cor contritum quasi cinis

On May 14, 1935, his sixty-seventh birthday, Magnus Hirschfeld died in his apartment in Nice. He had settled in the South of France the previous November, exiled from Germany after the rise of the Third Reich. Most of his library and archives at the Institute for Sexual Science in Berlin had been looted two years earlier, when Nazi groups stormed the building. Heike Bauer describes the event in this way:

> It happened in three stages: in the morning, Nazi students entered the institute and began to destroy its interior. In the afternoon, members of the Sturmabteilung—the paramilitary wing of the Nazi Party known as the SA—joined the fray to conduct a more systematic search. Together they removed large parts of the institute's library, which were then loaded onto trucks, ready for stage three of the attack, the destruction of the materials four days later in what would be the first in the series of infamous Nazi book burnings.[1]

Although he did not know it then, when Hirschfeld departed Germany for a speaking tour on November 15, 1930, he would never again set foot in his native land. He sailed first to New York and traveled for four months across the United States giving lectures and readings. He then sailed to Japan, and from there traveled to China, where he first met a young man who would become his companion for the remainder of his life: Li Shiu Tong. Li was a student in philosophy and medicine, but after attending one of Hirschfeld's lectures, he became fascinated by sexology and, with the approval of his family, withdrew from his university to accompany Hirschfeld on the remainder of his world tour. They traveled to the Philippines, Thailand, Bali, Java, Singapore, Sri Lanka, and India, and from there to Egypt and Palestine.[2] While in India in autumn 1931, Hirschfeld received communications from Berlin conveying the seriousness of the situation there, and he began to suspect that he would not be able to return. When he sailed back to Europe in March 1932—arriving in Athens on a ship from Damascus—he was met with such intense hostility and harassment that he abandoned any thought of returning to Berlin. "If Germany doesn't want me," he wrote, "I don't want it either."[3]

Hirschfeld's longtime lover Karl Giese met him and Li when they disembarked in Athens. The news from Berlin was so grim that it became clear that Hirschfeld's life would be in danger if he attempted even to cross the German border. And so after several weeks in Greece, the three traveled to Vienna. Giese was able to return to Berlin to manage the institute in Hirschfeld's absence, and Li was able to visit its facilities. In August of that year, Hirschfeld moved to Zurich, and apart from a brief trip with Li and Giese for a conference in Brno, Czechoslovakia, he stayed in Switzerland until the following year. In May 1933, as the Nazis were raiding the institute and after receiving numerous death threats, Hirschfeld hid by lying on the floor of a car as Li and Giese drove him to Paris.[4] He wrote in his journal of this move, noting that "the French are kind to me, and friendly toward refugees."[5] In a cinema in Paris, Hirschfeld watched with horror as newsreels showed the raid on the institute and the book burning at which so much of his archive was destroyed; he wrote that this left him "under the deepest psychic shock."[6] Later that summer, Giese was arrested for indecency in a Parisian bathhouse and deported from France.[7] Worried that his expired passport would be discovered in Paris, Hirschfield moved to Nice with Li, who in early 1935 went to Zurich to continue his formal medical training, promising to return to Hirschfeld's side during intersessions and summers.[8]

The materials remaining in the institute after the raid—those that had not been destroyed, including some manuscripts, medical records, and objects from the Museum of Sex—were auctioned off by the Nazi attorney who had been appointed to administer the institute's dissolution. From France, Hirschfeld arranged to obtain as many of these materials as he could, with Giese acting as the primary caretaker. Giese hid some of them in locations "known to him" in Germany, while the rest were stored at the Bedel & Co. furniture storage facility in Paris. In Hirschfeld's will, all of these materials were bequeathed to Giese, while all of the materials in his possession—including everything from his international travels—were bequeathed to Li. In both cases, Hirschfeld's will directed that these bequests be used in the interests of developing the field of sexology rather than for Giese's and Li's personal benefit.[9] But despite Hirschfeld's hopes that all of his collections would eventually outlive the Nazis, and would form the basis of a new institution focused on research and support for gay, lesbian, and transgender people, the materials were further dispersed, and many lost, in the decades that followed. Giese had moved to Brno after his deportation from France. He had never completed secondary school in Germany, and so found himself dependent on the diaspora of people formerly associated with Hirschfeld's work. Despite the heroic efforts of an attorney named Karl Fein—who would be deported to the Theresienstadt Ghetto when Czechoslovakia fell to the Germans in 1942, and murdered by the Nazis the following year[10]—Giese was never able to acquire the materials left to him in Hirschfeld's will.[11] He died by suicide in Brno in 1938.[12]

After Hirschfeld's death, Li stayed in Zurich until 1940, when he moved to the United States to study at Harvard.

After a brief stint working at the Chinese Embassy in Washington, DC, he then returned to Zurich to continue his studies, which he never completed. He moved to Hong Kong in 1960, at which point, according to Hirschfeld biographer Charlotte Wolff—a lesbian psychologist who escaped Nazi Germany in 1936—he fell "out of sight, and [was] no longer in touch with any of the surviving admirers of Hirschfeld."[13] But long after Wolff published the 1986 biography that included this line, historian Ralf Dose discovered that in 1974 Li had moved from Hong Kong to Vancouver, Canada, where some of his family members had immigrated. There he lived in a small apartment, continuing to write about Hirschfeld and conducting his own interviews and surveys of gay men. When he died in 1993, his younger brother gathered his belongings—which included some of Hirschfeld's possessions thought to have been lost, as well as Li's own writing about their international tour and the studies he had been conducting in Vancouver—and deposited them in a dumpster outside the complex. A neighbor happened to see the boxes and suitcases full of these materials and "literally rescued [them] from the trash heap," sending them on to the Magnus Hirschfeld Society—although, as Heike Bauer later discovered, many of them would be lost again en route to their permanent archival home.[14] In Bauer's reckoning, the story of these records—and all of the otherwise forgotten queer lives documented within them—is "a testament to the queer dead whose existence left little trace in the historical archive but whose collective suffering nevertheless caused emotional shockwaves that reverberate across time and continue to haunt the present."[15]

* * * * *

During the summer of 1935, two years after his brother Reggie jumped in front of an underground train, Cecil Beaton was staying in Paris. On June 19, one month after Magnus Hirschfeld died, Cecil was meeting friends for a luncheon at the home of Marie-Laure de Noailles, a Viscomtesse and patron of artists including Jean Cocteau, Salvador Dali, Francis Poulenc, and Man Ray. Just before the meal was served, Marie-Laure received a telephone call informing her that during the previous evening, the gay Surrealist writer René Crevel had closed himself in his kitchen and turned on the unlit gas stove. She left the luncheon and rushed to the hospital to sit by René's side as he lay unconscious. Cecil and the others continued with their meal, and then worked on their plans for a ball the following day, for which Cecil was designing several gowns. That evening, back at the hotel, they were joined by a Chilean diplomat named Tony Gandarillas. Tony had been the longtime lover of the English painter Christopher (Kit) Wood, who had leaped into the path of an oncoming train five years earlier. Before arriving at the hotel, Tony had spent several hours at René's bedside, and he was distraught: "it is too much," he said. "I've been through this too many times before. All my friends commit suicide." Later that night, they received a telephone call informing them that "the attempted suicide had succeeded: after dying all day long, René eventually expired."[16] He was thirty-four years old.

René was no stranger to suicide. When he was fourteen years old, his father hanged himself after being discovered having an affair with another man. Ten years later, in 1924, René published his first novel, *Détours*, which included a description of a death identical to the one he would later choose:

> A pot of tea on the gas stove; the window tightly
> closed, I turn on the gas; I forget to light the match.
> Reputation safe and the time to say one's *Confiteor*
> [confession].[17]

That same year, René had responded to the following *enquête* (inquiry) published in the first edition of André Breton's new magazine *La Révolution Surréaliste*:

> We live, we die. What is the part of the will in all of this? It seems as if we kill ourselves the same way we dream. This is not a moral question we are asking: Is Suicide a Solution?[18]

Responses to the *enquête* were published in the magazine's second issue the following month. They ranged from moral disgust to poetic rumination to philosophical embrace. René Crevel's response begins with a simple declaration: "Yes [*Oui*]." He recalls the suicide of his father, "the being who was dearest and closest to my heart" [*l'être, alors, le plus cher et le plus secourable à mon Coeur*] and rails against the "soporific" [*soporifique*] and "timid habit" [*timide habitude*] of "the life I accept" [*la vie que j'accepte*], which he calls "the most terrible argument against myself" [*le plus terrible argument contre moi-même*].[19] This was not an especially uncommon line of thought for young men of this generation, who had survived the Great War in the previous decade but in doing so had witnessed the deaths of so many others. As Robin Walz asserts in her book *Pop Surrealism*, with this provocative query, the Surrealists were

> railing against a hypocritical society that praised the millions of men who had voluntarily marched into slaughter during the course of the war but morally condemned anyone who died by his or her own hand. ... Beyond the easy target of the European conflagration of war, the surrealist inquiry into suicide drove toward irreducible paradoxes of modern existence as experienced at the level of everyday life.[20]

To underscore this latter contention, the Surrealists included a series of *fait divers* (unclassifiable information, or miscellany) in the issue that contained the original *enquête*: short reports of suicides reprinted from various newspapers, where they often appeared as brief accounts "empasiz[ing] the fundamentally sensational and fragmented nature of modern identity."[21] Among the many tiny melodramas scattered across the pages of daily newspapers, a middle-aged woman holding a lantern and an umbrella threw herself down a neighbor's well; a tailor slashed his own throat; a teenage boy asphyxiated himself with gaslights; a young woman wearing lingerie embroidered with the single letter W drowned herself in the Seine late one night; and a young man shot a bullet through his temple after writing three letters, including one to be left at the local *poste restante* for an unknown man.[22]

* * * * *

The period between Robin's death in June 2019 and the memorial we planned for him in an Oakland redwood forest that September was defined by its rolling vagueness. I was unmoored from the habits of daily life. Unable to focus on work or play, and initially unsure why I was doing this, I began to write about objects from my childhood, adolescence, and young adulthood that I had forgotten still existed. These objects had been packed away in boxes that were falling apart, boxes that had followed me for many years, accompanying me through moves to various homes in various cities. Once I settled in San Diego, they had finally been shoved to the back corner of an attic in my house, near the place where the rafters end. During that discontented summer in 2019, I pulled them down one by one, carefully peeled back the packing tape whose ancient adhesive had hardened, and unwrapped items that I had not seen or touched in many years. Every day I wrote about the objects I found and the stories I recalled while holding them. When I first climbed up to the attic and pulled down a box, I thought that it was just busy-work to keep my mind occupied, an attempt to anchor myself again to the demands of the present: I was clearing out *stuff* I no longer needed, stuff that was just taking up space. But I eventually realized that this intimate archaeology with the ruins of my own queer past had become a form of mourning.

As I continued this melancholic unboxing through the fall and winter, I also began to seek out and read everything I could find about queer suicide: magazine articles, newspaper stories, clinical studies, case reports, pulp fiction, and narratives from the published diaries of people who had experienced this kind of sudden loss. I watched countless films that incorporated narratives—or, often, just brief mentions—of a queer person who had chosen to die. I found, as Heather Love has written, that "the history of Western representation is littered with the corpses of gender and sexual deviants," especially those who had killed themselves.[23] This was not an entirely sorrowful practice. I had always "known" that queer people were more likely to die by suicide than others, but I wanted to understand where that *knowing* came from. I began collecting records of specific incidents—obituaries, memoirs, news reports, eulogies—and built an archive of everyday queer people who had died by suicide and whose deaths had been written about, however briefly or expansively.

These two activities—recovering my own queer past from crumbling, forgotten boxes, and compiling my own collection of *fait divers*—structured my mourning for Robin and for the suddenly present-again deaths of Bud and Lana and Alec. I found purchase on my own grief, anchored to losses that almost dared not to speak their own names. Seeking, remembering, and writing evolved into funerary rituals all their own, cathartic (if not reparative) in their transformations. This archive—of a deeply personal queer past, and of an expansive history of queer death—began to shape itself into a cobbled-together map of queer kinship, its lines of attachment drawn by loss.

ii. When from the dust shall rise

Qua resurget ex favilla

Here is an impossibly soft blue baby blanket with a football patch sewn into one corner. One of my very earliest, disorganized memories is an image of that patch. I remember turning my head and seeing it, and how large it seemed. This is the first remembered icon of my little life, no symbol less suited to the person I am than a football. And yet every time I find it again, I notice how soft this blanket is, and how warm: sometimes the affect of otherness brings both comfort and pain.

* * * * *

In 1860, a seventeen-year-old man named Augustin Bedouin, whom we would today identify as transgender, was arrested for robbery. At the prison where he was being held, he was forcibly outed and sent to the women's wards. He hanged himself from an "iron bar with a pocket handkerchief."[24]

* * * * *

Here is a crayon portrait of me drawn by a boy I knew when we were in the first grade. My face, crowned with bright yellow hair, takes up most of the page; I am wide-eyed and smiling. In the background, arranged so as to give an unusually astute (for a six-year-old artist) sense of perspective, is a green pasture. At the top of the drawing, written in bright red, "I love you." And here is a black-and-white photograph of this friend and me in our first-grade classroom. I sit at a kidney-shaped table, bending to look beneath it. He is climbing the chair behind me, mouth opened as if singing. I have a distinct memory of this table: around the time this photo was taken, this friend and I were sitting beneath it, and as I stared at him I wondered: do all boys feel this way?

* * * * *

In 1892, Katie Tipton shot herself in the heart in Nashville. She left a letter for her girlfriend, who had recently told her "that she would soon have to leave her."[25]

* * * * *

Here is a notebook of writing—occasional reflections and angst-filled poetry—from my junior year of high school. On one page I wrote: "will I ever find them?" This was all I felt that I could inscribe of my obsession with the ACT UP poster pinned to a wall in the counselor's meeting room at my school. Designed by the Gran Fury collective, the poster is horizontally long and vertically squat. There are three pairs kissing: a heterosexual couple on the far left, a gay couple in the center, and a lesbian couple on the far right. Text at the top of the poster reads, "Kissing Doesn't Kill: Greed and Indifference Do." The first time I saw this poster I was transfixed by it until I realized that I was not alone; my staring was being seen. I looked across the room filled with other students and saw the counselor, who was looking straight at me. I felt a sudden shock of shame. Her eyes softened with compassion as she smiled, gently nodded, and mouthed the words "I see you. You're safe."

* * * * *

Jean Cocteau's father killed himself in 1898. He did not leave a note, and his reasons were never explicitly conveyed. But in the lightly fictionalized autobiography *The White Paper*, Jean would later write,

> It has always seemed to me that my father and I too closely resembled each other not to have this essential feature in common. He was probably unaware of his true bent; at any rate, instead of pursuing it, he struggled along another path without knowing what it was that made the way so dreary and life to hang so heavy upon him. Had he discovered the tastes he never had the chance to cultivate and which his phrases, his gestures, certain of his movements, a thousand details about his person revealed to me, he would have been thunderstruck. . . . But no; he lived, living in ignorance of himself, and he accepted his burden.[26]

* * * * *

Here is a small stuffed bear. He is about twelve inches long, and he is wearing a green-checked bow tie. His arms and legs are sewn so that they do not lie flat; if you hold him right, he seems to be stuck mid-stride. He has hard black eyes and a small embroidered nose, but no mouth. This is the bear given to me by my very first boyfriend, Mark. Here is a photograph of Mark wearing a kilt, his hair tied back in a ponytail. He wore Paco Rabanne and could recite the entirety of "I am the very model of a modern Major General" on demand. We found each other through another friend who, on our first date, drove us to the state park that bordered the campus of my school, where there was an outdoor aviary surrounded by a wooden deck. That was where we first explored one another, making out as the predatory birds in their giant cage hunted tiny rodents in the dark and as our friend blasted Sinéad O'Connor's second album from her car. When he gave me this bear, he had sprayed it with his cologne, but the scent has long since gone.

* * * * *

On April 1, 1950, scholar Francis Matthiessen leaped from a twelfth-floor window of the Hotel Manger in Boston. Francis was a professor at Harvard and a socialist activist. He had recently been targeted by the House Un-American Activities Committee, hounded for his left-wing politics. He was forty-eight years old.[27] Twenty-eight years later, the letters between Francis and his lover, the painter Russel Cheney, were published in a single volume. The letters reveal that their pet names for one another were Rat and Devil.[28]

* * * * *

Here is a Polaroid from a trip to New Orleans for a debate tournament my senior year of high school. A group of us are sitting on outdoor steps, watching others as they perform some devised melodrama. Most of us are smiling or laughing. But there in the back is Lana, hunched over and hugging herself. She looks tentative, lost, out of place. She is looking forward but her eyes seem veiled, as if she is remembering something that none of the rest of us knew.

* * * * *

On June 7, 1954, Alan Turing died after eating an apple that he had laced with cyanide, "an apparent nod to the poisoned apple in one of his favorite films, the Disney version of *Snow White and the Seven Dwarfs*." He had been arrested for "homosexual offenses" and convicted of indecency several years earlier. His sentence included probation and forced chemical castration. Shortly before he died, he sent the following sardonic syllogism to his friend Norman Routledge:

Turing believes machines think
Turing lies with men
Therefore machines cannot think[29]

Turing's suicide is one of the rumored origin stories, perhaps apocryphal, for the bitten-apple icon emblazoned on the ubiquitous products sold by Apple, one of the richest corporations in the world.

* * * * *

Here is a small blue carnival ticket, the kind sometimes used for raffles, torn from a massive roll of others identical to it but for the number printed in black. This one was used, as were many others in similar sites elsewhere, to identify the blood drawn for an HIV test in a queer clinic, without requiring that blood's owner to provide their name or other identifying details. It was handed to me by a woman sitting at a reception desk, its twin clamped to a clipboard along with forms I had to out fill out: they asked about my age, my sexual practices, my sexual partners. The clipboard also included two brochures, one about the virus and one about safer sex practices. When my number was called, I followed another person—I do not remember anything about them—down a flickering, fluorescent-hued hall to a small, sterile room. The person asked me questions I had never been asked before, and I trembled as I responded. When my blood was drawn, my nerves kicked in; as I watched the vial fill, I thought about everything that had led me here. Two weeks later, I returned to the clinic, waiting in the same uncomfortable chairs in the same long hall, sitting next to others who, when they caught my eye, would smile and nod. By the time the number printed on this ticket was called, I was sweating with anxiety. As I followed the person who collected me down to the same small room, I thought I might faint. When I heard those four words for the very first time—"your test was negative"—and as the person reminded me of the test's limitations, I stopped breathing, fixed between a sense of momentary relief and awareness that this sitting and waiting for a number to be called, this filling out of forms and rereading brochures, this tense procession down a starkly lit hall, would now be a regular part of my life, a ritual that required not a onetime performance but an ongoing, perpetually repeating enactment. I pocketed the ticket, later affixing it to the inside cover of a journal I kept, like a talisman of luck for every future walk I would take down every long hall.

* * * * *

In March 1975, a young man stood on the edge of Golden Gate Bridge. He threw his journal over the side, and then two books, and then himself. "I knew him well," said counselor James Stoll. "I am angry at the waste of his death. [. . .] There was not enough time for the few of us who work with such persons to counteract his 22 years of societally induced self-hate."[30]

* * * * *

Here is a chewed and twisted plastic strip. It was once a red coffee stirrer, plucked from a bin in a coffeeshop on the second floor of a bookstore in Evanston. In March 1993, I was smitten with a floppy-haired boy who worked there. My oboist friend Sarah would go for coffee with me, sitting at those tables for hours while I stole glances of him over whatever book I was pretending to read. On the third or fourth time we went, I chewed this stirrer into oblivion as I nervously worked up the nerve to go talk to him. I finally did, and he gave me his number, and so began a springtime romance that now seems like an idyllic parable about young love. Here is a photograph of us washing dishes in his apartment; we have spent this day, the first warm day after a long winter, flying kites on the beach, followed by a long nap in his bed. My hair in the picture is long, draping down to my shoulders, and I am smiling as if I have never been so alive.

* * * * *

On October 28, 1976, Quentin Hubbard, the "swishy" son of and successor to L. Ron Hubbard, was found dead in Las Vegas. He was unconscious in his car with a hose leading from the tailpipe to a window. He was taken to a hospital, but he was not carrying identification, and was listed as John Doe. He never regained consciousness and died two weeks later, on November 12. Several days after his death, investigators found a smog sticker from Florida on his car along with the vehicle's identification number. They contacted the Florida Department of Motor Vehicles, and he was finally identified.[31]

* * * * *

Here is a small photograph of Alec from the last time I saw him. It is sealed in a silver frame. I was taking this picture right after hearing him laugh his utterly eccentric laugh. I would remember this moment years later, when I read this description of René Crevel by his friend Philippe Soupault: "even his laugh, so tremendous, so tragic, so unbearable, was a revolt. Intense and quick."[32] In the photograph, Alec's hair is pulled back from his face, and he is staring straight at the camera, daring it to capture him.

* * * * *

On August 29, 1978, Harvey Milk's lover Jack Lira hanged himself on the back porch of their apartment in San Francisco. According to Harvey, he had recently watched a documentary about gay victims of the Holocaust and "thought the same situation was coming to America."[33] He left a note saying "I tried. . . . I loved you." He was twenty-five years old.[34]

* * * * *

Here is a ball-chain necklace made of shiny metal; its clasp still holds. It loops through six aluminum rings of different colors: red, orange, yellow, green, blue, and violet. These are freedom rings, icons of protests and pride parades from the early 1990s, invented by a New York jewelry designer who would later die of AIDS. This set was purchased in April 1993 from a vendor at the March on Washington. I had traveled there with the floppy-haired coffeeshop boyfriend, his sister, and her girlfriend. We drove through the night from Chicago to Washington in an old white van. When we arrived, we slept for a few hours in someone's apartment and then ventured out. I wore my favorite pair of jeans with holes in the knees, a long-sleeved tee, and scuffed Doc Martens; Matt wore a vivid plaid flannel whose mismatched colors I still see in dreams. Neither of us had ever seen so many queer people—more than a million, they later said—gathered together. Neither of us had ever seen the whole AIDS quilt laid out on a lawn. We soaked it all in together, clasping hands for the first time in public. The night after the march, we followed the crowds down into a Metro station, everyone en route to the bars of Dupont Circle. Our side of the platform was packed, thousands of sweaty, exhausted queers waiting for the train. We were boisterous and loud, aflame with the pride of so many of us being here together. But suddenly, everyone grew silent. I looked across the tracks to the other side of the platform, where I saw the PFLAG contingent. They were parents and grandparents, still decked out in their "I Love My Lesbian Daughter" and "Gay Is Good" T-shirts and carrying their "Silence = Death" placards. Just as suddenly as we had grown quiet, people on our side of the platform erupted into a massive ovation. "Thank you," some screamed. "We love you, too." People around me were crying with gratitude—some wept uncontrollably—and I, who had trained myself never to cry in public, started sniffling.

* * * * *

On August 23, 1983, Linda Brogan died by suicide in Durham, North Carolina. She was thirty-nine years old. Her death is noted on a single piece of typed paper in a thin file labeled "Death and Dying" at the Lesbian Herstory Archives. She had been a member of lesbian activist groups in Georgia and North Carolina, and a phone number is listed for one of her friends, or perhaps her surviving partner—the name is Elizabeth. No other details are included. However, in the 2015 book *Out of the Closet, into the Archives*, Linda Brogan and Elizabeth Knowlton are described as being members of a lesbian-feminist commune in the Chapel Hill area in North Carolina. With their housemates Leslie Kahn and Nancy Blood, they collectively wrote and produced the *Feminist Newsletter* in the 1970s. It was distributed through lesbian networks and communities throughout the South.[35]

* * * * *

Here is a small plastic bottle of bubbles printed with German text and an image of a small bear. It is sealed in a clear plastic bag with a tie at the top. And here is a pair of black plastic sunglasses, lenses tinted bright yellow. During my last summer in Chicago, before I moved to Sri Lanka, I worked as a houseboy in the home of a middle-aged gay couple who were foster parents to two children. I was also dazzled by a brief but wondrous summer romance with tall, lanky Kevin, whose eyes were perpetually locked in a faraway gaze. In the halcyon days of late summer, we lounged on the beaches bordering Lake Michigan, reading books to one another. In the halcyon nights, we wandered through the city, sometimes stopping at fortune teller shops, whose readings we collected and later compared before wrapping ourselves around one another, thick with salt and sweat. The night before I boarded the flight that would carry me halfway around the world, he gave me three gifts while we sat on the beach in Lakeview. The first was a plastic green compass, "so you'll always find your way home"; it is now lost. The second, was this pair of sunglasses with yellow-tinted lenses, "so the world will always look golden." And the third was this bottle of bubbles, "so you'll remember our time together, beautiful but brief, like life itself."

* * * * *

On August 27, 1983, twenty-year-old Bobby Griffith jumped from the bridge of a highway overpass in Portland, Oregon. He had been out dancing that night, and left the club around midnight. He had been raised in a conservative, evangelical home in California, and he struggled for most of his life to reconcile his sexuality with his inherited religion. The story of his death and his mother's eventual turn to advocate for gay and lesbian rights was told in the book *Prayers for Bobby*, which was later adapted into a film starring Sigourney Weaver and Ryan Kelley.[36] In diary entries from the winter before he died, Bobby wrote,

LIBERA ME

> Sometimes I sense that life is very fragile and that at any given moment it could be snuffed out the way a candle is by a sudden draft. I get this feeling deep within my bones, and I just want someone to protect me. . . . Please don't send me to hell.[37]

* * * * *

Here is a Polaroid of me and my first partner, David, with a picture he drew of my going-away party. I was leaving Chapel Hill, where I'd just finished a master's degree, for Berkeley, where I was starting my doctorate. After dropping me off in California, David was leaving for Germany, where he was shooting a film, and then for New York. We didn't know how the distance would work, but we decided just to let it unfold. It did, eventually, into a friendship that is a touchstone for both of us. Several days after the little party depicted in his drawing, we left for the long, slow cross-country drive. It was a week that felt, in retrospect, like an extended disentangling. And after we arrived at my new home and he had left for Berlin, I stayed up all night writing a poem that I never sent to him.

> *The driving across takes*
> *five days, four if you rush: somehow*
> *scenery seems more lush when*
> *traveling at high speeds, more full*
> *despite its passivity, its willingness*
> *to be driven across. And leaving is wildfire,*
> *I mean it really grows, gets ferocious*
> *towards the end, leaves you thirsty*
> *for it, thirsty to get going, thirsty, too,*
> *to stay.*
> *Roads in Arkansas are like roads*
> *across Alaska, desperate for anything*

*to happen, like saying
"It did occur. It did occur,"
over and over to make yourself believe,
despite all prior knowledge, despite
everything you think,
that memory works,
that the body feels, that you are
capable of realizing any lasting trace.
And this, the diving in, the
long haul into Texas, where
turning around is suicide—another
eight hours of nothing again—is
the point past which
there is no revolution, no spinning
on axis to reclaim that which you have
left behind.
It is here where scenery changes,
overcomes the immediacy of travel,
of moving your life from one unknown
to another, defies that sense that your life
really is travel, a trip across ages, across
breathing to death. Because this moment,
this tic of untiring void, this shift amid
one being-here and another, this gap between
history and promise, is most sincere. It is
here where Southwest starts,
land itself named in relation to farther shores,
landing itself further down and further over.
Something about this sand, something
about this greater sense of sky, that
warms the heart to speech. You can't stay
silent in the desert; either claustrophobia
flees or insignificance sets in: the sheer immensity*

gets you rolling.
The settling down is hardest, because driving
makes you weary but anxious to move your feet.

* * * * *

On March 23, 1989, in the neighborhood where I now live, two employees at the university where I now work died in a double suicide. Robert Markworth, who was forty-one, and his longtime lover Robert Simmons, who was thirty-seven, had recently been diagnosed with AIDS. They swallowed barbiturates with alcohol, and then one placed a plastic bag over the head of the other in their bedroom before hanging himself in their garage. They had first met and fallen in love in Michigan, and moved together to San Diego in the late 1970s. Their colleagues and neighbors spoke of how pleasant and kind they were. They left a suicide letter that they had written together, with instructions for selling their home.[38]

* * * * *

Here is a photograph of my first San Francisco boyfriend. We are in a nightclub, and he has his arms wrapped around me. Our affair was brief but intense: a winter and spring mostly consisting of very late nights. He lived a very fast life; and years later, when he died in his sleep, still far too young, I would remember this particular night and the sharp anticipation I felt as I first glanced across the dark room and was met with a smile, a nod, an approach. But by the time I heard about his death, other lovers and friends had also died young, and there were so many nights to remember. And so I folded this picture away into a box that I knew I might never open again.

iii. That which is hidden will appear

Quidquid latet apparebit

Throughout his career, as he was working and corresponding with hundreds of homosexual and transgender people, Magnus Hirschfeld kept notes on those who contemplated and attempted suicide. Many of these stories were documented in his book *Die Homosexualität des Mannes und des Weibes* (*The Homosexuality of Men and Women*), which was originally published in German in 1914 and first translated into English in 1920. In addition to the suicide letter he received from that young gay soldier the night before his wedding—the one that Hirschfeld credits with prompting him into a career in sexology—he describes people he has counseled who, within hours of their last meeting, have killed themselves, and others who have sent him letters from afar, describing their imminent self-inflicted deaths. He explains that he regularly reads newspapers for stories about the suicides of people who are either explicitly identified as, or subtly implied to be, homosexual; "those who scan newspapers for such things," he writes, "will very often encounter similar notices."[39] He describes keeping "a file which I made for the one hundred suicides of homosexuals about which I came to know," and that he "was personally acquainted with more than half of them."[40] He narrates some stories at length: people who hanged themselves, shot themselves, stabbed themselves, or poisoned themselves because of blackmail, police persecution, parental or religious disapproval, failed love affairs, or (especially for teenagers and young adults) their overwhelming feeling of despair for the future once they realized their sexual desires.

Hirschfeld also describes seeing scars from previous suicide attempts on the bodies of his patients: "While giving homosexuals physical examinations, I very frequently saw suicidal wounds, such as those from cuts near arteries, or gunshot wounds in the region of the heart or temple."[41] In the *Suicide* film shot by Andy Warhol in 1965, Rock Bradett bared his arms for the camera, which centered on the scars of his previous suicide attempts: more than a dozen on each wrist in "different shades of purple."[42] Rock relives those previous attempts in short vignettes throughout the film. "I open my arms like I open a beer." "I open my arms with the razor." "I open again on the same track not yet healed."[43] Diane di Prima writes of Freddie Herko before his leap from the Cornelia Street apartment window that the "scars had left his flesh but not his mind. Or his heart either, questing in a kind of eternal pain."[44] Writing about Hirschfeld's notes on the scars of his patients, Heike Bauer argues that this fleshy archive "documents the deadly effects of homosexual persecution and how social ostracization could make queer lives feel unlivable":

> The image of suicidal scarring not only bears witness to the damage caused by social norms but indicates how such damage touched Hirschfeld's sexological practice. It suggests that the body in the clinic is . . . a repository of experience, which sometimes imprints itself onto the skin, making legible what language fails to articulate. With this in mind, the data collected by Hirschfeld on homosexual suicide can be seen as an attempt to make visible the queer scar tissue that marks modern homosexuality. By counting homosexual suicides within a statistical framework, Hirschfeld emphasized the collective shape of the individual suffering.[45]

In his response to the *enquête* from the inaugural 1924 issue of *La Révolution Surréaliste*, theatre artist Antonin Artaud wrote, "No, suicide is still a hypothesis," before expounding on the dubitable nature of life itself. "It is absolutely certain," he wrote, "that I have long been dead: I already committed suicide."[46] In 1925, in an issue of *La Disque Vert* also focused on suicide, Artaud wrote, "If I commit suicide, it will not be to destroy myself but to put myself back together. . . . I shall for the first time give things the shape of my will."[47] In a similar vein, for the original Surrealist *enquête*, writer Léon Baranger offered what was perhaps the most elegiac of the published responses:

> Sometimes when the door is closed we encounter another adventure. We dive to the depths of the Atlantic and continue via the Pacific, but it's all over for the side from which we departed.[48]

This is what I want for them, for all of them: a dive from which they emerge into a new Pacific, freed of the scars that shaped a collective out of suffering, hearts unbroken, lives flush and livable again.

X
In Paradisum

In fact, death made him more present, more evenly distributed in everything he left behind him, more meaningfully remembered.

PETRU POPESCU,
THE ENCOUNTER: AMAZON BEAMING (1991)

The fallen curtain lent an unexpected intimacy to the stage.
EMILY ST. JOHN MANDEL, *STATION ELEVEN* (2014)

i. Eternal light

Lux aeterna

"There is a very powerful relationship between empathy and proximity," Simon McBurney intoned in a 2018 performance of Theatre de Complicité's *The Encounter* at the Barbicon Theatre in London, "and I would like to get closer to you now."[1] This small invocation became especially poignant in the context of empty performance venues and widespread social distancing during pandemic lockdowns in 2020, when Complicité made a video of the production available for viewing from home. Tender, too, was the intensity of one particular moment near the end of McBurney's performance, an adaptation of Petru Popescu's 1991 book *The Encounter: Amazon Beaming*, about the twentieth-century photojournalist Loren McIntyre's experiences with the indigenous Mayoruna community as he was seeking the furthermost source of the Amazon River.[2] Participating in a ritual for which strong psychedelics were used to communicate with ancestors, McBurney-as-McIntyre describes the sensation of believing he was about to die: "Death is a bank of lights being switched off. It's a vast theatre in my head that grows like a cacophony, on and on and on. And then it dims."[3]

I watched this performance from my couch on a foggy afternoon that May, two months after the governor of California issued stay-at-home orders in response to the still-escalating pandemic. At that time, it was not clear how long the lockdown would continue, but there was still general optimism that summer might return some sense of normalcy. We did not know that the stay-at-home orders would remain in effect for eight more months, until January 2021, nor that successive waves of viral variants would provoke further lockdowns. In May 2020, social distancing was relatively novel, as was the extreme isolation of stay-at-home orders, especially for those who live alone. When I watched the Complicité performance, I was also one month away from the first anniversary of Robin's death. I was hungry for connection, hungry to be with other people again, and—still aching from the loss of my friend—hungry for the world of theatre that we had both loved. In the book from which the Complicité production was adapted, McIntyre learns from a Mayoruna elder named Barnacle about a local conception of history grounded in cycles, a "succession of 'darks' and 'brights,' like the days and nights," where "dark periods mean strife, hardship, and retreat, and the bright ones relative peace and relaxation." Barnacle tells him that "we can escape the dark . . . by moving back to the beginning."[4] It is Barnacle whom McIntyre is describing when he reflects that "death made him more present, more evenly distributed . . . more meaningfully remembered"; death was Barnacle's "last trick and ritual."[5]

After watching the performance, I kept hearing echoes of the lines about empathy, about history, and about saturated remembrances of those who have died. I thought of Robin's absence as a palpable presence with me, the way his death had distributed him throughout my days and nights. And I began to wonder: What happens to empathy when a given proximity is lost? What happens to empathy when the lights of a loved one's life have dimmed for good? Can empathy survive—can empathy thrive and grow—in the darkness of loss? Can the depth of *feeling for* a loved one who has died even be called empathy, or does it become something else, something like imagination, something like fantasy, something even like *ritual*? Perhaps this is what grief is: an evolution of empathy after the empathized-for loved one is gone, empathy without a recipient. And perhaps, in the end, this is what *theatre* is, too: not simply play or make-believe, but the *feeling-for* that survives a loss, that circulates around a loss, that orients itself to repetitive rehearsals and endless stagings of a lost original source. Maybe grief *needs* theatre; maybe theatre needs grief.

In December 2021—almost two years into the pandemic—HBO began broadcasting the miniseries *Station Eleven*, a screen adaptation of the novel by Emily St. John Mandel. The series, like the novel, documents the sudden onset, grave escalation, and long aftermath of a global pandemic caused by a swine flu with a 99 percent mortality rate. The opening scene of the first episode begins with animals scavenging within a dark theater, which has been flooded and overgrown with vines, small trees, and ferns. A portion of the theater's roof has collapsed so that a beam of light from outside shines down upon the stage. We see a pig rooting through the undergrowth and then, in a pool of water, a Playbill from what we later learn was the final production staged in this place: William Shakespeare's *King Lear*, headlined by an actor named Arthur Leander. In a flash, the scene toggles back in time, though we do not know how far. From a camera situated somewhere at the back of the audience, we see the darkened auditorium with rows of filled seats and a lit stage. The set includes several piles of boulders and stones and an illuminated backdrop depicting a cloudy sky. The stage lighting is muted and cold: a chilly, fog-filled day. We watch as a man walks into the ring of a spotlight shining down from above, a visual echo of the beam of sunlight leaking through the collapsed roof in the opening shot.

In a gravely tone, the man begins to perform lines from *King Lear*. The lines are from act 4, scene 6, just after Gloucester has attempted to kill himself by leaping from the Dover cliffs. He and his disguised son Edgar meet Lear, who has been wandering the heath in an increasing state of madness and despair. Lear speaks:

Ay, every inch a king.
When I do stare, see how the subject quakes.
I pardon that man's life. What was thy cause?
Adultery? Thou shalt not die! . . .
Gloucester's bastard son was kinder to his father
Than my daughters got 'tween the lawful sheets.
To't, luxury, pell-mell, for I lack soldiers.
Behold yond simp'ring dame,
Whose face between her forks presages snow,
That minces . . .[6]

And then, without finishing his lines, the man playing Lear—Arthur Leander from the Playbill—turns to lean on one of the stones. Gloucester sputters a line from further down in the script in an attempt to prompt Arthur back into the scene—"Dost thou know me?"—but Arthur wheezes and collapses onto the stage floor. An audience member named Jeevan, who has realized before anyone else that something is seriously wrong, rises from his seat and climbs onto the stage. Thinking that Arthur is displaying the signs of a heart attack, Jeevan shouts for a doctor. As the curtain is lowered, the camera toggles to an overhead view and centers on the fallen actor's face: his eyes have lost focus. We watch as Arthur dies.

In the novel from which the series was adapted, the theater's stage shifts palpably in this moment: the curtain has dropped, blocking the audience's view and "lend[ing] an unexpected intimacy to the stage." Jeevan is unmoored by these changed conditions, no longer a spectator but uncertain as to what his role may be. From this point onward, the social world within and beyond the theatre also begins to crumble. In the series adaptation, Jeevan helps a young girl who is part of the cast, Kirsten, make her way home. On the way, his sister, who is a doctor working in a hospital's overflowing emergency room, calls to tell him that the flu outbreak in Europe recently in the news has arrived in the United States, and is much more serious than is being publicized. "We've never seen a flu like this before," she says. "It's too late to run. You need to get to [their brother] Frank. Don't believe a word the news says. . . . People are walking around already exposed, and they don't even know it. Avoid contact with anyone."

"OK, but this happens, right? This happens," Jeevan says. "This is happening?"

"Lock yourselves in, build a barricade. It's your best chance at surviving."[7]

When Jeevan and Kirsten arrive at her house and find it dark, and her parents do not answer the door, he takes her with him to gather supplies from a grocery store and then to his brother's apartment. Within weeks, all social infrastructure has collapsed, and the vast majority of the human population has died.

The remainder of the series toggles between several timelines: the period before the outbreak, the days and months immediately following it, and two decades after the catastrophe. In the after-times, the world is in shambles, and most of the survivors and their descendants live either in small encampments or in nomadic groups. But theatre has survived: the series's narrative is centered on an itinerant theatre troupe, the Traveling Symphony, that cycles through small settlements along a tour path called the Wheel. In this postapocalyptic world, no electronic devices and few books remain. The members of the troupe have memorized Shakespeare's canon of plays, from which they select each season's productions. No other genre has survived the catastrophe—no film, no television, no recorded sound—and so the Traveling Symphony is enormously popular, and every community along the Wheel keenly anticipates their annual visits. Now a young woman, Kirsten is their star.

IN PARADISUM

The series delights in these theatrical stagings. When the Traveling Symphony performs, their portable stage is assembled with intricately designed structures, elaborate scavenged sets, and baroque patchwork costumes. They surround their stage with candles and other small flames to light the nighttime shows. The actors' performances range from subtle psychological realism to showy melodrama, the Elizabethan lines rolling off the actors' tongues as if it were everyday speech. One night, while performing the role of Hamlet, Kirsten has flashbacks to an evening shortly after the performance of *King Lear* when Arthur Leander died. She and Jeeven are with Frank, barricaded in his apartment, when she receives the last text messages that she will ever receive, one from each parent's phone. "The body of the owner of this phone is located in the morgue at Lakeview Memorial Hospital," each message reads. "Do not come here."

Kirsten relives this moment while playing Hamlet during act 1, scene 2, when Hamlet is first confronted by his mother and stepfather about his unending melancholy over his father's death. Gertrude says,

> Do not for ever with thy vailed lids
> Seek for thy noble father in the dust:
> Thou know'st 'tis common; all that lives must die,
> Passing through nature to eternity. . . .
> Why seems it so particular with thee?

As flashes of that day twenty years earlier pass before her eyes, Kirsten is overcome with the memory of her original shock as she performs Hamlet's monologue describing the depths of his grief:

> *Seems*, madam! nay it *is*; I know not "seems."
> 'Tis not alone my inky cloak, good mother,
> Nor customary suits of solemn black,

> Nor windy suspiration of forced breath, . . .
> Together with all forms, moods, shapes of grief,
> That can denote me truly: these indeed *seem*,
> For they are actions that a man might play:
> But I have that within which passeth show;
> These but the trappings and the suits of woe.[8]

These moments in the series are rich with layered complexity. Gertrude accosts Hamlet for continuing to mourn the loss of his father by describing the banality of death and the ability of others to accept and move on from such losses. In response, Hamlet's monologue distinguishes between the guttural experience of unrelenting grief—"that within which passeth show"—and the embodied enactments, the "trappings and suits of woe," that merely symbolize mourning. All of this is taking place within a scene in which Kirsten is performing a role on a stage, taking on the "forms, moods, and shapes of grief" while simultaneously re-experiencing the primal scene of her own catastrophic loss, the death of her parents. The stage gives Kirsten both access to and an outlet for her own powerful grief, and this grief gives Kirsten's theatrical performance its power. Her grief needs theatre; her theatre needs grief.

The Traveling Symphony's motto, painted on the side of its caravan, is this: "Because Survival Is Insufficient." As the pandemic continued into 2022 and another variant wreaked havoc on the world, I watched and rewatched *Station Eleven* greedily, transfixed by its vision of a postdisaster world in which theatre becomes a beacon not just for survival but for human resilience, for the warmth of togetherness, and for the power of creativity and the arts. I imagined watching it with Robin, how he would have wept at the delicacy of its tragedies and loved its centering of friendship as the most important human relationship, how his eyes would have gleamed with an actor's pride during all of the theatrical scenes. I imagined watching it with Alec, also a theatre lover: we performed together in high school, and he directed a scandalous production of *Hair* at his college. He would have scrutinized the show's dramaturgy—the precision of its historical accuracy, the narrative arc of its concept of the future—and carefully appraised the cast's performances, particularly when their characters emoted. I imagined watching it with Lana, who would have seen herself in Kirsten. She would have grown very quiet during the Hamlet scene thinking about her own mother, who died by suicide when she was young. She would also have become distracted at some point, wrapping herself into a ball and falling asleep, or leaving in a rush to some other more vivid and daring endeavor. And Bud, though I knew him only from my father's stories: I imagined him with me too, all done up in his dandiest suit. What would he make of this era he never knew? What would he make of me?

There they all were with me on my couch, surrounding me in my quarantined isolation, watching me, a survivor of their catastrophes, as I learned something from grief about theatre and something from theatre about grief.

ii. Perpetual light

Lux perpetua

The film begins with a dark screen and the sound of a video camera whirring as its lens is zoomed and retracted. We hear a videocassette being removed and another being inserted. We see a shaky, handheld shot of a man jumping and twisting in a series of awkward dance moves. He is standing in front of the windows of a sliding patio door. "Oh my God, what even is that" a young girl asks from behind the camera.

"These are my moves," the man replies.

"Dad, that's so embarrassing."

"That's not embarrassing," he says, sounding slightly hurt as he walks out onto the balcony. They talk some more: we learn that she has just turned eleven, and that his thirty-first birthday is two days away.

"When you were eleven, what did you think you think you would be doing now?" she asks him.

He stills and looks at the floor. The camera zooms and the video freezes as he begins to turn away. In the upper edge of the frozen frame, we just can make out the silhouette of a viewer, someone whose image is being reflected in the screen on which she is watching this video, someone who has paused it precisely on this image of the man slowly turning away. She adjusts how she is sitting, tilts from one side to the other.

The image shifts to a darkened club scene. As a strobe light flashes, it captures a room of people dancing, their bodies moving in syncopated rhythm. The camera centers on a woman who is standing in the midst of the dancers. She is alone, her arms at her sides, her eyes closed. We later learn that this is Sophie. It is she who was watching old videos of herself on vacation in Turkey with her father Calum. The videos have captured the last time that she would ever see or be with him: Calum will die shortly after their vacation. And although the film never makes this explicit, it implies that he will die by suicide.

Charlotte Wells's 2022 film *Aftersun* is a narratively sparse collection of Sophie's childhood vacation videos interspersed with other scenes: her memories of the trip, her attempts to imagine moments when her father was alone, and the mysterious strobe-lit club—the setting of a fantasied reunion.[9] Sophie, who now lives with her wife and their new baby, has awakened on her birthday morning—perhaps she is turning thirty-one, Calum's age on the vacation—and is reconstructing the last time she saw her father by watching these videos, seeking to fill in the gaps of what she sensed as a child and what she now knows of his fate. Throughout the film, we watch young Sophie as she witnesses her father struggling with waves of longing, self-recrimination, and despair. The two have a loving, playful relationship, and he is tender with her in a way his own parents never were: the scene that opens the film is later revealed to end with him confessing that they had forgotten his eleventh birthday, an indication of his lifelong dejection. We learn that he asked her to stop recording before he would answer her question of what he had foreseen for his life when he was eleven. "I'll just record it in my little mind camera," she responds; and from her memory, we see a partial reflection of him in the corner of a mirror as he tells her the story.

One evening, young Sophie asks her father if he'll ever return to his native Scotland, where she lives with her mother. His response gives voice to the alienation that we have sensed throughout the film:

> There's this feeling, once you leave where you're from, like where you grew up, that you don't totally belong there again. Not really. But Edinburgh was never . . . I never felt like I really did belong there.

Calum's queerness is an open question throughout the film, never explicitly named but strongly implied. In one scene, he tells her that he and someone named Keith are thinking of renting a house together on the outskirts of London, a house that would have a room for her when she came to visit. In another scene, while they are taking a boat out to snorkel and scuba dive, a handsome young instructor helps Calum with his wetsuit. Calum smiles as he talks to him, his gaze lingering. And on the final night of their vacation, Calum pulls Sophie onto a dance floor at their hotel as Queen's

"Under Pressure" is playing. Asked in an interview about this nuanced but inconclusive portrait of Calum, the film's director commented that her "characters are always going to be queer by default."[10]

Calum's death is left similarly unexplained, but the suggestion that it is self-inflicted appears throughout the film. In the most direct reference, one evening Calum leaves Sophie, who is hanging out with a group of new teenage friends at the hotel. We see him wandering through the resort and to the beach. We watch as he marches determinedly into the surf, disappearing as the waves crash around him; the camera lingers, waiting for a reemergence that does not come. In a later scene, we learn that he has left a note for Sophie in the room before going alone to the beach: "I love you very much. Never forget that." But he does return, and we watch him from behind as he sits in their room, naked and alone, sobbing uncontrollably. And in an earlier scene, while talking with the scuba instructor on the boat, he confesses, "I can't see myself at forty, to be honest. Surprised I made it to thirty." We learn that he lied about having a scuba license before diving—and are left wondering if this risky deception was an indirect attempt to disappear and fade away.

In the film's sequences drawn from Sophie's memories, Calum often appears in indirect and fragmentary ways: she watches him through half-closed eyes one night as she falls asleep; he is barely visible in a dark haze. She watches him while swimming, his form rippled and distorted by the water. We see him reflected in the polished top of a breakfast table, and in the concave mirror of a dark television screen, and in the transparent glare of a window pane. He is a liminal figure, both partial and whole in her memory. Sometimes he engages deeply with her, emotionally open and seemingly happy. But just as often he threatens to slide out of view entirely, appearing only as fragmented body parts: a shoulder, an arm, the back of his head. He is both present and absent throughout the film, his gaze sometimes direct, but always clouded by an interior life that shines through in its vivid turmoil. When he says goodbye to her at the airline gate where she boards a plane to fly home to Edinburgh, he holds the camera, recording her hesitation as a flight attendant guides her away. Adult Sophie lingers over this footage, slowing it down to watch it carefully, pausing the video at the moment when, before she disappears down the jetway, her childhood self turns back to him, smiles broadly, and waves goodbye. This image captures the very final moment he laid eyes on her, and she on him: adult Sophie stares at her own young eyes gazing back at her father, behind the camera, for the last time.

This is a haunted frame, thick with its mournful layering of final gazes. The camera pans away from the screen on which Sophie is watching until it finds her, sitting alone on her sofa. We then see the scene that she is imagining, immediately after she last saw him: Calum at the airport, standing alone in a beige space lit by fluorescent bulbs. He closes the video camera with which he was recording his daughter's departure, turns around, and walks away through distant double doors, indelibly gone for good. But immediately before this sequence, Sophie was remembering their final dance to "Under Pressure" the night before that departure. Memories of them dancing are interwoven with Sophie's fantasy of the dark, strobe-lit club where she as an adult has been trying to approach her father as he dances on the other side of the room. In this last iteration, she has finally reached him, and as the flashes of light freeze everyone's motions—like a camera shutter extracting still images from action, embalming split-seconds from the flow of time—we seem them locked in an embrace as they dance. Those pulsing beams of light have returned him to her, however momentarily, restoring him from the darkness of his oblivion. This has been her dream all along: to find him there as he dances—forever young in each flash of light—and having found him, to hold and be held by him again.

This is the scavenging work of mourning, the desire to find something new among the relentless recollections, the longing to restore the lost beloved. And these are the ways I see them still, illuminated as if by a strobe: Robin outside near a roundabout, bouncing from leg to leg with barely bridled glee; Lana near the lake, laughing as the swan chases someone who got too close; Alec in the tsunami of one of his soapbox monologues, voice sharpening as his intensity builds; Robin in the flush of another new love, the one he called *my angel*; Alec on the ground cross-legged, reading Joyce aloud; Lana in the rain, stomping the puddles just as they'd gathered their shallow depths; Alec in a flash of anger, eyes like javelins; Robin on his porch with a drink, lost in the telling of some old lovers' squall; Lana the first time she told me of her mother's death, drenched with the weight of it; Alec in a stuffy suit, and again in shorts and sandals; Robin with a feather boa and his too-small kimono robe singing "Sledgehammer"; Lana asleep on the grass, and the miracle of her slack, dreaming face. And Bud in my father's stories, laughing as he sings near a piano, or bent over the engine of a car that wouldn't start, or climbing a neighbor's windmill to grease its gears, or splashing as he swims in a nearby creek. These are the beams of light.

For two hundred days in 1964, my best friend, Robin, and my grandfather, Bud, were both alive. Shortly after this span of time, in the fall of that year, James Baldwin published the essay "Nothing Personal" in a book of photographs by his friend Richard Avedon. The essay begins with a reflection on despair, which Baldwin finds everywhere in the popular culture, mass media, and everyday interactions of midcentury American life. Much of this despair, for Baldwin, is rooted in the violence of both American history and the American present, and the numbness with which most Americans decline to confront it, turning away from the suffering of others and the deaths of others with a dispassion that both isolates and dehumanizes their very selves. Midway through the essay, Baldwin turns to the question of one's own mortality. He situates this provocation at a specific time: the "devastating hour" of four o'clock in the morning. In the dusky half-light of that early hour,

> The day, no matter what kind of day it was, is indisputably over; almost instantaneously, a new day begins: and how will one bear it? Probably no better than one bore the day that is ending, possibly not as well. Moreover, a day is coming which one will not recall, that last day of one's life, and on that day one will *oneself* become as irrecoverable as all the days that have passed.[11]

Baldwin, who flirted with suicide throughout his life and attempted it several times, composed this essay as his own disavowal of that inclination. He follows the lines above with an invocation to use the liminal nature of four o'clock in the morning as a basis for fragile hope:

> It is a fearful speculation—or, rather, a fearful knowledge—that, one day one's eyes will no longer look out on the world. One will no longer be present at the universal morning roll call. The light will rise for others, but not for you. Sometimes, at four AM, this knowledge is almost enough to force a reconciliation between oneself and all one's pain and error. Since, anyway, it will end one day, why not try it—life—one more time?[12]

In the second half of the essay, Baldwin centers on what he calls the "only . . . passionate achievement which can outlast death, which can cause life to spring from death":

love, a love that gathers from the "light in the eyes, which is the only light there is in the world."[13] He continues,

> One discovers the light in darkness, that is what darkness is for; but everything in our lives depends on how we bear the light. It is necessary, while in darkness, to know that there is a light somewhere, to know that in oneself, waiting to be found, there is a light.[14]

This is the light—the light of love—that saves us from all of the four-o'clock-in-the-mornings, when we face the inevitable transition from one day into another day, and also encounter our movement toward the moment of our own inevitable end. Baldwin then stages a proposition, framed as a little parable: imagine that "some convulsion, sometimes called accident, throws you" so that you, a resident of someplace like Chicago, fall in love with someone who lives in Hong Kong.

> Hong Kong will immediately cease to be a name and become the center of your life. And you may never know how many people live in Hong Kong. But you will know that one [person] lives there without whom you cannot live. And this is how our lives are changed, and this is how we are redeemed. . . . If your lover lives in Hong Kong and cannot get to Chicago, it will be necessary for you to go to Hong Kong. . . . And you will, I assure you, as long as space and time divide you from anyone you love, discover a great deal about shipping routes, airlines, earthquake, famine, disease, and war. And you will always know what time it is in Hong Kong, for you love someone who lives there. And love will simply have no choice but to go into battle with space and time and, furthermore, to win.[15]

Baldwin ends this parable, and shortly thereafter the essay, with these invocations: "The light. The light. One will perish without the light. . . . The moment we cease to hold each other, the moment we break faith with one another, the sea engulfs us and the light goes out."[16]

It is 1964 in Fort Worth and LaBelle, and I am not yet a dreamed-of thing. It is 1994, late at night on a Birmingham highway, and the sirens have started to blare. It is 1997, early fall in North Carolina, and the thick exhaust is stifling a pleasant breeze. It is the summer solstice in Oakland in 2019, and a door is hanging open on its hinges as two cats run amok. It is 1964 again, and a shadow stills on the porch of a Florida home. There are thousands of miles and many ways to travel between all of these sacred places. It is eight o'clock in the evening in San Diego as I write these final lines, and I know what time it is elsewhere: it is also eight o'clock in Oakland and San Francisco; it is ten o'clock in Birmingham and Chicago and Fort Worth; it is eleven o'clock in North Carolina and old LaBelle. It is late July, and the air in all of these places is thick with the warmth of a midsummer night. And I can still see them all, radiant and gleaming. They are all there, shining forth across the earthquakes and famines and shipping routes of time and distance and loss. I can see them dancing in a darkened nightclub, bursts of light pulsing down from the strobe. They are all there. And they are not alone.

Requiem aeternam dona eis	*Grant them eternal rest*
Et lux perpetua luceat eis	*And let eternal light shine upon them*
Requiescant in pace	*Rest in peace*
Requiescant in pace	*Rest in peace*
Requiescant in pace.	*Rest in peace.*

Coda

No, darling, mourn no longer for Malone. He knew very well how gorgeous life is—that was the light in him that you, and I, and all the queens fell in love with. Go out dancing tonight, my dear, and go home with someone, and if the love doesn't last beyond the morning, then know I love you.
　　ANDREW HOLLERAN, DANCER FROM THE DANCE (1978)

Do we not become others after the moment we've done writing? A posthumous book? . . . Antehumous?
　　　　　　JEAN COCTEAU, THE WHITE PAPER (1958)

Every November, in a little nook across the canyon behind my house, amid a sea of succulents and evergreens, one little deciduous tree dresses its leaves in the most glamorous shades of purple and red. Like a call to its kin in distant geographies where entire forests take on these hues, this tree's little gesture takes center stage and insists on being seen. I watch for the change every autumn, calling out, "Still green, friend, but I know your big show is coming." And when it does I stand and look, taking account of how, in such extreme isolation—such intense and solitary difference from its neighbors—this queer little tree has found a way to shout its fabulous winsomeness across the wide canyon and, in so doing, has sought and seen me. When the leaves inevitably brown and fall, I mourn how brief their beauty was, how fleeting their call for recognition, how ephemeral those too-few days of seeing and being seen.

This little tree reminds me every year of the beauty and the risk of being queer. Native to lands far away from the coastal region of Southern California where I, too, have transplanted myself, it nonetheless insists on flaming up and flaming out each November when the fog rolls back in after the warmth of late summer, chilling the nighttime air. Every year it insists on flamboyance, dressing itself in plum-red hues despite the hostile climes of its adopted geography. This is what it means to be queer in a world like ours.

In the time it has taken me to write this book, two of these cycles have come and gone, and a third will soon begin. Now when I watch the tree's November transformation, I think of Bud and Lana and Alec and Robin and all of the other people whose stories I have told in these pages. I remember them while I watch across the canyon as the tree slowly emerges from the indistinguishable green of its summer surroundings, bursts into its eccentricity, and then fades again from view. Someone planted it there on the crest of the canyon's far ledge, choosing it for the very foliage that I now seek each

November. Someone—who?—is the custodian for this tree, watering its thirsty roots and occasionally trimming back its spindly branches. Someone cares for it, someone who knows all to well that not every lonesome tree is able to change its leaves; not every tree survives.

"The world does not stop and wait for us to understand it," wrote Bernard Mayes in his 2001 autobiography *Escaping God's Closet: The Revelations of a Queer Priest*, and yet "life does not continue in the same way regardless of our explanation of it."[1] Ordained by the Anglican Church in the 1950s, Bernard had been sent to the United States to serve first as a chaplain at New York University and later as a mission priest in a rural town north of San Francisco. He had long accepted that he was queer, but while living near Washington Square Park in Manhattan, Bernard allowed his queerness to blossom: "new flowers and shoots were budding within me. I met and was made love to by a poet, a painter, a playwright, and an actor."[2] Even so, Bernard felt the risk, the shame, and the suffocating sense of isolation that queer people face. "It's a wonder we survived," he wrote. "Once discovered, we were doomed."[3]

After he had made his way to California, Bernard began to shift his attention away from the dramaturgies of Anglican dogma and toward the suffering of suicidal people. He had lost several friends and colleagues to suicide, and was troubled especially by "the stigma that has traditionally attached to those who take their own lives and are henceforward the 'unquiet dead,'" which

> still colors nearly all explanations, medical as well as religious, of suicide. Condemnation of them has remained largely inflexible and absolute, as if they have committed an unnatural act whose implications other humans cannot tolerate. . . . Even when pain is

the cause of the act, the suicide is liable to be accused of impatience or selfishness. The argument that there can be no reasonable justification for taking one's life because things eventually improve is spurious. One has every right to choose not to wait. Life is uncertain.[4]

He was particularly concerned about the extremely high rate of suicide among his fellow queer people:

Unable to change their sexual orientation, condemned not to a week or a moment, but to an entire life of frustration by an ignorant and unsympathetic majority, they must suffer a situation that neither medical opinion nor religious dogma are able to ameliorate.... So far as gay people were concerned, professional advisers, too often being what we now describe as "homophobic," were likely to be causing, if not suicides, at least as much misery as they were preventing.[5]

Bernard realized that the only services in existence for people experiencing suicidal thoughts and ideation were organized by medical professionals who still understood queerness as an illness, religious counselors who understood queerness as a sin, and the police, who devoted much of their time to harassing and arresting queer people. Just as disconcerting, all three of these constituencies also understood suicide strictly in pathological, immoral, and criminal terms. And so he decided to open what would become the first suicide hotline in the United States, staffed by trained volunteers from the public and operating around the clock.

After an exhaustive search for a space from which he could run his hotline, Bernard eventually found a small basement room in the Marquette Building at 965 Geary Street in San Francisco's Tenderloin district. He had been living in the

Tenderloin, where a vibrant queer community had begun to thrive, since his arrival in the city, so the location was convenient. He tells this story of finding the room where the hotline would make its first home:

> [The building manager] looked me up and down. . . . He was holding the papers of the lease in one hand and his eyes narrowed suspiciously. What was someone like me taking a little room like this for? . . . I decided to come clean. More days of fruitless searching stretched before me. This tiny place was becoming more important, more appropriate, the more we talked. It was warm, a bit smelly perhaps, but there was a space for files. . . . "It's for a service [to] help suicidal people." The dreadful word had been uttered. . . . He said nothing; just looked at me. Then, extending his arms, he slowly turned over his hands. "You mean like this?" he asked. Two ragged scars ran across both wrists. . . . Drawing out a pen, he said, "You can have it for half price."[6]

The room was initially outfitted with a desk, a couch, and a small red phone. Bernard consulted medical and social work professionals and developed a training guide for volunteers, who were screened for homophobia and "suicidophobia."[7] He advertised in newspapers and on city buses with a pseudonym chosen for its stolid simplicity and a phone number: "Thinking of ending it all? Call Bruce, PRI-0450." The hotline began operations in 1961 and is the hotline mentioned as receiving numerous calls from people with HIV in the 1988 news program *AIDS and Suicide* described in the Benediction section of this book; it is also the hotline where the character Mary Ann Singleton briefly volunteers in Armistead Maupin's beloved book *Tales of the City*. Bernard received a single call on the hotline's first night in 1961; by the time of his death in 2014, the hotline received more than two hundred calls per day.[8]

Almost exactly fifty years after Bernard Mayes's suicide hotline took its first call, on a small hill outside of a house overlooking the Pacific Ocean in Ōtsuchi, Japan, garden designer Itaru Sisaki refurbished an old telephone booth and painted it white. Inside the booth, he placed a black rotary phone, unconnected to any wires, on a small shelf. Sisaki's cousin had recently died after a diagnosis of terminal cancer, and he was bereft. He installed his Telephone of the Wind (風の電話) to allow him to speak to this cousin: "Because my thoughts couldn't be relayed on a regular phone line, I wanted them to be carried on the wind."[9] In 2011, the year after the booth's installation, the massive Tōhoku earthquake and tsunami devastated Ōtsuchi and surrounding areas, leading to innumerable deaths and other losses. Sisaki opened his Telephone of the Wind to the public, and thousands of people began visiting to summon and speak to the loved ones they mourned. In a 2020 documentary, visitors can be heard speaking into the phone: "Are you thinking of me? I don't know if the way I'm living is right. I think a lot. I don't know if you can hear me." And: "I can't tell you everything or you'll worry. I often think about what you would do in my shoes." And: "Grandfather, I hope you're well. I'm trying my best. Think of me." And: "I really thought you'd get away." When asked by the filmmakers about the overwhelming response to the telephone, Sisaki comments,

> Generally, when people die because of an illness, they're in a hospital first and have enough time to spend with their family. But in a tsunami or a sudden accident or a suicide, there's no time for people to say goodbye. It's sudden. Then one is overcome by the deepest sadness, real despair. I would like to

stimulate people's self-healing powers. Here, everyone faces their pain before moving forward in life.[10]

Writing this book has been my own version of building a Telephone of the Wind: I have written it to face and to dwell with the unmooring effects of my own grief, but also to explore, for the benefit of others who have survived the suicides of people they love, the profundity of that unmooring. I suspect—or rather, I *hope*—that the experience of reading this book might provoke a kind of unmooring, too. This is, after all, what it means to mourn the sudden loss occasioned by a suicide: one can no longer trust the flow of time, or the stability of the everyday, or the forward-motion of narrative form. This has complicated my turn to the archives of the queer past, including both the testaments to previous eras of queer life inscribed in novels, plays, and films, and the ephemera—newspapers articles, letters, photographs, and other materials—of queer lives that are only partially and momentarily reflected in archival collections. This, too, is representative of the experience of mourning a sudden loss, which is characterized by fleeting impressions, intrusive partial memories, and other hauntings of the dead.

In his 1978 novel *Dancer from the Dance*, Andrew Holleran tells the story of Malone, a beautiful young gay man who entrances the countless other gay men who populate the queer spaces of New York nightlife of the era: the bars, clubs, bathhouses, parks, and back alleys in which queer life was lived in the decade after the Stonewall Riot and before the arrival of HIV. Initially naive to the intricate choreographies of these spaces, Malone eventually gives himself over to them. He is especially enlivened by the dark, sweaty dance floors where he is immersed in the erotics of queer kinship: "Of all the bonds between homosexual friends, none was greater than that between friends who danced together. The friend you danced with, when you had no lover, was the most important person in your life."[11] Though he revels in immersing himself in such networks of belonging and in the fleeting sexual encounters that come to define his days and nights, he is ultimately driven by his desire to find a man with whom he can nurture a deep and abiding love. This he does not find; "we're completely free," he comments to a friend in a park while cruising late one night, "and that's the horror."[12] In his final gesture of disappointment, at the end of a summer on Fire Island, Malone leaves a party with a friend, says goodbye, and walks out into the ocean. He disappears beneath the water, never to be seen again.

Holleran's novel begins and ends with a series of letters between two friends who had known Malone. The final letter—which, unlike all of the others, is signed not with a campy pseudonym but with its author's actual name, Paul—muses on the queer scene of the early and middle 1970s, the subterranean parties and sweaty club nights and other ecstasies that had felt so much like freedom, and that would soon—with the arrival of a new viral threat—seem like an impossible, utopic past. "Love, in the best of circumstances, is hard to find," Paul writes, before urging his friend to "mourn no longer for Malone. . . . Go out dancing tonight, my dear, and go home with someone, and if the love doesn't last beyond the morning, then know I love you."[13]

I can think of no better ending to this book than to invoke these final lines as if I had spoken them in those final hours to those I have lost. I will write them instead to you, whoever you are, wherever you are—on the far side of the canyon off the backyard of my house, or across an ocean, or thousands of miles and many years away. Go out dancing tonight. Go home with someone. And know that I love you.

Acknowledgments

I have been buoyed by the support and care of many people while writing this book. Thank you to everyone who shared their memories of the four people whose deaths are at the center of this work and who listened as I retold my own—especially Catherine Burriss, Renu Cappelli, Katie Gough, Nicole Green, Kelly Johnson, Gaije Kushner, Cody Kyber, George Porter, Jill Russell, Monica Stufft, Heather Warren-Crow, and those who knew my grandfather while he was alive. Thank you to Mona Bower, Julie Burelle, Peter Goodwin, Patricia Ybarra, the friend who asked that his name remain private, and two anonymous reviewers for reading early versions of this manuscript and offering your generous feedback. Thank you to Vandhana Ravi for providing invaluable research assistance as I delved into the depths of the far-flung archives of queer suicide. Thank you to Caroline Collins, Kali Boston, Christina Aushana, and Sarah McGovern for a collaboration that expanded well beyond our individual lives. In addition to all of these friends, thank you to many others who have given me more than I could ever describe here:

Brent Anctil, Marlon Bailey, Sarah Balian, Robin Bernstein, Chris Berry, Boatema Boateng, Angela Booker, Doug Case, Joshua Chambers-Letson, Kelly Chung, Nishea Clark, Laurie Beth Clarke, Dwight Conquergood, Bard Cosman, Pamela Cosman, Renee Alexander Craft, Tracy Davis, Jackie Dean, Dan Deforge, Jill Dolan, Kirstie Dorr, Kate Drabinski, Laura Edmondson, Fatima El-Tayeb, Ariana Federico, Gary Fields, LeAnn Fields, Poppy Fitch, Matthew Frum, José Fusté, Ruthie Gilmore, Yelena Gluzman, Julie Gordon, Nitin Govil, Aaron Gozum, Sharon Greene, Joseph Hankins, Val Hartouni, Ari Heinrich, Jeremy Hoisak, Sheila Holtrop, Mitchum Huehls, Lindsay Brandon Hunter, Tina Hyland, Shannon Jackson, Kristina Jacob, Caroline Jack, Tara Javidi, Jenefer Johnson, E. Patrick Johnson, Andrew Jolivétte, Priya Kandaswamy, Sara Clarke Kaplan, Kerry Keith, Tarek Khan, Roshanak Kheshti, Larissa Kiel, Ashvin Kini, Georgina Kleege, Sookyong Ko, Cathy Kudlick, Eng-Beng Lim, Marissa Lopez, Lisa Lowe, D. Soyini Madison, Curtis Marez, Mazdak Mazarei, Paige McGinley, Jisha Menon, Koritha Mitchell, Joe Nugent, Tavia Nyong'o, Yasmeen Obeid, Mary Frances O'Connor, Jules Odendahl-James, Yumi Pak, Roy Perez, Michael Peterson, Aaron Piziali, Della Pollock, Jack Isaac Pryor, Hannah Raleigh, Ivan Ramos, Ramón Rivera-Servera, Dylan Rodríguez, Kelly Rowett-James, Sue Schweik, David Serlin, Jared Sexton, Kaja Silverman, Mark Simonton, Amanda Smith, Erin Palmer Snyder, Jade Power Sotomayor, Michael Spinella, Andrea St. Julian, Andy Steadham, Shelley Streeby, Thea Quiray Tagle, Ernesto Tanjuan, David Teague, Jennifer Terry, Cesar Torres, Nikki Vangelisti, Nancy Vaughn, Shane Vogel, Kalindi Vora, Ossy Werner, Frank Wilderson, Stacy Wolf, Diana Worman, Bill Worthen, Hentyle Yapp, Kate Yavenditti, Linnea Zeiner, and Oumelbanine Zhiri.

Thank you to my colleagues at UC San Diego in and beyond the departments of Communication, Ethnic Studies,

ACKNOWLEDGMENTS

and Critical Gender Studies, and to colleagues in Theatre and Performance Studies at many other universities, for helping to nurture supportive environments in which to work.

Thank you to the curators and archivists at the Musée Louis-Hémon in Péribonka, Quebec; at the Davidson College Libraries in Davidson, North Carolina; and at the University of California, San Diego Libraries—especially the fabulous Lia Friedman—for assistance with archival research.

Thank you to everyone at Fordham University Press—especially the wondrous John Garza, who has been the most supportive editor an author could dream of, and the fabulous copyeditor Bob Land—for bringing this book into the world.

I am grateful to Antony Gormley, who granted permission for me to use the photograph on the cover of this book. I first saw the piece depicted in this photograph, *Blind Light*, at its original 2007 installation at the Hayward Gallery in London. I was transfixed by that mist room enclosed in glass, both formally and, for lack of a better word, emotionally. Formally, I was entranced by the way it played with visuality; three years before visiting the exhibition (and as narrated in part of this book) I had experienced a sudden and unexpected medical collapse that resulted in, among other things, a significant amount of retinal damage. The changes to my visual field, which were so difficult to describe in casual conversation, were almost perfectly represented by the mists in that room: the shifting figures of people around me fading in and out, only partially apparent even as they were fully present. This was also the emotional content of the work to me: its ability to infuse the space of the gallery with a representation—almost an allegory—of my changed vision, and I wept with something like empathy for myself when I returned to my hotel that evening. Years later, after the 2019 suicide of my best friend, I came across this image and immediately, viscerally recalled my experience of seeing the installation in

2007. But this particular photograph, with the faintly visible image of a person behind the glass, suddenly obtained a second level of significance: I saw Robin, so recently departed, hovering within the image's frame, both present and absent, both here and gone. I kept this image in the background of my computer desktop through the two years of writing this book, and every time I began to feel the overwhelm of writing about loss, I would look at it again, prompting myself to remember that there is presence within absence, too.

While writing this book, I received a fellowship from the John Simon Guggenheim Foundation. Although the fellowship was awarded for another ongoing project, it nonetheless provided time to focus and, equally importantly, acknowledgment of my work, just as I was finishing the first draft of this manuscript. I received additional support for this project from the Academic Senate and the Department of Communication at the University of California, San Diego.

Finally, thank you to all of the queer people I have ever met, no matter how brief or fleeting our meeting was. This book is for all of us.

Notes

Prologue

1. McDaniel, "Mesquite High School Counselor Commits Suicide: Newspaper Blamed," 9–11.
2. Texas Penal Code Title 5, Chapter 21, Section 21.06.
3. McDaniel, 10–11.
4. "Counselor Faces Lewdness Charge," 1.
5. Baril, *Undoing Suicidism*, 3.
6. Ibid., 7.
7. Ibid., 8.
8. Didion, *The White Album*, 200.
9. Ibid., 11.

I. Introitus

1. "LaBelle Man Shoots Self," 11.
2. Ball, dir., *Uncle Frank* (2020).
3. *Anders als die Andern*, directed by Richard Oswald (1919; Edition Filmmuseum, 2006), DVD.
4. Bauer, *The Hirschfeld Archives*, 21.
5. Cited in Bauer, 40–41nn.17, 21.

6. Huneke, "Death Wish," 129.
7. Ibid., 157.
8. Ibid., 138.
9. Gentry, "Ode to Billie Joe."
10. Baer Jr., dir., *Ode to Billy Joe* (1976).
11. Konnikova, "The Power of Once upon a Time," n.p.

II. Dies Irae

1. Beaton, *The Wandering Years*, 262–63.
2. Ibid., 265.
3. "'Dive' under a Tube Train," 11.
4. Beaton, *The Wandering Years*, 263.
5. Ibid.
6. Ibid., 267.
7. Ibid., 263.
8. Ibid., 267.
9. Ibid.
10. Ibid., 268.
11. Ibid., 273.
12. Ibid.
13. Mariani, *The Broken Tower*, 420.
14. Pitkethly, dir., *Voices & Visions: Hart Crane* (1988).
15. "Poet's Death Linked with Loss of Father," 4.
16. Auden, *Another Time*, 107–10.
17. Muñoz, *Cruising Utopia*, 148.
18. Quoted in Watson, *Factory Made*, 172.
19. Ibid.
20. Warhol and Hackett, *POPism*, 85.
21. Di Prima, *Recollections of My Life as a Woman*, 398.
22. Ibid., 120.
23. Di Prima, *Freddie Poems*, n.p.
24. Ibid., n.p.
25. Di Prima, *Recollections of My Life as a Woman*, 396–97.
26. Ibid., 397–98.
27. Di Prima, *Spring and Autumn Annals*, 18–19.
28. "Choreographer Dies in Fall," 91.

III. Kyrie Eleison

1. "Two Pathetic Songs Found in Last-Ride Car," 1.
2. Berlin, "Remember."
3. Cowels and Kavanagh, "Forgotten."
4. "Murder and Suicide Bared in Love Pact of Two S.L. Girls," 1, 5.
5. Ibid., 5.
6. "Co-Ed at Utah 'U' Was Witness to Quarrel, Claims," 4.
7. "Murder and Suicide Bared in Love Pact of Two S.L. Girls," 5.
8. Ibid.
9. "Poison Takes Lives of Two Girls," 1.
10. "Ruth Drake's Tragic Death Stirs Payson," 1.
11. "Ardent Letters of Love between Girls Are Found," 5.
12. Ibid., 1.
13. Ibid., 5.
14. "Divorce Decree on Nonsupport Charge Given Sarah in 1925," 1.
15. "Co-Ed at Utah 'U' Was Witness to Quarrel, Claims," 4.
16. "Ruth Drake Is Suicide, Says Inquest Jury," 1.
17. "Abnormal Love May Have Caused Double Tragedy," 1.
18. "Tragedy Probe States Cause," 20.
19. "Murder and Suicide Bared in Love Pact of Two S.L. Girls," 5.
20. "Ardent Letters of Love between Girls Are Found," 5.
21. "Murder and Suicide Bared in Love Pact of Two S.L. Girls," 5.
22. "Veiled Threat May Be Clue to Girls' Deaths," 2.
23. "Abnormal Love May Have Caused Double Tragedy," 1.
24. Bourdet, *The Captive*, 145.
25. Ibid., 146, 148–49.
26. Ibid., 149–50.
27. Ibid., 152.
28. Ibid., 250.
29. Ibid., 162–63.
30. Atkinson, "Trenchant Tragedy," 1.

31. Atkinson, Introduction to *The Captive*, vii.

32. Frankfeld, "From the Second Balcony: *The Captive*," 2.

33. Curtin, *We Can Always Call Them Bulgarians*, 53.

34. "Police Raid Three Shows, Sex, Captive, and Virgin Man; Hold Actors and Managers," 1.

35. Hellman, "The Children's Hour."

36. Roughead, *Bad Companions*, 114.

37. Ibid., 122.

38. Ibid., 126.

39. Ibid., 127.

40. Ibid., 135.

41. Faderman, *Scotch Verdict*, 15.

42. Ibid., 17.

43. Ibid., 18.

44. Ibid., 60.

45. Wyler, dir., *These Three* (1936).

46. Wyler, dir., *The Children's Hour* (1936).

47. Spencer, "Sex, Lies, and Revisions," 47.

48. Ibid.

49. Bullough and Bullough, "Lesbianism in the 1920s and 1930s," 896–97.

50. Ibid., 897.

51. Ibid.

52. Ibid., 903.

53. Ibid.

54. Williams, *A Streetcar Named Desire*, 49.

55. Ibid., 114.

IV. Lacrimosa

1. Viola, *The Raft*.

2. Warhol, *Suicide* (1965), 16mm.

3. "Picture of the Week," 42–43.

4. "Evelyn McHale," n.p.

5. Jones, "The Soup Can Artist," 51.

6. Gopnik, *Warhol*, 409.

7. Tavel, "Introduction, Interview Notes, and Script for *Suicide*," 68.

8. Ibid., 69.
9. Ibid., 70.
10. Ibid., 70–71.
11. Ibid., 72.
12. Fellini, dir., *Nights of Cabiria* (1957).
13. Baldwin, *Going to Meet the Man*, 43.
14. Ibid., 51.
15. Ibid., 57.
16. Miller, *The Drama of the Gifted Child*, 12.
17. Ibid., 86.
18. Middlebrook, *Anne Sexton: A Biography*, 397.
19. Kumin, "How It Is," 38.
20. Kumin, "Splitting Wood at Six Above," 34.
21. Kumin, "Itinerary of an Obsession," 45.
22. Kumin, "The Ancient Lady Poets," 111.
23. Kumin, "Apostrophe to a Dead Friend," 24.
24. Kumin, "October, Yellowstone Park," 215–17.
25. Kumin, "New Year's Eve 1959," 69–70.
26. Sexton, "Wanting to Die," 142–43.
27. Kumin, "Oblivion," 115–16.
28. Cortázar, *Cronopios and Famas*, 6.
29. Dumbadze, *Bas Jan Ader*, 154.
30. Ibid., 153.
31. Christie, *The Crying Book*, 34.
32. Ibid., 68.
33. Kalin, "*Suicide*, 1965," 301.
34. Vaughan, "Superpop, or a Night at the Factory," 7.
35. Cocteau, *Hommage à Rock Bradett* (ink on paper, 1967).

V. Offertorium

1. Stillman, "'Truth House' to Be Built," 8.
2. Ibid., 8.
3. Hitchcock, dir., *Vertigo* (1958).
4. For a beautiful, nuanced discussion of the further implications of the specifically racialized myth of Carlotta Valdes, see Ben-Oni, "Temporary Passings/Possessions: On Hitchcock's Vertigo and Carlotta Valdes."

5. Di Prima, *Recollections of My Life as a Woman*, 396–97.

6. Warhol, dir., *Freddie Herko Screen Test* (1964).

7. Muñoz, *Cruising Utopia*, 161–62.

8. Di Prima, *Recollections of My Life as a Woman*, 119.

9. Watson, *Factory Made*, 57.

10. Glueck, "Art Notes: Viewers; At the Guggenheim International, They Know What They Don't Like," 22.

11. Warhol and Hackett, *POPism*, 58.

12. Barthes, *Camera Lucida*, 95.

13. Ibid., 26–27. My emphasis.

VI. Sanctus

1. "Harvey Woodward's Dream School Beginning to Take Form and Shape as Building Contracts Are Awarded," 35.

2. Jones, "Where There's a Will: The Story of Indian Springs School," 28–29.

3. Taylor, "New Boys School in Shelby County," 27.

4. Wells and Wall, "Gay Social Life Centers on the Traditional Bars," 1–2.

5. Dallas, "Bars Are Important to Social Life," 6A.

6. Griffin, "Bar Looks Like an Ordinary Place, and Strictly Run," 1B, 9B.

7. Wells, "Low Profile Keeps Gays Powerless in PB County," 5.

8. Fuller, "Gays Say Disco Important Place to Socialize, Get Away from Straights." 4.

9. Irons and Forte, "'Gay' Subculture Loses Social Inhibitions," B3, B18.

10. "Jury Report Links 2 More Cops to Payoffs," 11.

11. Waas, "Deviates Difficult to Ferret Out," 1–2.

12. Waas, "Homosexual Problem Growing in County," 1.

13. Weisbecker, "Town Fights Private Club It Calls Gay," 1.

14. Negri, "Gays Charge Harassment," 21.

15. Barbaro, "Gay Bars Are Havens, until They're Not," 8.

16. Peregrin, "Berlin Owners Celebrate 30 Years as Chicago's Best Non-gay Gay Club," n.p. During the final preparations of this manuscript, I learned that Berlin would be permanently

closing its doors on November 19, 2023, shortly before its fortieth anniversary. For all the nights when so many of us found ourselves embraced by your dark convivialities, thank you, Berlin.

17. White, *Nocturnes for the Kind of Naples*, 22.

18. Browning, *Culture of Desire*, 23.

19. Faulkner, *As I Lay Dying*, 163.

20. Ibid., 164.

VII. Benedictus

1. Gay, Lesbian and Straight Education Network, "GLSEN, PFLAG, The Trevor Project Release Statement on Recent Tragedies," n.p.

2. Parker, "The Story of a Suicide," 36–51.

3. Hawkins, "Bullying Gay and Lesbian Kids: How a School District Became a Suicide Contagion Area," n.p.

4. Ibid.

5. Zhao et al., "Suicidal Ideation and Attempt among Adolescents Reporting 'Unsure' Sexual Identity or Heterosexual Identity Plus Same-Sex Attraction or Behavior: Forgotten Groups?," 104.

6. Huneke, "Death Wish," 159.

7. Ibid., 144.

8. Rofes, *I Thought People Like That Killed Themselves*, 11–12.

9. Ibid., 1.

10. Ibid., 9.

11. Merloo, *Suicide and Mass Suicide*, 57.

12. Rofes, *I Thought People Like That Killed Themselves*, 14.

13. Hoffman, *The Gay World: Male Homosexuality and the Social Creation of Evil*, 189.

14. Rofes, *I Thought People Like That Killed Themselves*, 18.

15. Ibid., 19.

16. Jay and Young, *The Gay Report*, 728.

17. Rofes, *I Thought People Like That Killed Themselves*, 23–24.

18. Jay and Young, *The Gay Report*, 728–29.

19. Saunders and Valente, "Suicide Risk among Gay Men and Lesbians: A Review," 5.

20. Paul et al, "Suicide Attempts Among Gay and Bisexual Men: Lifetime Prevalence and Antecedents," 1340.

21. Rofes, *I Thought People Like That Killed Themselves*, 16.

22. Rofes, "A Gay Issue That Cannot Be Ignored: An End to the Silence about Suicide," 15.

23. Rofes, *I Thought People Like That Killed Themselves*, 124.

24. Nelson, "Outbreaks of Pneumonia among Gay Males," 3.

25. Altman, "Rare Cancer Seen in 41 Homosexuals," 20.

26. Lorch, "KS Diagnosis, Takes Life," 1.

27. Centers for Disease Control, "Current Trends Update on Acquired Immune Deficiency Syndrome (AIDS)—United States," 513–14.

28. Lorch, "KS Diagnosis, Takes Life," 15.

29. Ibid.

30. "A Hospital Patient, 35, Leaps to His Death from 17th Floor," 4.

31. Kandel, "2 Men Tied Together Die in 35-Story Plunge," 6; Randazzo and Weiss, "AIDS 2 End Lives," 4.

32. Kendel, "2 Men Tied Together Die in 35-Story Plunge," 6.

33. Marzuk et al, "Increased Risk of Suicide in Persons with AIDS," 1335.

34. Ibid., 1336.

35. Centers for Disease Control, "Current Trends Update: Acquired Immune Deficiency Syndrome—United States," 17–21.

36. Kolata, "AIDS Patients Are Found to Have an Extremely High Suicide Rate," 5.

37. "AIDS and Suicide," *Nightline*, ABC News, March 31, 1988.

38. Rarick, "AIDS Adding to Ranks of Hemlock Society, Death-With-Dignity Lobby," 28.

39. "A Question of Mercy," *60 Minutes*, CBS News, April 16, 1989.

40. Glass, "AIDS and Suicide," 1369.

41. Ibid., 1369–70.

42. Ibid., 1370.

43. Ibid..

44. Pelton et al., "Rates and Risk Factors for Suicidal Ideation, Suicide Attempts and Suicide Deaths in Persons with HIV: A Systematic Review and Meta-analysis," 1.

45. Altman, "Rare Cancer Seen in 41 Homosexuals," 20.

46. Oliver, "Marty James; Gay Activist Aided Suicides," 6.

VIII. Agnus Dei

1. Huie, "The Kids Are Too Straight: Translating Qiu Miaojin's *Notes of a Crocodile*," n.p.

2. Sasseen, "The Death of the Author," n.p.

3. Nathan, *Mishima: A Biography*, 98, 141–42.

4. Mishima, *Confessions of a Mask*, 38.

5. Ibid., 40.

6. Ibid., 43–44.

7. Mishima, *Forbidden Colors*, 21.

8. Ibid., 22.

9. Qiu, *Last Words from Montmartre*, 139.

10. Ibid., 7.

11. Ibid., 15, 17.

12. I describe this mysterious illness and year of recovery in Anderson, *Autobiography of a Disease*.

13. Beaton, *The Unexpurgated Beaton: The Cecil Beaton Diaries as He Wrote Them, 1970–1980*, 490–91.

14. Ibid., 490.

15. Stanislavski, *An Actor Prepares*.

16. "Theatre and performance respond to a psychic need to rehearse for loss, and especially for death." Phelan, *Mourning Sex*, 3.

17. Blau, "Universals of Performance," 156.

IX. Libera Me

1. Bauer, *The Hirschfeld Archive*, 92.

2. Charlotte Wolff describes Hirschfeld's "World Tour" in great detail in her 1986 biography: Wolff, *Magnus Hirschfeld*, 284–362.

3. Quoted in Dose, *Magnus Hirschfeld*, 64.

4. Marhoefer, *Racism and the Making of Gay Rights*, 159.

5. Quoted in Dose, *Magnus Hirschfeld*, 65.

6. Quoted in Marhoefer, *Racism and the Making of Gay Rights*, 159.

7. Dose, *Magnus Hirschfeld*, 66.

8. Marhoefer, *Racism and the Making of Gay Rights*, 163.

9. Hirschfeld's attempts to salvage materials from the institute, and the bequests in his will, are discussed in all four of the biographies previously cited (Wolff, Dose, Bauer, and Marhoefer). An English translation of portions of Hirschfeld's will is available on the website of the Magnus Hirschfeld Society: https://magnus-hirschfeld.de/gedenken/historisches/institut/hirschfelds-testament-en/.

10. Institut Terezínské Iniciativy, "Karl Fein," n.p.

11. Dose, *Magnus Hirschfeld*, 80.

12. Dose, *Magnus Hirschfeld*, 15; Wolff, *Magnus Hirschfeld*, 416; Bauer, *The Hirschfeld Archive*, 104; Marhoefer, *Racism and the Making of Gay Rights*, 162.

13. Wolff, *Magnus Hirschfeld*, 416–17.

14. Dose, *Magnus Hirschfeld*, 81; Bauer, *The Hirschfeld Archive*, 4; Marhoefer, *Racism and the Making of Gay Rights*, 181–82.

15. Bauer, *The Hirschfeld Archive*, 134.

16. Beaton, *The Wandering Years*, 276.

17. The original French reads: "Une tisane sur le fourneau à gaz; la fenêtre bien close; j'ouvre le robinet d'arrivée; j'oublie de mettre l'allumette. Réputation sauve et le temps de dire Confiteor." Crevel, *Détours*, 29. The English translation included here is from Alvarez, *The Savage God*, 252.

18. Naville and Péret, *La Révolution Surréaliste* 1, 2. The translated version cited here is from Walz, *Pop Surrealism*, 115.

19. Naville and Péret, *La Révolution Surréaliste* 2, 13.

20. Walz, *Pop Surrealism*, 115.

21. Ibid., 116.

22. Translations for the *fait divers* appear in ibid., 141–43.

23. Love, *Feeling Backwards*, 1.

24. "Miscellaneous Reading," n.p.

25. "A Woman's Strange Love," 1.

26. Cocteau, *The White Paper*, 16–17.

27. "Professor's Leap Laid to Worries," 10.

28. Matthiessen and Cheney, *Rat and the Devil*.

29. Levitt, *The Man Who Knew Too Much*, 5.
30. "The Homosexual and Suicide," 28.
31. Miller, *Bare-Faced Messiah*, 303, 344–45.
32. Soupault, *Lost Profiles*, 31.
33. "World Briefs," 12.
34. Melnick, "Supervisor Milk's Roommate a Suicide," 1, 14.
35. Cantrell, "SUBSCRIBE to Feminary!," 320–21.
36. Aarons, *Prayers for Bobby*.
37. Maguen, "Teen Suicide," 43–44.
38. "Double Suicide Believed AIDS Related," A-15.
39. Hirschfeld, *The Homosexuality of Men and Women*, 1022.
40. Ibid., 1011.
41. Ibid.
42. Vaughan, "Superpop, or a Night at the Factory," 7.
43. Tavel, "Introduction, Interview Notes, and Script for *Suicide*," 87, 89, 90.
44. Di Prima, *Recollections of My Life as a Woman*, 153.
45. Bauer, *The Hirschfeld Archive*, 48.
46. Naville and Péret, *La Révolution Surréaliste* 1, 12. The original text reads, "Non, le suicide est encore une hypothèse. . . . Et très certainement je suis mort depuis longtemps, je suis déjà suicidé."
47. Artaud, *Artaud Anthology*, 56. The original text reads, "Si je me tue ce ne sera pas pour me détruire, mais pour me reconstituer. . . . Je donne pour la première fois aux choses la forme de ma volonté."
48. Naville and Péret, *La Révolution Surréaliste* 1, 10. The original text reads, "Parfois la porte fermée on rencontre l'autre aventure. On plonge au fond l'Atlantique et on continue par le Pacifique, mai c'est fini pour le côté du départ."

X. In Paradisum

1. Theatre de Complicité, *The Encounter*, directed by Simon McBurney. In the published version of the script, this line reads: "It seems empathy and proximity are connected, so I'd like to get closer to you." Theatre de Complicité, *The Encounter*, 7.

2. Popescu, *The Encounter*. For the original *National Geographic* story about McIntyre's Amazon experience, see McIntyre, "Amazon—The River Sea," 456–94.

3. In the published version of the script, this line reads: "Death is a bank of lights being switched off, a vast theatre in my head, it grows like a cacophony, dims, and then black." Complicité, *The Encounter*, 41.

4. Popsescu, *The Encounter*, 227.

5. Ibid., 269.

6. Shakespeare, *King Lear*, act 4, scene 6, lines 127–37.

7. Somerville and Mandel, *Station Eleven*, Episode 1, "Wheel of Fire."

8. Shakespeare, *Hamlet*, act 1, scene 2, lines 72–89. Emphasis added.

9. Wells, dir., *Aftersun* (2022).

10. Vaillancourt, "Out There, Now Up Here," 28.

11. Baldwin, "Nothing Personal," 55. Reprinted from Baldwin and Avedon, *Nothing Personal*.

12. Ibid., 55.

13. Ibid., 56, 57.

14. Ibid., 59.

15. Ibid.

16. Ibid., 59, 60.

Coda

1. Mayes, *Escaping God's Closet*, 284.

2. Ibid., 92.

3. Ibid., 91.

4. Ibid., 127.

5. Ibid., 128, 30.

6. Ibid., 137–38.

7. Ibid., 142–44.

8. Yardley, "Bernard Mayes, 85, Dies; Started First U.S. Suicide Hotline," A30.

9. Hester, "The Phone Booth for Japanese Mourners."

10. Simon and Popuri, dirs., *After Fukushima: A Telephone to the Afterlife* (2020).
11. Holleran, *Dancer from the Dance*, 111.
12. Ibid., 146.
13. Ibid., 249–50.

Bibliography

Aarons, Leroy F. *Prayers for Bobby: A Mother's Coming to Terms with the Suicide of Her Gay Son*. New York: HarperCollins, 1995.
"Abnormal Love May Have Caused Double Tragedy." *Salt Lake Tribune*, November 30, 1926, 1.
"A Hospital Patient, 35, Leaps to His Death from 17th Floor." *New York Times*, October 31, 1985, B4.
"AIDS and Suicide." *Nightline*. ABC News, March 31, 1988.
Altman, Lawrence K. "Rare Cancer Seen in 41 Homosexuals." *New York Times*, July 3, 1981, A20.
Alvarez, Alfred. *The Savage God: A Study of Suicide*. New York: Norton, 1990.
Anderson, Patrick. *Autobiography of a Disease*. New York: Routledge, 2017.
"A Question of Mercy." *60 Minutes*. CBS News, April 16, 1989.
"Ardent Letters of Love between Girls Are Found." *Salt Lake Telegram*, November 29, 1926, 5.
Artaud, Antonin. *Artaud Anthology*, edited and translated by Jack Hirschman. San Francisco: City Lights Books, 1965.
Atkinson, J. Brooks. Introduction to *The Captive*, by Édouard Bourdet, vii–x. New York: Brentano's, 1927.

———. "Trenchant Tragedy." *New York Times*, October 10, 1926, X1.

Auden, W. H. *Another Time.* London: Faber & Faber, 1940.

"A Woman's Strange Love." *York Dispatch* (York City, PA), May 3, 1892, 1.

Baer, Max, Jr., dir. *Ode to Billy Joe.* 1976; Warner Brothers, 2020. DVD.

Baldwin, James. *Going to Meet the Man.* New York: Vintage, 1995.

———. "Nothing Personal." *Contributions in Black Studies* 6 (1983): 49–60.

Baldwin, James, and Richard Avedon. *Nothing Personal.* New York: Atheneum, 1964.

Ball, Alan, dir. *Uncle Frank.* Amazon Prime Video, 2020, https://www.amazon.com/Uncle-Frank-Paul-Bettany/dp/B08KZCMFRQ.

Barbaro, Michael. "Gay Bars Are Havens, until They're Not." *New York Times*, June 19, 2016, ST8.

Baril, Alexandre. *Undoing Suicidism: A Trans, Queer, Crip Approach to Rethinking (Assisted) Suicide.* Philadelphia: Temple University Press, 2023.

Barthes, Roland. *Camera Lucida.* New York: Hill & Wang, 1982.

Bauer, Heike. *The Hirschfeld Archives: Violence, Death, and Modern Queer Culture.* Philadelphia: Temple University Press, 2017.

Beaton, Cecil. *The Unexpurgated Beaton: The Cecil Beaton Diaries as He Wrote Them, 1970–1980*, edited by Hugo Vickers. New York: Knopf, 2003.

———. *The Wandering Years; Diaries 1922–1939.* Boston: Little, Brown and Company, 1961.

Ben-Oni, Rosemary "Temporary Passings/Possessions: On Hitchcock's Vertigo and Carlotta Valdes." *The Kenyon Review*, January 17, 2016, https://kenyonreview.org/2016/01/temporary-passings-possessions-on-hitchcocks-vertigo-and-carlotta-valdes/.

Berlin, Irving. "Remember." New York: Irving Berlin Music Publishers, 1925.

Blau, Herbert. "Universals of Performance, or, Amortizing Play." *SubStance* 11, no. 4 / 12, no. 1 (1982–83): 140–61.

Bourdet, Édouard. *The Captive*, translated by Arthur Hornblow Jr. New York: Brentano's, 1927.

Browning, Frank. *Culture of Desire: Paradox and Perversity in Gay Lives Today*. New York: Vintage, 1993.

Bullough, Vern, and Bonnie Bullough, "Lesbianism in the 1920s and 1930s: A Newfound Study." *Signs* 2, no. 4 (July 1977): 895–904.

Cantrell, Jaime. "SUBSCRIBE to Feminary! Producing Community, Region, and Archive." In *Out of the Closet, into the Archives: Researching Sexual Histories*, edited by Amy L. Stone and Jaime Cantrell, 311–36. Albany, NY: SUNY Press, 2015.

Centers for Disease Control. "Current Trends Update: Acquired Immune Deficiency Syndrome—United States." *Morbidity and Mortality Weekly Report* 35, no. 2 (January 17, 1986): 17–21.

———. "Current Trends Update on Acquired Immune Deficiency Syndrome (AIDS)—United States." *Morbidity and Mortality Weekly Report* 31, no. 37 (September 24, 1982): 507–8, 513–14.

"Choreographer Dies in Fall." *New York Times*, October 28, 1964, 91.

Christie, Heather. *The Crying Book*. New York: Catapult, 219.

Cocteau, Jean. *Hommage à Rock Bradett*, ink on paper, 1962, Musée Louis-Hémon, Péribonka, Quebec, accession number 1987.6.1.

———. *The White Paper*. New York: Macauley, 1958.

"Co-Ed at Utah 'U' Was Witness to Quarrel, Claims." *Salt Lake Telegram*, December 2, 1926, 4.

Cortázar, Julio, *Cronopios and Famas*, translated by Paul Blackburn. New York: Random House, 1969.

"Counselor Faces Lewdness Charge." *Mesquite Daily News* (Mesquite, TX), October 17, 1979, 1.

Cowels, Eugene, and Mary Kavanagh. *Forgotten*. Boston: Oliver Ditson Company, 1894.

Crevel, René. *Détours*. Paris: Éditions de la Nouvelle Revue Française, 1924.

Curtin, Kaier. *We Can Always Call Them Bulgarians: The Emergence of Lesbians and Gay Men on the American Stage*. Boston: Alyson Books, 1986.

Dallas, John. "Bars Are Important to Social Life." *Journal-News* (Rockland County, NY), February 19, 1973, 6A.

Death and Dying, April 7, 1963–May 23, 2000, and undated. Subject Files: Part 2: Breasts, Fem Folder No.: 04130. Lesbian Herstory Archives, New York.

Didion, Joan. *The White Album*. New York: Farrar, Straus and Giroux, 2009.

Di Prima, Diane. *Freddie Poems*. Point Reyes, CA: Eidolon Editions, 1974.

———. *Recollections of My Life as a Woman: The New York Years*. New York: Penguin, 2002.

———. *Spring and Autumn Annals: A Celebration of the Seasons for Freddie*. New York: City Lights Books, 2021.

"'Dive' under a Tube Train." *Liverpool Echo*, October 20, 1933, 11.

"Divorce Decree on Nonsupport Charge Given Sarah in 1925." *Salt Lake Telegram*, November 29, 1926, 1.

Dose, Ralf. *Magnus Hirschfeld: The Origins of the Gay Liberation Movement*, translated by Edward H. Willis. New York: Monthly Review Press, 2014.

"Double Suicide Believed AIDS Related." *Update* (San Diego, CA), March 29, 1989, A15.

Dumbadze, Alexander. *Bas Jan Ader: Death Is Elsewhere*. Chicago: University of Chicago Press, 2013.

"Evelyn McHale." Codex 99, October 8, 2009, http://www.codex99.com/photography/43.html.

Faderman, Lillian. *Scotch Verdict: Miss Pirie and Miss Woods v. Dame Cumming Gordon*. New York: William Morrow and Company, 1983.

Faulkner, William. *As I Lay Dying*. New York: Vintage, 1964.

Fellini, Federico, dir. *Nights of Cabiria*. 1957; Criterion Collection, 1999. DVD.

Frankfeld, Dorothy. "From the Second Balcony: *The Captive*." *Barnard Bulletin* (Barnard College, NY), February 18, 1927, 2.

Fuller, Chris. "Gays Say Disco Important Place to Socialize, Get Away from Straights." *Daily Tar Heel* (University of North Carolina, Chapel Hill), December 5, 1978, 4.

Gay, Lesbian and Straight Education Network. "GLSEN, PFLAG, the Trevor Project Release Statement on Recent Tragedies."

News release, September 30, 2010, https://web.archive.org/web/20101004195050/http://www.glsen.org/cgi-bin/iowa/all/news/record/2634.html.

Gentry, Bobby. "Ode to Billie Joe." Track 10 on *Ode to Billie Joe*. Capitol Records, 1967.

Glass, Richard M. "AIDS and Suicide." *Journal of the American Medical Association* 259, no. 9 (March 4, 1988): 1369–70.

Glueck, Grace. "Art Notes: Viewers; At the Guggenheim International, They Know What They Don't Like." *New York Times*, January 26, 1964, X22.

Gopnik, Blake. *Warhol*. New York: Ecco, 2020.

Griffin, Leo. "Bar Looks Like an Ordinary Place, and Strictly Run." *Evening Press* (Binghamton, NY), April 25, 1973, 1B, 9B.

"Harvey Woodward's Dream School Beginning to Take Form and Shape as Building Contracts Are Awarded." *Birmingham News*, December 24, 1950, 35.

Hawkins, Beth. "Bullying Gay and Lesbian Kids: How a School District Became a Suicide Contagion Area." *MinnPost*, December 7, 2011, https://www.minnpost.com/politics-policy/2011/12/bullying-gay-and-lesbian-kids-how-school-district-became-suicide-contagion-a/.

Hellman, Lillian. "The Children's Hour." In *The Collected Plays*, 1–71. Boston: Little, Brown and Company, 1972.

Hester, Jessica. "The Phone Booth for Japanese Mourners." *Bloomberg*, January 10, 2017, https://www.bloomberg.com/news/articles/2017-01-10/japan-s-wind-phone-is-a-site-to-mediate-on-life-and-loss.

Hirschfeld, Magnus, *The Homosexuality of Men and Women*, translated by Michael A. Lombardi-Nash. Amherst, NY: Prometheus Books, 2000.

Hitchcock, Alfred, dir. *Vertigo*. 1958; Universal Pictures Home Entertainment, 2014. DVD.

Hoffman, Martin, *The Gay World: Male Homosexuality and the Social Creation of Evil*. New York: Basic Books, 1968.

Holleran, Andrew. *Dancer from the Dance*. New York: William Morrow, 1978.

"The Homosexual and Suicide." *Vector* 11, no. 2 (February 1975): 28–29.

Huie, Bonnie. "The Kids Are Too Straight: Translating Qiu Miaojin's *Notes of a Crocodile*." *Kyoto Journal*, April 8, 2013, https://www.kyotojournal.org/in-translation/notes-of-a-crocodile/.

Huneke, Samuel Clowes. "Death Wish: Suicide and Stereotype in the Gay Discourses of Imperial and Weimar Germany." *New German Critique* 46, no. 1 (136) (February 2019): 127–66.

Institut Terezínské Iniciativy. "Karl Fein." Database of Holocaust Victims in Czechoslovakia, https://www.holocaust.cz/en/database-of-victims/victim/10165-karl-fein/.

Irons, Ken, and Mike Forte. "'Gay' Subculture Loses Social Inhibitions." *Greensboro (NC) Record*, September 28, 1971, B3, B18.

Jay, Karla, and Allen Young. *The Gay Report: Lesbians and Gay Men Speak Out about Sexual Experiences & Lifestyles*. New York: Summit, 1979.

Jones, Margaret. "The Soup Can Artist." *Sydney Morning Herald*, October 10, 1965, 51.

Jones, Pam. "Where There's a Will: The Story of Indian Springs School." *Alabama Heritage* 77 (Summer 2005): 26–35.

"Jury Report Links 2 More Cops to Payoffs." *San Francisco Examiner*, section 1, 11.

Kalin, Tom. "Suicide, 1965." *The Films of Andy Warhol Catalogue Raisonné, 1963–1965*, edited by John G. Handhar, 300–304. New York: Whitney Museum of American Art, 2021.

Kandel, Bethany. "2 Men Tied Together Die in 35-Story Plunge." *Fresno Bee*, October 26, 1985, A6.

Kolata, Gina. "AIDS Patients Are Found to Have an Extremely High Suicide Rate." *New York Times*, March 4, 1988, B5.

Konnikova, Maria. "The Power of Once upon a Time: A Story to Tame the Wild Things." *Scientific American*, May 8, 2012, https://blogs.scientificamerican.com/literally-psyched/the-power-of-once-upon-a-time-a-story-to-tame-the-wild-things/.

Kumin, Maxine. "The Ancient Lady Poets." In *The Long Marriage: Poems*, 111–12. New York: Norton, 2002.

———. "Apostrophe to a Dead Friend." In *Our Ground Time Here Will Be Brief*, 24. New York: Viking/Penguin, 1982.

———. "How It Is." *The New Yorker*, March 3, 1975, 38.

———. "Itinerary of an Obsession." *The American Poetry Review* 8, no. 6 (November/December 1979): 45.

———. "New Year's Eve 1959." In *Connecting the Dots*, 69–70. New York: W. W. Norton, 1996.

———. "Oblivion." In *The Long Marriage: Poems*, 115–116. New York: W. W. Norton, 2002.

———. "October, Yellowstone Park." *Ploughshares* 18, no. 1 (Spring 1992): 215–17.

———. "Splitting Wood at Six Above." *The New Yorker*, February 2, 1976, 34.

"LaBelle Man Shoots Self." *News-Press* (Fort Myers, FL), September 23, 1964, 11.

Levitt, David. *The Man Who Knew Too Much: Alan Turing and the Invention of the Computer.* New York: Norton, 2006.

Lorch, Paul. "KS Diagnosis, Takes Life." *Bay Area Reporter* (San Francisco, CA), December 23, 1982, 1, 15.

Love, Heather. *Feeling Backwards: Loss and the Politics of Queer History.* Cambridge, MA: Harvard University Press, 2009.

Maguen, Shira. "Teen Suicide: The Government's Cover-Up and America's Lost Children." *The Advocate*, September 24, 1991, 40–47.

Marhoefer, Laurie. *Racism and the Making of Gay Rights: A Sexologist, His Student, and the Empire of Queer Love.* Toronto: University of Toronto Press, 2022.

Mariani, Paul. *The Broken Tower: The Life of Hart Crane.* New York: W. W. Norton & Co., 1999.

Marzuk, Peter M., et al. "Increased Risk of Suicide in Persons with AIDS." *Journal of the American Medical Association* 259, no. 9 (March 4, 1988): 1333–37.

Matthiessen, F. O., and Russell Cheney, *Rat and the Devil: Journal Letters of F. O. Matthiessen and Russell Cheney,* edited by Louis Hyde. Hamden, CT: Archon Books, 1978.

Mayes, Bernard. *Escaping God's Closet: The Revelations of a Queer Priest.* Charlottesville: University Press of Virginia, 2001.

McDaniel, Ann. "Mesquite High School Counselor Commits Suicide: Newspaper Blamed." *This Week in Texas*, November 16, 1979, 9–11.

McIntyre, Loren. "Amazon—The River Sea." *National Geographic* 142, no. 4 (October 1972): 456–94.

Melnick, Norman. "Supervisor Milk's Roommate a Suicide." *San Francisco Examiner*, August 29, 1978, 1, 14.

Merloo, Joost. *Suicide and Mass Suicide*. New York: Grune & Stratton, 1962.

Middlebrook, Diane. *Anne Sexton: A Biography*. New York: Vintage, 1992.

Miller, Alice. *The Drama of the Gifted Child*, translated by Ruth Ward. New York: Basic Books, 1981.

Miller, Russell. *Bare-Faced Messiah: The True Story of L. Ron Hubbard*. New York: Henry Holt and Company, 1987.

"Miscellaneous Reading." *Alexandria (VA) Gazette*, January 14, 1860, https://www.digitaltransgenderarchive.net/files/p5547r52m

Mishima, Yukio. *Confessions of a Mask*, translated by Meredith Weatherby. New York: New Directions, 1958.

———. *Forbidden Colors*, translated by Alfred H. Marks. New York: Knopf, 1968.

Muñoz, José Estéban. *Cruising Utopia: The Then and There of Queer Futurity*. New York: NYU Press, 2009.

"Murder and Suicide Bared in Love Pact of Two S.L. Girls." *Salt Lake Telegram*, November 29, 1926, 1, 5.

Nathan, John. *Mishima: A Biography*. New York: Hachette, 2000.

Naville, Pierre, and Benjamin Péret. *La Révolution Surréaliste* 1. Paris: Éditions Gallimard, December 1, 1924.

———. *La Révolution Surréaliste* 2. Paris: Éditions Gallimard, January 15, 1925.

Negri, Sam. "Gays Charge Harassment." *Tucson Citizen*, June 15, 1976, 21.

Nelson, Harry. "Outbreaks of Pneumonia among Gay Males." *Los Angeles Times*, June 5, 1981, 3.

Oliver, Myrna. "Marty James; Gay Activist Aided Suicides." *Los Angeles Times*, January 5, 1992, B6.

Oswald, Richard, dir. *Anders als die Andern*. 1919; Edition Filmmuseum, 2006. DVD.

Parker, Ian. "The Story of a Suicide." *The New Yorker*, February 6, 2012, 36–51.

Paul, Jay P., et al. "Suicide Attempts among Gay and Bisexual Men: Lifetime Prevalence and Antecedents." *American Journal of Public Health* 92, no. 8 (August 2002): 1338–45.

Pelton, Matt, et al. "Rates and Risk Factors for Suicidal Ideation, Suicide Attempts and Suicide Deaths in Persons with HIV: A Systematic Review and Meta-analysis." *General Psychiatry* 34, no. 2 (March 2021), https://gpsych.bmj.com/content/34/2/e100247.

Peregrin, Tony. "Berlin Owners Celebrate 30 Years as Chicago's Best Non-gay Gay Club." *Chicago Tribune*, November 4, 2013, https://www.chicagotribune.com/redeye-berlin-owners-celebrate-30-years-as-chicagos-best-nongay-gay-club-20131104-story.html.

Phelan, Peggy. *Mourning Sex: Performing Public Memories*. London: Routledge, 1997.

"Picture of the Week." *Life*, May 12, 1947, 42–43.

Pitkethly, Lawrence, dir. *Voices & Visions: Hart Crane*. New York Center for Visual History, 1988, https://www.learner.org/series/voices-visions/hart-crane/.

"Poet's Death Linked with Loss of Father." *New York Times*, April 29, 1932, 4.

"Poison Takes Lives of Two Girls." *Evening Herald* (Provo, UT), November 29, 1926, 1.

"Police Raid Three Shows, Sex, Captive, and Virgin Man; Hold Actors and Managers." *New York Times*, February 10, 1927, A1.

Popescu, Petru. *The Encounter: Amazon Beaming*. New York: Viking, 1991.

"Professor's Leap Laid to Worries." *New York Times*, April 2, 1950, A10.

Qiu, Miaojin. *Last Words from Montmarte*, translated by Ari Larissa Heinrich. New York: New York Review Books, 2014.

Randazzo, John, and Murray Weiss. "AIDS 2 End Lives." *New York Daily News*, October 25, 1985, 4.

Rarick, Ethan. "AIDS Adding to Ranks of Hemlock Society, Death-with-Dignity Lobby." *Los Angeles Times*, August 26, 1990, A28.

Rofes, Eric. "A Gay Issue That Cannot Be Ignored: An End to the Silence about Suicide." *The Advocate*, August 9, 1979, 15–19.

———. *I Thought People Like That Killed Themselves: Lesbians, Gay Men and Suicide*. San Francisco: Grey Fox Press, 1983.

Roughead, William. *Bad Companions*. New York: Duffield and Green, 1931.

"Ruth Drake Is Suicide, Says Inquest Jury." *Ogden (UT) Standard-Examiner*, December 3, 1926, 1.

"Ruth Drake's Tragic Death Stirs Payson." *Evening Herald* (Provo, UT), November 29, 1926, 1.

Sasseen, Rhian. "The Death of the Author." *Los Angeles Review of Books*, January 23, 2016, https://lareviewofbooks.org/article/the-death-of-the-author/.

Saunders, Judith M., and S. M. Valente. "Suicide Risk among Gay Men and Lesbians: A Review." *Death Studies* 11, no. 1 (1987): 1–23.

Sexton, Anne. "Wanting to Die." In *The Complete Poems of Anne Sexton*, 142–43. Boston: Houghton Mifflin, 1981.

Shakespeare, William. *Hamlet*, edited by Susanne L. Wofford. Boston: Bedford Books, 1994.

———. *King Lear*, edited by Grace Ioppolo. New York: Norton, 2008.

Simon, Constantin, and Aruna Popuri, dirs. *After Fukushima: A Telephone to the Afterlife*. ARTE Reportage, 2020, https://www.arte.tv/en/videos/099478-000-A/arte-reportage/.

Somerville, Patrick, and Emily St. John Mandel. *Station Eleven*. Episode 1, "Wheel of Fire." Directed by Hiro Murai. Aired December 16, 2021, HBO, https://play.max.com/show/5f205b2b-80b6-47db-be11-35baa657eb4c

Soupault, Philippe. *Lost Profiles: Memoirs of Cubism, Dada, and Surrealism*, translated by Alan Bernheimer. San Francisco: City Lights Books, 2016.

Spencer, Jenny. "Sex, Lies, and Revisions: Historicizing Hellman's The Children's Hour." *Modern Drama* 47, no. 1 (Spring 2004): 44–65.

Stanislavski, Constantin. *An Actor Prepares*, translated by Elizabeth Reynolds Hapgood. New York: Routledge, 2003.

Stillman, Jack. "'Truth House' to Be Built," *Florence (AL) Times*, October 18, 1960, 8.

Tavel, Ronald. "Introduction, Interview Notes, and Script for *Suicide*." https://www.ronaldtavel.com/wp-content/uploads/2020/10/suicide.pdf.

Taylor, Fred. "New Boys School in Shelby County." *Birmingham (AL) News*, November 16, 1949, 27.

Theatre de Complicité. *The Encounter*. London: Nick Hern Books, 2016.

———. *The Encounter*, directed by Simon McBurney. Performed and recorded at the Barbicon Theatre (London, UK), 2016. http://www.complicite.org/productions/TheEncounter.

"Tragedy Probe States Cause." *Salt Lake Tribune*, December 3, 1926, 20.

"Two Pathetic Songs Found in Last-Ride Car." *Salt Lake Telegram*, November 29, 1926, 1.

Vaillancourt, Daniel, "Out There, Now up Here." *Los Angeles Times*, December 8, 2022, S28–31.

Vaughan, Roger. "Superpop, or a Night at the Factory." *New York Herald Tribune*, August 8, 1965, 7.

"Veiled Threat May Be Clue to Girls' Deaths." *Salt Lake Tribune*, November 30, 1926, 2.

Viola, Bill. *The Raft*, video and sound installation, 2004, 10:33 minutes. National Portrait Gallery, Washington, DC.

Waas, George. "Deviates Difficult to Ferret Out." *Fort Lauderdale News*, March 9, 1967, B1–2.

———. "Homosexual Problem Growing in County." *Fort Lauderdale News*, March 8, 1967, B1.

Walz, Robin. *Pop Surrealism: Insolent Popular Culture in Early Twentieth-Century Paris*. Berkeley: University of California Press, 2000.

Warhol, Andy, dir. *Freddie Herko Screen Test*. 1964. 16mm.

———, dir. *Suicide*. 1965. 16mm.

Warhol, Andy, and Pat Hackett. *POPism: The Warhol Sixties*. New York: Penguin, 1980.

Watson, Steven. *Factory Made: Warhol and the Sixties*. New York: Pantheon Books, 2003.

Weisbecker, Lee. "Town Fights Private Club It Calls Gay." *Charlotte Observer*, October 4, 1978, C1.

Wells, Betty, and Don Wall. "Gay Social Life Centers on the Traditional Bars." *Wichita Eagle and Beacon*, May 26, 1974, 1–2.

Wells, Charlotte, dir. *Aftersun*. 2022; A24, 2023. DVD.

Wells, Ken. "Low Profile Keeps Gays Powerless in PB County." *Miami Herald*, February 11, 1979, AA5.

White, Edmund. *Nocturnes for the King of Naples*. New York: St. Martin's, 1978.

Williams, Tennessee. *A Streetcar Named Desire*. New York: New Directions, 1947.

Wolff, Charlotte. *Magnus Hirschfeld: A Portrait of a Pioneer in Sexology*. London: Quartet Books, 1986.

"World Briefs." *Campaign Australia*, September 1978, 12.

Wyler, William, dir. *The Children's Hour*. 1961; British Film Institute, 2018. DVD.

———. *These Three*. 1936; Warner Archive Collection, 2016. DVD.

Yardley, William. "Bernard Mayes, 85, Dies; Started First U.S. Suicide Hotline." *New York Times*, November 1, 2014, A30.

Zhao, Yue, et al. "Suicidal Ideation and Attempt among Adolescents Reporting 'Unsure' Sexual Identity or Heterosexual Identity plus Same-Sex Attraction or Behavior: Forgotten Groups?" *Journal of the American Academy of Child & Adolescent Psychology* 49, no. 2 (February 2010): 104–13.

Index

Aaberg, Justin (student), 133
ACT UP (LGBTQ organization), 184
Ader, Bas Jon (artist), 89–91
Aftersun (film), 207–12
Albee, Edward (playwright), 160, 166–67
Alec (author's friend), 15–18, 26–30, 40–43, 48, 77–78, 94–96, 100–101, 106–7, 131, 182, 189, 207, 212, 215, 218
Amos, Stanley (friend of Andy Warhol), 104
Anders als die Andern [*Different from the Others*] (film), 22–23, 25, 26, 118
Artaud, Antonin (theatre artist), 197–98
Atkinson, J. Brooks (theatre critic), 61–62
Auden, W. H. (poet), 31, 42–43, 172
Avedon, Richard (photographer), 212

Baer, Max, Jr. (film director), 25–26
Baker, Donald (litigant), 3
Baldwin, James (author and essayist), 75, 82–83, 212–15
Baranger, Léon (author), 198
Baril, Alexandre (author), 9–10
Barker, Cody (student), 133
Barnacle (Mayoruna elder), 201
Barthes, Roland (theorist), 104–5
Bauer, Heiki (author), 24–25, 175–78, 197
Beale, Edie (socialite), 93
Beaton, Cecil (designer and diarist), 33–36, 38, 165–66, 178–79
Beaton, Reggie (brother of Cecil), 33–36, 38, 49–50, 109, 165–66, 178
Bedouin, Augustin (1860 suicide), 183
Bell, Alan (psychologist), 137
Bell, Jamarcus (student), 133–34
Berlin (nightclub), 117–28
Berlin, Irving (composer and lyricist), 52

Berlioz, Hector (composer), 7
Bettany, Paul (actor), 20
Bitner, Brandon (student), 134
Björk (musical artist), 7
Black Cat Tavern Protest (uprising), 114
Black Nite Brawl (uprising), 114
Bourdet, Édouard (playwright), 58–63
Boyd, Stephen (medical examiner), 148
Bradett, Rock (performer and model), 80–82, 91–92, 197
Bradley, Ed (journalist), 149–50, 152
Brando, Marlon (actor), 72
Breton, André, 180–81
Britten, Benjamin (composer), 7
Brogan, Linda (activist), 191
Brown, Asher (student), 134
Brown, Harrison (student), 134
Browning, Frank (author), 122–23
Brumel, Antoine (composer), 7
Bryars, Gavin (composer), 7
Bud (author's grandfather), 15–18, 26–30, 36–38, 43, 47, 77–78, 95–96, 105–7, 130–31, 182, 207, 212, 215, 218
Bullogh, Bonnie and Vern (sexologists), 70–72
Burrell, Alfred (friend of Ruth Drake), 52–58

Cabiria (author's cat), 163–65
Cadieux, David (patient), 147–48
Caiazza, Stephen (physician), 145
Callahan, Daniel (medical ethicist), 149
Casey, Robert (politician), 133
Cash, Johnny (musical artist), 7
Cats (film), 156–57
Centers for Disease Control (governmental organization), 142, 146, 162

Chase, Raymond (student), 134
Cheney, Russel (painter), 186
The Children's Hour (film), 69, 72
The Children's Hour (play), 63–70
Christie, Heather (author), 90–91
Clementi, Tyler (student), 133
Cline, Patsy (musical artist), 7
Cocteau, Jean (artist and author), 91–92, 179, 184–85, 217
Compton's Cafeteria Riot (uprising), 114
Conundrum (memoir), 5
Corlin, Richard (physician), 149
Coronation Mass (composition), 43–44
Cortázar, Julio (author), 88–89
Cowles, Eugene (composer and lyricist), 51, 52
Cowley, Peggy (friend of Hart Crane), 38–40
Crane, Hart (poet), 1, 38–40, 49–50, 93, 109
Crevel, René (author), 179–81, 189
Cunningham, Merce (choreographer), 44

Dancer from the Dance (novel), 5, 217, 223–24
David (author's lover), 193–95
Delon, Alain (actor), 91
Didion, Joan (essayist), 1, 10–11
di Prima, Diane (poet), 44–46, 99–100, 197
Dodd, Johnny (friend of Freddie Herko), 43–44, 46
Dose, Rafe (historian), 178
Drake, Ruth (girlfriend of Sarah Lundstedt), 52–58, 71–72
The Drama of the Gifted Child (book), 83–85
Dumbadze, Alexander (art historian), 90
Dykes to Watch Out For (comic strip), 5

INDEX 257

Ellis, Havelock (sexologist), 65, 71
The Encounter (novel), 199–201
The Encounter (play), 200–201
Everything but the Girl (musical group), 7
Exodus International (right-wing organization), 134

Faderman, Lillian (historian), 65–68
Faulkner, William (author), 20, 108, 129
Fauré, Gabriel (composer), 7, 131
Fein, Karl (attorney), 177
Food and Drug Administration (governmental organization), 146
"Forgotten" (song), 51, 52
Frankfeld, Dorothy (student), 62
Freddie Herko Screen Test (film), 101–5
The Front Runner (novel), 5
Fury, Gran (artist collective), 184

Gandarillas, Tony (diplomat), 179
Gardner, Alexander (photographer), 104
Gay, Lesbian and Straight Education Network [GSLEN] (LGBTQ organization), 133–35
Gay Men's Health Crisis (LGBTQ organization), 144, 146
Gentry, Bobbie (musical artist), 25–26
Giese, Karl (archivist), 176–78
Giovanni's Room (novel), 4, 82
Giselle (ballet), 44
Glass, Richard (physician), 150–53, 162
"Good Morning Heartache" (song), 113
Gopnik, Blake (biographer), 80
Griffin, Leo (journalist), 113
Griffith, Bobby (student), 192–93

Hall, Radclyffe (author), 51, 71
Hamlet (play), 205–7
Harrington, Zach (student), 134
Heakin, Richard (gay-bashing victim), 116
Hellman, Lillian (playwright), 63–70
Hemlock Society (advocacy organization), 148–49
Herms, George (photographer), 104
Hepburn, Audrey (actor), 69, 72
Herbaugh, Richard (horticulturist), 142–44
Herko, Freddie (dancer), 43–46, 49–50, 78, 80, 99–100, 101–5, 197
Hirschfeld, Magnus (sexologist), 23–25, 71, 118, 175–79, 196–97
Hitchcock, Alfred (film director), 97–99
Hoffman, Martin (psychologist), 137
Holiday, Billie (musical artist), 7
Holleran, Andrew (author), 217, 223–24
Hommage à Rock Bradett [*Homage to Rock Bradett*] (painting), 91–92
Hubbard, Quentin (1976 suicide), 189
Hudson, Jennifer (musical artist), 157
Humphrey, Derek (activist) 148–49
Huneke, Samuel Clowes (author), 24–25, 135–36

I'm Too Sad to Tell You (conceptual artwork), 87–91
In Search of the Miraculous (conceptual artwork), 87–91
Institut für Sexualwissenschaft [Institute for Sexual Science] (research institute), 23–25, 118, 175–78

Institute for Sex Research, Indiana University (research institute), 137
Izzy (author's cat), 47, 164, 168–73

Jack's Waterfront Hangout (nightclub), 115
Jackson, Corey (student), 134
James, Marty (activist), 148–50, 152–54
Jay, Karla (author), 138–39
Johnson, Timothy (physician and journalist), 147
Jones, Margaret (journalist), 80
Jones, Samantha (student), 134
Joyce, James (author), 13, 212

Kafka, Franz (author), 42
Kanengiser, Steven (partner of Marty James), 153–54
Kavanagh, Mary (composer and lyricist), 51, 52
Kelley, Ryan (actor), 192
Kelly (author's friend), 40, 42
Kevin (author's lover), 191–92
Khalifé, Rami (composer), 7
King Lear (play), 202–7
Krafft–Ebing, Richard (sexologist), 65, 71
Kumin, Maxine (poet), 85–87, 166

Lana (author's friend), 15–18, 26–30, 40–43, 48, 77–78, 94–96, 99–101, 106–7, 131, 182, 186, 207, 212, 215, 218
Lance, Montana (student), 134
La Prisonniére [*The Captive*] (play), 58–63, 68
La Révolution Surréaliste (magazine), 180–81, 197–98
Leigh, Vivien (actor), 72
Lira, Jack (Harvey Milk's lover), 190
Lorde, Audre (author and poet), 45–46

Lucas, Billy (student), 134
Lum (author's great–grandfather), 128–31
Lundstedt, Sarah (girlfriend of Ruth Drake), 52–58, 71–72

MacLaine, Shirley (actor), 69, 72
Magnetic Fields, the (musical group), 7
Mandel, Emily St. John (author), 199, 202
Mariani, Paul (biographer), 39
Mark (author's lover), 185
Markworth, Robert (1989 suicide), 195
Marzuk, Peter (psychiatrist), 145–47, 150–52, 162
Matt (author's lover), 188–89, 190–91
Matthiessen, Francis (scholar), 186
Maupin, Armistead (author), 221
Mayes, Bernard (priest and activist), 219–22
Mazdak (author's friend), 161
McBurney, Simon (theatre artist), 200–201
McCullers, Carson (author), 20
McHale, Evelyn (photograph subject), 78–79
McIntyre, Loren (photojournalist), 200–201
"Memory" (song), 157
Merlot, Joost (psychologist), 136
Miller, Alice (psychologist and author), 83–85
Milk, Harvey (politician), 190
Minnesota Family Council (right wing organization), 134
Mishima, Yukio (author), 132, 158–59
Monica (author's friend), 47, 156, 162–64
Mooney, Shirley (nightclub owner), 118

INDEX 259

Mozart, Wolfgang Amadeus (composer), 7, 43
Muñoz, José Estéban (theorist), 102–3

National Gay Task Force (LGBTQ Organization), 144–45
Nights of Cabiria (film), 82
Nocturnes for the King of Naples (novel), 5, 108, 118–19
Nolt, Caleb (student), 134
Novak, Kim (actor), 97–99

O'Connor, Sinéad (musical artist), 7, 185
Ode to Billy Joe (film), 25–26
"Ode to Billie Joe" (song), 25–26
Odetta (musical artist), 7
Olmsted, Frederick Law, Jr. (landscape architect), 110
Oranges Are Not the Only Fruit (novel), 5
Oswald, Richard (film director), 22
"The Outing" (story), 82–83

Parents Action League (right wing organization), 134
Parents and Friends of Lesbians and Gays [PFLAG] (LGBTQ organization), 133, 191
Parker, Charlie (musical artist), 7
Patch Bar Protest (uprising), 114
Payne, Lewis (conspirator), 104
"People" (son), 113
Pilsner, the (bar), 49, 128
Pirie, Jane (teacher), 64–68
The Play about the Baby (play), 160, 166–67
Popsecu, Petru (author), 199–201
The Price of Salt (novel), 5
Prince (musical artist), 7
Pulse (nightclub), 116–17

Qiu, Miaojin (author), 157–60
Queen (musical group), 209–10

The Raft (video installation), 76
Ransom, Todd (health worker), 134
Reagan, Ronald (politician), 152
"Remember" (song), 52
Renaissance, the (nightclub), 114
Reni, Guido (painter), 158–59
Robin (author's friend), 15–18, 26–30, 32–33, 38, 46–49, 72–74, 76–78, 82–85, 87–89, 95–96, 100–101, 106–7, 127–28, 131, 156–57, 160–65, 166–68, 170–72, 181–83, 201, 206–7, 212, 215, 218
Robins, Eli (psychiatrist), 137–38
Rodriguez, Gilbert (artist), 144–45
Rofes, Eric (author), 135–41
Romeo and Juliet (play), 53
Ross, Diana (musical artist), 113
Roughead, William (attorney and criminologist), 64–66

Sacco, Felix (student), 134
Sade (musical artist), 7
Saghir, Marcel (psychiatrist), 137
Sánchez, Linda (politician), 133
Schuman, Jim (nightclub owner), 118
Scientific–Humanitarian Committee (LGBTQ organization), 23
Scotch Verdict (novel), 65–68
Sego, Robert (high school teacher), 2–3
Sex (play), 63
Sexton, Anne (poet), 85–87, 166
Shakespeare, William (playwright), 31, 202–7
Shankar, Ravi (musical artist), 7
Shanti Foundation (LGBTQ organization), 154
Sigur Rós (musical group), 7
Simmons, Robert (1989 suicide), 195
Simone, Nina (musical artist), 7
Sisaki, Itaru (designer), 222–23
Sister Outsider (book), 5

"Sledgehammer" (song), 212
Spencer, Jenny (theatre historian), 69–70
Standley, David (student), 134
Stanislavski, Konstantin (theatre practitioner), 167
Stanley, Charles (friend of Freddie Herko), 45
Station Eleven (novel), 199, 202–7
Station Eleven (television series), 202–7
Stewart, James (actor), 97–99
Stone Butch Blues (novel), 5
Stonewall Riot (uprising), 114, 115
A Streetcar Named Desire (play), 72–74
Streisand, Barbra (musical artist), 113
Suicide (film), 78–82, 91, 197
"Suicide (Fallen Body)" (silkscreen), 78–80
"Suicide (Purple Jumping Man)" (silkscreen), 79–80
Sullivan, Tim (nightclub owner), 118
Sylvester (musical artist), 7

Tales of the City (novel), 5, 221
Tarek (author's lover), 195
Tavel, Ronald (scriptwriter and performer), 80–82
Taylor, Christian (student), 134
Theatre de Complicité (theatre group), 200–201
These Three (film), 69
The Thirteen Most Beautiful Boys (film), 101
Tilley, Tim (student), 134
Timothy (Cecil Beaton's cat), 165–66
Tipton, Katie (1892 suicide), 184
Tong, Li Shiu (sexologist), 175–78
Trevor Project, the (LGBTQ organization), 133
Turing, Alan (scientist), 186–87

Uncle Frank (film), 19–22, 25, 26
"Under Pressure" (song), 209–11

Veidt, Conrad (actor), 22
Vertigo (film), 97–99
Villalonga, Charles (agriculturist), 144–45
Viola, Bill (artist), 76
Vulcan (Roman god), 16–17

Walker, Jimmy (politician), 63
Wallace, Mike (journalist), 13
Walsh, Seth (student), 134
Warhol, Andy (artist), 44, 78–82, 91, 101–5, 197
Watson, Steven (friend of Andy Warhol), 44
Weaver, Sigourney (actor), 192
Webster, Jo (nightclub owner), 118
Weinberg, Martin (sociologist), 137
The Well of Loneliness (novel), 51, 71
Wells, Charlotte (filmmaker), 208, 210
West, Mae (performer), 63
White, Edmund (author), 108, 118–19
Whitman, Walt (poet), 43
Wiles, Robert (photographer), 78
Williams, Tennessee (playwright), 72–74
Wolff, Charlotte (psychologist), 178
Wood, Christopher (painter), 179
Woods, Marianne (teacher), 64–68
Woodward, Harvey (industrialist), 109–11
The Virgin Man (play), 63

Yeats, W. B. (poet), 31, 42–43, 155
Young, Allen (author), 138–39
Youskevitch, Igor (dancer), 44

Patrick Anderson is professor in the Departments of Communication, Ethnic Studies, and Critical Gender Studies at the University of California, San Diego, and a 2023 Guggenheim Fellow. His previous books include *Violence Performed: Local Roots and Global Routes of Conflict* (Palgrave, 2009), *So Much Wasted: Hunger, Performance, and the Morbidity of Resistance* (Duke, 2010), and *Autobiography of a Disease* (Routledge, 2017).

www.ingramcontent.com/pod-product-compliance
Lightning Source LLC
Chambersburg PA
CBHW031145020426
42333CB00013B/511